Latin America and the
U.S. National Interest

Also of Interest

The Caribbean Challenge: U.S. Policy in a Volatile Region, edited by
H. Michael Erisman

FOREIGN POLICY on Latin America, 1970-1980, edited by the staff of
Foreign Policy

Colossus Challenged: The Struggle for Caribbean Influence, edited by
H. Michael Erisman and John D. Martz

U.S.-Panama Relations, 1903-1978: A Study in Linkage Politics, David
Farnsworth and James McKenney

Political Change in Central America: Internal and External Dimensions,
edited by Wolf Grabendorff, Heinrich-W. Krumwiede, and Jörg Todt

Controlling Latin American Conflicts: Ten Approaches, edited by Michael
A. Morris and Victor Millán

Mexico's Oil: Catalyst for a New Relationship with the U.S.? Manuel R.
Millor

The New Cuban Presence in the Caribbean, edited by Barry B. Levine

Revolution in Central America, edited by Stanford Central America
Action Network, Stanford University

Latin American Nations in World Politics, edited by Heraldo Muñoz and
Joseph Tulchin

PROFILES OF CONTEMPORARY LATIN AMERICA:

Nicaragua: The Land of Sandino, Thomas W. Walker

The Dominican Republic: A Caribbean Crucible, Howard J. Wiarda and
Michael J. Kryzanek

Colombia: Portrait of Unity and Diversity, Harvey F. Kline

Mexico: Paradoxes of Stability and Change, Daniel Levy and Gabriel
Székely

Honduras: Caudillo Politics and Military Rulers, James A. Morris

*Available in hardcover and paperback.

Westview Special Studies on Latin America and the Caribbean

Latin America and the U.S. National Interest:
A Basis for U.S. Foreign Policy
Margaret Daly Hayes

Arguing for a new and sober look at the nature of U.S.-Latin American relations, Dr. Hayes addresses the question: Does the United States have compelling national interests in maintaining close relations with Latin American countries? Her conclusion is yes, but for reasons different from those offered in the traditional literature or espoused by many policy analysts. She maintains that U.S. interests in relations with Latin America are primarily political, secondarily economic—though economic ties are the basis of the relationship—and only marginally military. Proper emphasis on these long-term interests may be critical to U.S. national security in a global, as well as regional, context.

Dr. Hayes points out that the Latin American countries—occupying a unique position among developing nations today because of their comparatively successful experiences in achieving economic growth and development—represent an increasingly important political influence in both the developed and developing worlds. Moreover, she argues, it is in the U.S. interest to give economic aid to the less-developed countries in the hemisphere, particularly in the Caribbean Basin: U.S. security is better preserved and enhanced by encouraging political and economic stability in the region than by promoting military alliances that Latin Americans may not really want.

Supporting the need for a revised rationale for U.S.-Latin American relations, Dr. Hayes focuses in detail on the regions and nations of special interest to the United States today: the Caribbean Basin, Mexico (in a chapter by Professor Bruce M. Bagley), Brazil, and the Southern Cone.

Dr. Margaret Daly Hayes is a member of the professional staff of the U.S. Senate Committee on Foreign Relations. Previously she was director of the Center of Brazilian Studies at the Johns Hopkins University School of Advanced International Studies.

The Western Hemisphere

Latin America and the U.S. National Interest: A Basis for U.S. Foreign Policy

Margaret Daly Hayes

Westview Press / Boulder and London

Westview Special Studies on Latin America and the Caribbean

Copyright © 1984 by Westview Press, Inc.

Published in 1984 in the United States of America by Westview Press, Inc.,
5500 Central Avenue, Boulder, Colorado 80301; Frederick A. Praeger, President
and Publisher

Library of Congress Cataloging in Publication Data
Hayes, Margaret Daly.
  Latin America and the U.S. national interest.
  (Westview special studies on Latin America and the Caribbean)
  Bibliography: p.
  1. United States--Foreign economic relations--Latin America. 2. Latin Amer-
ica--Foreign economic relations--United States. I. Title. II. Title: Latin
America and the US national interest. III. Series.
HF1456.5.L3H38 1984   337.7308   83-27389
ISBN 0-86531-462-4
ISBN 0-86531-547-7 (pbk.)

Composition for this book was provided by the author
Printed and bound in the United States of America

5 4 3 2 1

Contents

Tables and Figures

Figures

Acknowledgments

This study was initially undertaken for the Office of
the Assistant Secretary of Defense, International Security
Affairs, in response to a request to examine Latin America's national security importance to the United States.
The original manuscript was completed while I was Associ-
ate Director of the Center of Brazilian Studies at The
Johns Hopkins University School of Advanced International
Studies. That draft has been substantially updated and
changed both in response to new circumstances in Latin
America and to evolution in my own thinking about U.S. in-
terest in the region.

Acknowledgment is owed to many persons who have influenced my thinking on U.S.-Latin American relations and
the content of this study. Professor Albert Fishlow of
Yale University contributed valuable time to an intensive
discussion of the economics of U.S.-Latin American relations, and the lessons of that tutorial are reflected in
Chapter 2 and other economic discussions in the text. Ambassador John H. Crimmins read and offered detailed comments on Chapter 5 on Brazil and Chapter 6 on U.S. security
interests in the region. Dr. Robert D. Bond read Chapter
3 on the Caribbean basin and shared his valuable insights
into Venezuela's role in that region. Dr. Abraham F. Lowenthal read an early draft of Chapter 6 which led to the
publication of "Security to the South: U.S. Interests in
Latin America" in the summer 1980 issue of International
Security. Lt. Col. Jack Child, USA (Ret.), then of the
Inter-American Defense College faculty, made a number of
useful comments on Chapter 6 as well.

Professor Bruce M. Bagley of The Johns Hopkins School
of Advanced International Studies not only contributed
the chapter on Mexico, but also served as a sounding board
for the development of ideas in other chapters. Dr. A. W.

xiv

"Tony" Gray, Cdr., USN (Ret.), and the Latin American
seminar of the National War College have provided many
useful comments and critiques of the regional chapters,
as well as of the chapter on U.S. security interests.
All of these persons have contributed in no small part
to the substance of this report. However, I accept full
responsibility for errors of omission or commission in
the final product.

A number of persons helped in the preparation of this
manuscript. Several students of The Johns Hopkins University School of Advanced International Studies, including
Julia Michaels, John D. Greenman, Serge D'Adesky, Cindy
Steel, and Enid Miller-Amaya, assisted in the gathering of
data for this project. Dan Davis of Georgetown University
undertook the burden of updating all the economic and
trade data for this final version. Very special thanks
go to Ms. Priscilla Taylor of Editorial Experts, Inc.,
whose editing vastly improved my prose, and Ms. Jean Spen-
cer, also of EEI, who cheerfully and patiently waded
through multiple drafts and corrections. Patricia Wal-
bridge contributed the graphics work to the book. Lynne C.
Rienner of Westview Press encouraged me to undertake the
revision and redraft for publication and waited patiently
through many delays for the final product.

A special note of appreciation is due to several people without whose support the project would neither have
been started nor finished: Brigadier General (then Colo-
nel) Clarke M. Brintnall of the Office of the Secretary of
Defense, International Security Affairs, contributed both
special enthusiasm for the project and a close attention
to its findings; Rear Adm. Gordon J. Schuler, USN, then
director of OASD/ISA/Inter-American Region, originally re-
quested a full and open-ended examination of Latin America's importance to the United States. I also thank my
colleague Dr. Riordan Roett, director of the Latin American Studies Program at The Johns Hopkins University School
of Advanced International Studies, for his continuing encouragement to "carry on" when research and the business
of the Center of Brazilian Studies began to compete for my
time. Finally, my husband, Dr. Richard E. Hayes, has always been my best supporter and critic.

Amb. Frederick M. Chapin, while Deputy Assistant Secretary of Defense for International Security Affairs,
brought the manuscript to the attention of a great number
of U.S. government officials in the Department of Defense
and in U.S. embassies in the hemisphere. As a result of
his efforts, some of the ideas presented in the study were
incorporated into a revision of U.S. policy toward the

region and are reflected in a few additional lines about
Latin America in the Secretary of Defense's annual report.
To have even a small impact on policy formulation is an
uncommon reward for a researcher and I am especially
thankful for Ambassador Chapin's enthusiasm for this
project.

Margaret D. Hayes
Washington, D.C.

1
Latin America and the United States' National Interest

Latin America is a region of more than 30 countries ranging in size from Brazil, the world's fifth largest nation, to Barbados, one of the world's smallest states. The population of the region is approximately 360 million, with one-third of that number living in Brazil and nearly one-quarter in Mexico. The gross regional product in 1980 was approximately $722 billion, a figure that makes the economy of all of Latin America about equal in size to that of West Germany among the developed countries, or comparable to the combined national products of all of the developing countries of Asia and the Indian subcontinent, and twice the regional product of Africa.

The United States has a profound interest in the future of Latin American societies and in its relations with those societies. It is the United States' national interest that there exist in its hemisphere stable, friendly, prosperous nationstates that permit the free movement of goods and services in and through the region, and that no hostile foreign powers exercise influence there. This interest is being challenged today by political instability stemming from the region's own development struggles, by economic insecurity resulting from the region's backwardness and exacerbated by international economic trends, and by insurgency generated internally and encouraged and supported opportunistically from abroad.

The critical questions to be answered in reviewing U.S. political, economic, and security interests are not whether the United States has interests in the hemisphere, but rather, how to promote those interests more effectively. This chapter seeks to examine essential U.S. interests in Latin America in a realistic and pragmatic fashion. It also seeks to establish an order of priority for U.S. interests and a priority for actions promoting U.S. interests.

1

BACKGROUND

Historically, Latin American relations have had a relatively low priority on the agenda of U.S. Presidents and cabinet members. The low level of attention reflected Latin America's relative isolation from the main currents of international relations. The Monroe Doctrine, which sought to exclude foreign (i.e., European) powers from the Western Hemisphere, was successful. The low level of priority also reflected the tremendous development gap that separates Latin America from the developed world--Europe, the United States, and Japan. It reflected the United States' independence of imported raw materials as well. Unlike the European powers, the United States did not have to look abroad for resources to fuel its industrial growth. While U.S. corporations went abroad seeking opportunity for profits, and often called on the U.S. government to support their efforts, the United States did not establish colonies in its sphere of influence.

The principal U.S. concern in the hemisphere has been to secure it from the control or influence of hostile foreign powers. While that purpose has been self-serving, it has not been contrary to Latin America's own interests. Over time, though certainly not consistently, the U.S. has invested constructive energies in the hemisphere as well. The Point Four programs of the postwar period, the Alliance for Progress in the 1960s, and, most recently, the Caribbean Basin Initiative, are examples.

In spite of the emphasis on the United States' own security, and what Latin countries would regard as a failure to accommodate Latin America's greater interest in economic development, there has been a consistent concern for the quality of relations with the nations of the hemisphere. Nearly all U.S. Presidents have sent special emissaries to Latin America in the hope of understanding the region better and of developing better programs to deal with its problems. President Dwight D. Eisenhower sent his brother Milton Eisenhower to the region in 1953 and Vice President Nixon in 1959. John F. Kennedy, building on lessons learned in the 1950s, announced the Alliance for Progress during his presidential campaign.

U.S. attention to Latin America languished during the Johnson administration, which was preoccupied with the Vietnam conflict. However, Richard Nixon entered office promising a more "mature dialogue" with Latin America, and dispatched Nelson Rockefeller to tour the region in 1969 and report back on U.S. initiatives that might respond to Latin American needs. Jimmy Carter sent his closest confidant, the First Lady, on a series of visits to Latin America to explain U.S. policy to Latin

America and to report Latin American sentiments back to the President.

More recently, private commissions have also sought to contribute to better U.S. Latin American policy. In 1974, the Commission on United States-Latin American Relations (Linowitz Commission) issues its report, The Americas in a Changing World. Chairman Sol M. Linowitz noted "the fundamental changes which have taken place in the world, within Latin America, and in the United States in recent years make timely--and indeed urgent--a reordering of relationships in this hemisphere." The Linowitz Commission had an initial important impact on the Latin American policies of the Carter administration, and so other commissions were spawned. Whereas Linowitz had "not presumed to prescribe to Latin America," in 1981 the Aspen Institute convened a distinguished panel of public servants from the United States and Latin America to explore the problems of Governance in the Western Hemisphere (Aspen Institute, 1982). In 1982, Linowitz and former Secretary General of the Organization of American States Galo Plaza convened a "new dialogue" to discuss near-term problems of The Americas at a Crossroads (Wilson Center, 1983).

The messages of these successive special emissaries and commissions have been consistent. Relations between the United States and its Latin American neighbors are in dire need of attention and reevaluation. The United States and Latin America should consult more regularly and work more closely together, and the United States, as the power in the region, must accommodate Latin American preferences, priorities, and interests when developing policies for the region or on global issues that affect the region.

THE DEBATE OVER U.S. INTERESTS

The discussion of U.S. interests in its relations with Latin America and the Caribbean countries reflects a continuing absence of consensus about the basis for U.S. Latin American relations, the importance of Latin American relations to the United States in global context, and the benefits that derive from a strong "inter-American system." Lowenthal (1976) noted that "The idea of an inter-American 'community' of a natural harmony between the United States and Latin America, has also influenced U.S. rhetoric and policy toward the region throughout the country's independent history." However, he went on, "Latin American leaders from many countries and from various places on the political spectrum are coming to reject the idea of a special and exclusive relationship between their countries and the United States."

Latin Americanists have repeatedly called on the United States to "end America's hegemonic presumption"-- the belief that "the entire hemisphere was the rightful sphere of U.S. influence" (Lowenthal, 1979). Latin Americans have generally agreed with this position, for their own reasons. In reviewing the not always felicitous legacy of U.S. involvement in Central America and the Caribbean, serious scholars have argued that the United States should cease trying to influence the direction of events, should disengage from its "pro-consular" role, and let Latin leaders determine their own fates. In a similar vein, others maintain that the United States' overemphasis on security issues distorts policies toward the region and forecloses Latin America's opportunities for setting its own political course. Almost all critiques of U.S. policy toward Latin America call for greater U.S. attention to social and economic problems in the region while failing to offer compelling reasons for expending energies and resources in a region that may not be vital to U.S. security, that is determined to set its own independent course in regional and world affairs, and that has not been grateful for U.S. efforts toward it in the past.

TOWARD A BETTER DEFINITION OF THE U.S. INTEREST IN LATIN AMERICA

This book was undertaken with the assignment to give a candid assessment of whether Latin America is important to U.S. national security and to what degree. The conclusion of the investigation is that Latin America and the Caribbean are very important to the United States and will become even more important in the future as the international system continues to evolve into more diffuse power centers and as competing ideologies test the political balance. Once isolated from the mainstream of international politics, Latin America is now very much caught up in those competing and conflicting currents. The United States now has high stakes in fostering the political stability, institutional maturation, and economic development of Latin America and Caribbean countries. In order to develop policies that can contribute to those ends, there needs to emerge a broad-based consensus that the United States has a vital national interest in Latin America.

The most elementary U.S. interest in the hemisphere is in the region's contribution to U.S. national security. Security requires first and foremost that there be no direct military threat to the United States in the region. Latin America is secure from that perspective. Security also requires stable, predictable, and harmonious relations in the region, and Latin America--especially

its less developed regions--is far from secure on those
grounds.

In reassessing policy toward the region, a sober
evaluation of Latin America's economic prospects and capabilities is required. Latin America is important eco- (2)
nomically to the United States and will become more important as the region's potential is developed over time.
Nevertheless, some countries will always have difficulty
in sustaining economic growth, and the gap that separates
even the wealthiest and most diversified Latin American
countries from the United States or Western European powers will remain tremendous. Latin American countries
cannot contribute to the solution to world economic problems yet, though some may cease to be a part of those
problems in the near future.

It is also important to understand that Latin America has a tremendous political importance for the United
States. That importance becomes most visible when revolution threatens to upset the predictable order and perhaps to install an ideologically hostile government.
However, Latin America is important to the United States
on many less critical political dimensions. In weighing
U.S. strength and influence in the world, it is important
that values that the United States shares prevail in the
hemisphere; it is important that Latin America generally
line up with the United States on East-West questions.
Given the historic presumption of hemispheric solidarity,
it is important that the concept of regional consensus
remain viable.

These political interests acquire increased urgency
in the present-day climate of insurgency, revolution,
militant nationalism, political institutional decay, and
economic distress. The political order is often threatened long before vital security interests are placed in
jeopardy. For the most part, in its intermittent attention to Latin America, the United States has ignored its
more subtle political interests and failed to pursue a
sophisticated long-term policy toward the region. The
result has been periodic crisis often invoking the use of
military force which, in turn, has had negative political
consequences for relations in the region.

In his "inquiry into the American National Interest," Henry Kissinger noted that Americans have "historically shied away (from addressing) the essence of our
national interest and the premises of our foreign policy.... A mature conception of our interest in the world
would ... take into account the widespread interest in
stability and peaceful change. It would deal with two
fundamental questions: What is it in our interest to

6

prevent? What should we seek to accomplish?" (Kissinger, 1974).

The Special Relationship

The United States' principal goals for Latin America are that friendly, stable, prosperous nations prevail there; that no hostile foreign influences exercise power or influence there. It is the United States' interest that such conditions exist in the hemisphere and the goal of U.S. policy to see that they obtain. There are compelling reasons why Latin America should occupy a more important place in our national agenda. The most important is that, in spite of many efforts to deny it, the United States and Latin America do enjoy a special relationship. The relationship is special simply because all occupy the same geopolitical space--the Western Hemisphere--whose history is uniquely different and separate from that of Europe or Asia or Africa. The relationship is special because the United States is a superpower and unrivaled among the nations of the hemisphere. It is special, too, because over the course of years, the United States and Latin American countries have acted in concert on a large number of issues and have erected a framework of regional cooperation and expression--the inter-American system. The relationship is special because it has provided Latin American countries a unique shield against foreign intervention. Moreover, the friendship and collaboration of Latin American countries have enhanced the security of the United States, permitting it to meet threats and pursue its interests outside the hemisphere without concern for its immediate borders.

A special relationship does not necessarily entail an exclusive relationship, nor even always a happy relationship. Because of profound changes taking place internally in Latin America, because of the U.S. involvement in crises and alliances elsewhere in the world, and because of the gap in power and influence that historically has separated the U.S. from its Latin American neighbors, United States attention to Latin American problems has been sporadic and, as Latin Americans know well, has been stimulated by pending crises, not by a concern for Latin American preferences. Moreover, the United States has exercised its powerful influence over the region to manipulate outcomes it found convenient. It has often run roughshod over Latin American sensitivities and intervened in Latin American domestic politics to place in power governments of its own choosing. It has sought to dictate Latin American mores and to set limits to Latin American opportunities to acquire military weapons, nuclear, and other modern technologies.

It is time for a change to a more enlightened set of
relations with Latin America. However, any U.S.-Latin
American relationship must be predicated on a thorough
understanding of national interests involved. U.S. and
Latin American national interests will not always coincide. The United States should not be faulted for pursuing its interests, any more than Latin American nations
should be criticized for pursuing theirs. Each should
have a clear view of its own interests.

A NEGATIVE APPROACH TO SECURITY:
WHAT WE WOULD PREVENT

The United States' (and any nation's) most fundamental interest is in securing its borders against hostile enemies. No Latin American country is going to attack the United States. That is clear. However, it has
been the United States' historical concern to prevent
powers from outside the hemisphere from establishing a
base of power or influence within the region. Thus, even
though John Q. Adams initially argued against U.S. in-
volvements in the hemisphere, the Monroe Doctrine was
promulgated, making the entire region an area of U.S. security concern--to be defended by the British fleet, to
be sure, since the United States was not then powerful
enough to defend the region against the efforts of the
other major European powers. Slowly, over the course of
the nineteenth century, the United States reduced British
involvement in the region. The Spanish American War succeeded in eliminating the last remnant of Spanish influence. The completion of the Panama Canal made the U.S. a
maritime power with a vested interest in the unchallenged
right of passage throughout the Caribbean and Gulf of
Mexico.

The frequent U.S. interventions in Caribbean countries during the first quarter of the twentieth century
were undertaken in part to preclude the possibility that
European powers might send military forces to exact payment of debts to European creditors. In the years leading up to World War II, U.S. military planners developed
contingency plans for securing first the Caribbean and
access to it (South to approximately the bulge of Brazil), to the Panama Canal, and finally, to the hemisphere
(Child, 1979, 1980). Child notes that the debate over
the hemispheric defense concept was "complicated by the
fact that U.S. isolationist sentiment favored the Hemisphere Defense concept, because it suggested a self-
reliant (even autarchic) U.S.-Canadian-Latin American
alliance which could isolate itself from the ravages of
European and Asian wars." The self-reliant, isolationist viewpoint continues to influence U.S. thinking about
the hemisphere to this day.

8

During World War II, Latin American countries played an important role as U.S. allies--providing bases, airfields, and ports, and supplying raw materials to the war effort. Brazil sent troops to fight in Europe with the Allies.

Postwar defense planning continued to stress cooperation with Latin American militaries to enhance defense of the Panama Canal and the hemisphere, preservation of peace in the hemisphere, and avoiding unnecessary diversion of U.S. military resources to the Western Hemisphere (Child, 1980). However, the real challenge to U.S. security interests in the post-World War II environment came not from foreign military powers--the United States was the only nation still able to project power--but rather from a hostile ideology--Communism. In the aftermath of the world war, after watching Eastern European countries fall, one by one, behind the Iron Curtain, and seeing China move into the Communist camp, it became the primary U.S. security interest that the hostile ideology not take root in the Western Hemisphere.

Concern for revolutionary Marxism associated with the Soviet Union has been the key factor motivating U.S. policy in the hemisphere since the war. That concern was heightened following the Cuban revolution and that country's sudden turn toward the Soviet Union. The Missile Crisis in 1962 set the extreme limits of U.S. tolerance for Soviet involvement in the hemisphere. Nevertheless, the Soviet Union continues to test U.S. resolve in the region through its use of the Cienfuegos port facility and increasing numbers of visits by elements of its fleet and air force, as well as by steady arming of the Cuban forces with more and more sophisticated weapons. The ongoing debate over U.S. policy toward the Sandinista government in Nicaragua focuses on the possibility that other countries in the region might become politically and militarily allied with the Soviet Union and permit their territory to be used by the Soviets or other hostile powers.

The use of territory in the hemisphere by the Soviet Union for military purposes is clearly an intolerable threat to U.S. security. That point was made clear in the confrontation of the Missile Crisis. The United States also has a vital interest in assuring the political security and stability of nations in the hemisphere, especially in its immediate sphere of concern, the Caribbean basin. No superpower can permit its immediate surrounding neighborhood to be a source of insecurity and instability.

Historically, the United States has enjoyed a stable, predictable Southern border region without investing

large sums in its defense. U.S. forces deployed in the
Central American Caribbean region have been minimal and
largely concerned with extrahemispheric (NATO) issues.
The absence of major security assets in the region makes
potential threats more worrisome, heightens the severity
of reaction, and makes the preemptive use of military
force more likely. To have to engage in a major defense
effort in the region is a cost that is not readily or
willingly undertaken. Whereas the United States' chief
rival, the Soviet Union, maintains security on its borders with a large standing army and police state policies, the United States is dependent on positive support
from the countries in its sphere of influence. Because
U.S. security in Latin America is dependent on a positive
political climate in its immediate environment, revolutionary movements, governments with hostile foreign policies, alignment with Cuba, destabilizing arms races, and
the introduction of Soviet and East European weapons all
represent undesirable and perhaps unacceptable outcomes
for the United States in the region. These all represent
things the United States, acting in its national interest, would prevent in the hemisphere.

A POSITIVE APPROACH TO SECURITY:
WHAT WE WOULD PROMOTE

     Preventing what is politically and militarily unac-
ceptable may well depend on the success with which the
United States identifies and pursues that which we seek
to accomplish. The United States can no longer assure
its interests by use of military force in the Western
Hemisphere. The costs of U.S. use of military strength ①
against a Latin neighbor are excessive in terms of relations with other nations in the region and in terms of
U.S. prestige among developing nations. Moreover, the
United States has shown itself singularly ill-prepared ②
to battle wars of ideology that characterize the current
political instability. Finally, U.S. intervention in ③
affairs of politically weak, socially and economically
backward countries does not resolve key problems of those
countries' inadequacies to cope with and resolve their
own national problems. Whereas it was once easy to assume control over governments as in Haiti in 1915, or in
Nicaragua in 1912, neither international nor domestic
opinion can long support such interventions today. Nationalism is much stronger in Latin America today than it
was earlier in the century, and no foreign power can
dominate political processes as the United States once
did. Moreover, the instruments of opposition are no
longer primarily military. The Soviet Union uses general economic assistance terms, commercial and cultural
relations, or the facilities of diplomatic relations to
gain entrée and favor with nations it would like to lure

out of the U.S. sphere of influence. In addition to the
support it provides to insurgencies, Cuba uses technical, medical, and educational assistance to promote its
perspectives in Central America and the Caribbean. Cuban
assistance has positive benefits for most countries, and
political risks.

The challenge to the United States today is, as Kissinger noted in 1969, that it

> ...is no longer in a position to operate pro-
> grams globally. It has to encourage them. It
> can no longer impose its preferred solution; it
> must seek to evoke it. In the forties and fif-
> ties we offered remedies; in the late sixties
> and in the seventies our role will have to be
> to contribute to a structure that will foster
> the initiatives of others. We are a superpower
> physically, but our designs can be meaningful
> only if they generate willing cooperation. We
> can continue to contribute to defense and posi-
> tive programs, but we must seek to encourage
> and not stifle a sense of local responsibility.
> Our contribution should not be the sole or prin-
> cipal effort but it should make the difference
> between success and failure. (Kissinger, 1969)

In meeting the challenge of more mature nationalisms
in the hemisphere on the one hand and the ideological
challenges posed by a militant Communism, the United
States' public and policy community must achieve a
greater consensus and better understanding of the feasible and desirable outcomes that are consistent with U.S.
interests.

My proposition is that the United States' desires,
and for the long term, requires on its borders and in the
hemisphere stable, friendly, prosperous countries that
are not allied, formally or informally, with the Soviet
Bloc and that do not promote revolution in the region.
Cuba is the exception. Cuba will be tolerated, but only
within the confines of its island. Cuba's efforts to
export revolution to the hemisphere cannot be accepted
for the simple reason that instability in the region is
not consistent with U.S. interests.

The challenge to U.S. policy in the region is political. The United States must seek to evoke the responses it desires from its neighbors. In competition
among ideologies it must be better to be on the United
States' side. Latin Americans must perceive it in their
interest to choose that side.

note: does not say democratic

The Need for Hemispheric Unity

Regional support for U.S. values and policies is important on the one hand because we have long had it. Americans believe that there has been a commonality of interests and values in the hemisphere since the respective wars of independence. The concept of hemispheric solidarity may be a myth, but it has been an integral element of U.S. presence on the world scene. However, whereas in the past support from the region was automatic, or nearly automatic, today it is problematic, and must be cultivated. Building friendships with the nations in the hemisphere is not a simple, easy task. For some years, Latin American and other Third World countries have viewed their interests from different perspectives and have been defining and redefining their own foreign policies to accommodate those perspectives. Like Brazil, they prefer "not automatic alignment" with the United States. For the most part, Latin America's independent expressions of policy preferences are not incompatible with U.S. interests. They have been differences of degree, not of substance. In many cases, they have been rhetorical differences, not differences in practice, but the rhetoric has often made differences seem greater than they have been.

The danger in Latin America's more independent posture is that the region represents a real prize in U.S.-Soviet competition in the Third World. The Soviet Union does not necessarily create conditions of international instability that undermine regimes friendly to the United States, but it is eager to take advantage of such situations once a political vacuum obtains. Just as the Soviet Union challenges U.S. sensitivities and tolerances with military visits to Cuba, the USSR and Cuba are prepared to seek to tip the political balance in the hemisphere. Thus they have provided aid and advice to Nicaragua and to Grenada and established a presence in Guyana, Surinam, and even in Argentina, which now sells two-thirds to three-fourths of its exports to the USSR (see Leiken, 1981, for a description of other presence-establishing activities of the Soviet Union).

Hemispheric solidarity is also important because divisions among the countries of the region contributes to conflict and instability. Latin America is replete with border disputes which would be more difficult to resolve if countries were not committed to nonintervention and peaceful resolution of disputes. The principle of peaceful resolution has been violated only rarely. Moreover, if countries with competing ideologies emerge, the region will become more militarized, as has been seen already in Central America. Ideological differences among states make for unfriendly borders of necessity. By the same

token, U.S. military presence in the region would have to
be upgraded if regional military activities increase, and
particularly if one side is supplied by enemies of the
United States as has been the case in Nicaragua since the
coming to power of the Sandinista government. It is not
in the United States' interest that regional military
power be tipped in favor of countries over which it has
no influence.

The Need for Economic Growth and Prosperity

The United States also has a strong interest in the
future prosperity of the hemisphere. United States banks
and corporations have billions of dollars invested in or
lent to countries in Latin America and the Caribbean. In
the heady days of economic growth in the late 1970s, some
U.S. auto manufacturers and banks made their highest
profits on operations in the boom countries of Latin
America. The balance of trade with the region consistently has favored the United States. When Latin America
recovers from the 1980s economic crisis and begins to expand again, it will provide even larger and more diverse
markets for U.S. goods and services.

Economic problems in Latin America also are reflected in the United States. For years, the United
States has served as a safety valve for employment pressures in Mexico and the Caribbean. Illegal migration to
the United States increases dramatically when economic
conditions in Latin America deteriorate. Migrant populations place heavy burdens on local governments responsible for providing services to new constituents. There
are concerns that the illegal status of large numbers of
aliens invites exploitation in the labor market. While
the verdict is still out as to whether illegal migrants
take jobs from American workers, the periodic political
backlash against the migrants is real.

The U.S. and Latin American economies are increasingly interdependent. The symbiotic relationship between
the United States and Mexican economies is well-
documented. The United States is increasingly the key
to Caribbean economic recovery. The Caribbean Basin Initiative providing special concessions to Caribbean products was adopted in recognition that the United States
has an important stake in the economic development of its
neighbor region and that such development depends in
large part on access to credit from U.S. banks and firms
and to markets in the United States. Other similar arrangements that would create preferred economic opportunities for Latin American countries in the U.S. marketplace are attractive options for enhancing hemispheric
economic relations.

Economic pressures have caused regional wars, like the El Salvador-Honduras soccer war of 1969. However, economic pressures have more often contributed to the increasing appeal of revolutionary alternatives to present governments in the region. Given the high population growth rates in Latin America, growth is necessary just to keep up on employment. Without growth, there is no capital for investment in social infrastructure nor for diversification of investment in nontraditional areas that may offer greater protection against cyclical price trends that affect primary commodities.

Prosperity must be measured on two levels. On the macroeconomic level, growth is good for its own sake. It creates employment, permits investment in social services and necessary urban services such as sewage and electricity, but it does not necessarily improve the quality of life of the mass of population. The United States also has a strong interest in prosperity at the microeconomic level, for a key to more stable political systems lies in convincing the population that they have a stake in that system. That lesson has all too frequently been lost on Latin American regimes to date.

The United States has an interest in promoting growth even when the trickle down effect seems to operate too slowly in order to stem the pressures that lend support to radical revolutionaries. It has an obligation to insist on appropriate management of resources so that the benefits of growth are shared broadly.

The Need for Stable Regional Politics

The United States has a strong vested interest in the mature political stability of the hemisphere. Political stability does not require that governments are authoritarian, resistant to change, or slavishly supportive of U.S. policies. It does require mature political institutions and governments that can adapt to changing conditions at home and abroad, that can respond to the legitimate economic and social demands of their populations, and that can develop and implement policies that will contribute to greater prosperity and more equitable sharing in the resources of the country.

The United States has been accused rightfully of favoring regimes that are democratic in appearance but do not have meaningful democratic processes, for example, whose elections are substantively meaningless, or for favoring governments that respond positively to U.S. initiatives while ignoring or abusing the rights of citizens at home. Moreover, experience has shown that such regimes are reliable allies only in the short term. In the volatile political climate of rapid change that

14

characterizes Latin America today, governments and regimes that do not respond constructively to the demands
of their citizens are not likely to survive for long.
Throughout Latin America people have been politically
awakened and will no longer accept repressive or unrep-
resentative governments. In Central America, revolutionary insurgents have prepared to take advantage of incumbent governments' weaknesses, lack of support, and
repressive policies. Where insurgencies do not exist,
the Southern Cone, for example, exclusionary authoritarian governments have stifled the emergence of responsible leaders, parties, and institutions of the center,
making transition to civilian rule more difficult.

In devising policies that encourage political stability in its sphere of concern, the United States must
walk a fine line between supporting governments that are
capable of ruling and those that can only rule by exclud-
ing, eliminating, or repressing opposition voices. U.S.
policy makers must also be cautious of parties that have
leaders, but no following. We should not be satisfied
with imitations of democracy, whether from the right or
from the left. Policy makers and the public must recognize that representative democracy as known in the United
States is virtually unknown in Latin America. Political
institutions are not well-developed, especially at the
grass roots.

The United States' posture toward internal political
processes must be cautious and analytical. U.S. interests should be in results, not in people or symbols. The
United States must avoid becoming a pawn of local actors,
just as they resist becoming a pawn of U.S. policy.

The Impossibility of Disengagement

Some observers argue that the United States' overwhelming influence over Latin America precludes the region from developing in its own way. These commentators
argue that the United States should step back from the
region and cease trying to influence political and economic outcomes there. This is not a practical proposal
for a variety of reasons. In the first place, if the
United States ceases its activities in the area, some of
the more desirable outcomes pursued in U.S. policies
might be slowed. Rural development, strongly supported
by U.S. AID, might be one. Human rights would be another.
While the United States cannot make a system change its
human rights observances, it can exercise influence and
pressure to encourage the efforts of indigenous human
rights groups and discourage extreme behavior by governments. Success has been achieved in Argentina, Brazil,
and even in El Salvador and, to an extent, in Guatemala.
Without external pressures from governments and public

opinion, authoritarian governments are not likely to change. When they do not change, they risk becoming the targets of revolutionary change.

Second, the United States cannot withdraw from its close association with Latin American countries. To do so would create a vacuum that would invite exploitation by hostile countries seeking to divide the United States from its traditional sphere of influence. U.S. security interests would be threatened.

Finally, the United States' presence simply cannot be withdrawn from the region because too many facets of U.S. social and economic life are intertwined in the day-to-day business of nearly every country in the region. U.S. banks acted autonomously in lending billions of dollars to the region and are the key to international solutions to the financial crisis of the 1980s. U.S. businesses have maintained their operations in the region in spite of the severe economic recession. Reinvestment and recapitalization of plants by U.S. corporations will be a key to Central American and Caribbean economic recovery. U.S. firms will be sources of technology for Latin America's continued development. The U.S. market is the key to nearly every Latin American country's export-oriented economic recovery and expansion.

It is almost inevitable that U.S. influence in the region be enormous, particularly in comparison with the influence small Latin countries exercise over one another, or with the influence of the poorly organized political parties and interest groups that exist in the region. However, it is often overlooked that the United States is frequently called into Latin American issues and internal discussions by Latin American actors themselves. Nowhere has this been so evident as in the El Salvador civil conflict in which elements of the extreme right, the extreme left, and moderates all maintain active lobbies in Washington and across the nation to invoke U.S. influence on the outcome of ongoing political conflicts. No unilateral policy decision can remove the United States from involvement in hemisphere affairs.

LOOKING AHEAD

The remaining chapters of this book are intended to demonstrate that Latin America has become important to the United States on a great variety of dimensions--political, military, and economic--and to suggest that the region now merits the quality of attention that is accorded the United States' close allies and regions of important security interest, and a coherent policy that

better reflects U.S. political, economic, and security
interests.

Chapter 2 explores in detail Latin America's growing
importance in the international economy and its strategic
economic importance to the United States. The chapter
also reviews the limits on Latin America's current expansion, the dilemma of its crushing debt, and the details
of the enormous gap that still separates most of the region, including the most advanced countries, from the
major economies of Europe, or from the United States itself, and from Japan.

Chapter 3 discusses the importance to the United
States of the Caribbean basin, the region of immediate
concerns in the 1980s. The Caribbean's economic links to
the United States are examined, and the constraints on
Caribbean and Central American economic development, and
the implications of such constraints for the future political stability of the region are evaluated. The chapter explores Venezuela's role in the region as a potential economic and political leader. Finally, Cuba's
relations with the countries of the region and with the
United States are examined in detail. The prospects for
a U.S.-Cuba rapprochement in the near future are also
examined.

Chapter 4, by Bruce M. Bagley, examines the strong
U.S.-Mexico relationship. The variety of dimensions on
which the United States and Mexico are linked one to another as well as Mexico's efforts to grow out from under
its dependent relationship with the United States are
examined in depth. The history and motives behind Mexico's increasingly independent foreign policy in the region are reviewed. The problems that will confront Mexico in the future as a result of the "promise" of oil and
the implications for U.S.-Mexican relations are examined.
Finally, the chapter explores the prospects for continued
political stability in Mexico in light of its ongoing financial crisis, continuing income inequalities, high levels of population growth and unemployment, and the disparate rates of investment in capital and labor in the
national economy.

Brazil, the country touted as a future world power,
is studied in Chapter 5. Brazil's rapid growth in the
1970s, its increasingly independent foreign policies, and
its entry into the arms export market all point to Brazil's emerging as the political leader of South America,
and a major factor in Third World politics. Brazil's
difficult role between developed and developing world,
and its consequent resistance to efforts to make it a
Third World power, are reviewed and the constraints on
Brazil's continued expansion--debt, oil dependence,

population growth--are also enumerated. Brazil's remarkably successful shift away from authoritarian regime back
toward elected civilian government is explored in detail,
for Brazil provides a model for other countries seeking
to make the transition from military to civilian, authoritarian to democratic, governments.

In Chapter 6 U.S. military interests in Latin America are examined in detail. Strategic interests in the
Caribbean basin, in the South Atlantic, and in the West
Coast area are detailed. Latin American countries' own
security interests in these areas are documented. The
prospects for greater U.S.-Latin American military cooperation are discussed.

2
Latin America's Expanding International Economic Role

Latin America is the most important developing region in the world for the United States. However, in spite of their growing importance, the developing regions of the world, including Latin America, still contribute only a minor share of the gross world product (about 8 percent), play a minor role in overall world trade, and are separated from the major powers of the developed world by a gap that will not be overcome in the foreseeable future. The major economies in Latin America--Brazil and Mexico-- are most comparable to the smaller economies of Western Europe--Spain, Belgium, and the Netherlands, for example. The prospects that Latin American nations will develop capabilities comparable to those of the major powers, France, Germany or Japan, are very unlikely in the present century. This chapter focuses on the economic foundations of Latin America's expanding role in the international community: the size and structure of the region's economy, and the economic growth potential. The chapter examines Latin America's linkages to the world community: trade relations, supply of critical raw materials, and levels of overseas investment, particularly from the United States.

The economic linkages and development prospects examined here represent the principal national interests of the various members of the Latin American community. As Chapter 1 emphasized, economic development is the major focus of contemporary Latin American national security doctrine. Development is viewed as the key to domestic political stability, territorial security, world power projection, economic security, and social well-being. Different views on appropriate economic development models underlie competing ideological currents in the hemisphere. Differences over economic issues such as trade, investment, raw materials prices, and transfer of technology are the major items of dispute and discussion in bilateral relations between the United States and nearly all Latin American countries.

Economic issues are the chief determinants of Latin
American foreign policy at present and for the decade to
come. Therefore, an understanding of the Latin American
countries' current roles and positions in the international economy, as well as their future growth prospects
and the political and economic constraints on their growth
and development, is crucial to an evaluation of U.S. interests in the hemisphere and to the determination of appropriate U.S. policy toward individual countries and the
region as a whole.

LATIN AMERICA'S POSITION IN THE WORLD ECONOMY

Latin America has been one of the most rapidly developing and most economically advanced regions of the
developing world for the past two decades. In the next
ten years and beyond, it will gain increasing importance
in the world as an economic power base. Several countries
in the region have already begun to assume positions of
importance on the world scene. Brazil has the 6th-largest
population in the world, following the People's Republic
of China, India, the Soviet Union, the United States, and
Indonesia. Brazil's population rivals, but has surpassed,
that of Japan. Brazil is also the world's 9th-largest
economy, with a gross national product (GNP) of $119 bil-
lion in 1980. It stands between Italy and Canada in
terms of economic size. Mexico has become the world's
newest major source of oil with potential reserves greater
than those of any other oil-exporting country except Saudi
Arabia.

Latin America as a whole continues to have extraordinary resource potential, much of which is unexplored. In
addition to petroleum, Latin America supplies the United
States and its allies with important critical materials
including bauxite, iron ore, copper, and manganese. The
region has strong economic ties with the Western industrial world, with more than 70 percent of its foreign commerce taking place with the nations of Europe, Japan, and
the United States. Several of the countries of the region, including Brazil, Argentina, and Venezuela, are
emerging maritime powers. Mexico, Brazil, and Argentina
have large industrial bases, producing ships, automobiles,
steel products, and electric apparatus that compete on the
world market.

Latin America has developed rapidly over the past 10
to 15 years, building on a base of economic diversification and modernization that began well before World War II.
As a result, it has the most diversified and integrated
economic base as well as the greatest technical capabilities of the developing world regions. These factors should
permit Latin America to continue to grow for years to come.

In 1975 the regional economy was the size of Europe's in 1950. If recent growth rates continue, by 1985 it will be comparable in size to the European economy of 1970. Regional economic growth has been led by two countries, Brazil and Mexico, which together account for 60 percent of regional product.

Latin America's relative weight in the world community has increased substantially over the last two decades. Table 2.1 gives a comparative picture of the position of different world regions in terms of their contribution to global product for 1960, 1970, and 1980. The industrial countries of North America, Europe, and Japan continue to dominate the world economy, representing over 85 percent of the free world's gross national product. The Latin American economy, measured by gross national product, represented over one-third of the combined product of developing countries, exclusive of the OPEC members, in 1977. Asia's (less Japan) position declined substantially from 6 percent to 4.8 percent, while Africa's position improved slightly. Since the figures for Africa include South Africa (generally regarded as a developed/industrial economy) and oil-exporting countries such as Algeria, Nigeria, and Libya, whose national products increased dramatically between 1970 and 1980, this figure is surprisingly low. In contrast to these regions, Latin America's position in the world economy increased steadily from 6.2 to 7.4 percent without, in most cases, the assistance of extraordinary circumstances such as oil income.

Between 1960 and 1977, the gross regional product expanded from $129 billion to $334 billion in constant 1976 dollars, an expansion of nearly 160 percent (IDB, 1977). This represented a cumulative growth rate of approximately 5.8 percent a year, as compared with rates of approximately 3.8 percent for Africa and 2.9 percent for East and Southeast Asia, the other developing world regions. During the same period, the size of the industrial economies expanded by approximately 95 percent, with an average annual growth of 4.3 percent a year. Only the Eastern European economies grew more rapidly than did Latin America, approximately 6.6 percent per year in this time period. (World Bank: 1978).

In 1975, the Latin American regional economy was 70 percent the size of the Japanese economy, the third largest in the world. Brazil and Mexico accounted for nearly 60 percent of the regional product (Brazil, 34 percent, and Mexico, 22 percent) and four countries, Brazil, Mexico, Argentina, and Venezuela for 78 percent. These four nations are clearly the economic leaders of the region and their growth will shape the economic future of the hemisphere. This is demonstrated in Table 2.2, which gives the contribution to regional product of the major

TABLE 2.1
Shares of Gross World Product: Market Economies, 1960, 1970, 1975
(U.S. $ millions, market prices)

	1960		1970		1975	
North America	$546,600	49.4%	$1,064,000	43.8%	$1,690,400	34.5%
Europe	324,900	29.4	762,300	31.4	1,702,500	35.2
Latin America	69,400	6.2	160,100	6.6	357,400	7.4
Asia Less Japan	67,600	6.1	123,700	5.1	232,400	4.8
Japan	43,063	3.9	196,856	8.1	491,331	10.2
Africa	34,700	3.1	75,500	3.1	172,600	3.6
Middle East	19,700	1.8	45,900	1.9	189,100	3.9

Source: United Nations Yearbook of International Trade Statistics, 1977 and 1981.

TABLE 2.2
Gross National Product and Share of Regional Product of Latin American Countries, 1960, 1970, 1980 (Values in 1980 U.S. $ millions)

Country and Subregion	1960 GNP	%	1970 GNP	%	1980 GNP	%
Mexico	31,520.1	17.4	62,114.0	21.1	107,263.0	20.6
Central America[1]	8,322.7	4.6	14,988.9	5.1	23,178.4	4.5
Caribbean[2]	6,469.1	3.6	10,022.9	3.4	16,182.6	3.1
Venezuela	13,605.9	7.5	24,633.6	8.4	37,011.7	7.1
Subtotal	28,397.7	15.7	49,645.4	16.9	76,372.7	14.7
Colombia	8,240.2	4.5	13,712.7	4.7	24,068.0	4.6
Ecuador	1,841.9	1.0	3,148.4	1.1	6,310.8	1.2
Peru	9,454.7	5.2	15,450.8	5.3	20,925.5	4.0
Chile	8,558.4	4.7	13,241.8	4.5	17,661.4	3.4
Bolivia	1,260.0	7.0	2,049.3	.7	3,173.3	.6
Subtotal	40,695.2	22.5	47,603.0	16.2	72,139.0	13.9
Argentina	27,896.6	15.4	42,549.0	14.5	53,637.3	10.3
Uruguay	3,963.3	2.2	4,621.8	1.6	6,320.6	1.2
Paraguay	1,029.6	.6	1,588.7	.5	3,583.5	6.9
Subtotal	32,889.5	18.1	48,759.5	16.6	63,541.4	12.2
Brazil	47,759.7	26.3	86,088.6	29.3	200,176.7	38.5
Total	181,262.2	100.0	294,210.5	100.1	519,492.8	99.9

Source: Inter-American Development Bank, 1981.

[1]Central America--El Salvador, Guatemala, Honduras, Nicaragua, Panama, Costa Rica.

[2]Caribbean--Bahamas, Barbados, Dominican Republic, Guyana, Haiti, Jamaica, Trinidad and Tobago. Bahamas n.a. 1960, 1970. 1980 = 2,057.3.

countries and subregions. Mexico has retained an approximately constant share (20 percent) of the regional product.
By 1980 Venezuela's share of the regional product had declined to below its 1960 level. Argentina's position has
declined significantly from 15 percent in 1960 to only
10 percent in 1980. Clearly Brazil has been the most dynamic country. Its economy has more than tripled in size
and its share of regional product has grown from 26 to
38 percent.

Economic growth in Latin America has been the result
of a concerted policy of industrialization, which was
first promoted by the closing of national doors to foreign
goods and capital, forcing import substitution. More recently, growth has been encouraged by opening the economies to the international market and promoting exports of
both agricultural goods and manufactures to earn foreign
exchange for the purchase of high-technology industrial
goods from the developed world. This new strategy of expanding commercial relations is one of the most important
determinants of new and more aggressive Latin American
foreign policies.

As the most advanced of the world's developing regions, Latin American countries now demonstrate many of
the characteristics of both developed and developing
worlds. Between 1960 and 1976, the economic profiles of
the major Latin American countries came to look more and
more like those of the industrialized nations. Table 2.3
documents this shift on several indicators--agriculture's
share in gross national product, manufactures as a percentage of total exports, and labor force employed in
agriculture.

- In 1960, 9 percent of the gross national product
  of 19 industrial nations was derived from agricultural activities. This proportion declined
  to 6 percent by 1976. The average for Latin
  America in 1960 was 16.5 percent, down to 11 percent by 1976. Brazil derived only 8 percent of
  its GNP from agriculture in 1976, down from
  16 percent. For Mexico, the figures were 16 percent and 10 percent for 1960 and 1976 respectively.
  The production profile for these countries is approaching that of the developed industrial nations.

- Manufactures accounted for 76 percent of the 19
  industrial countries' exports in 1976, up from
  52 percent in 1960. In 1976, 52 percent of Mexico's exports were manufactures, up from 12 percent
  in 1960. Twenty-seven percent of Brazil's exports
  were manufactures in 1976, up from 3 percent in
  1960. Twenty-five percent of Argentina's exports

TABLE 2.3
Comparative Indicators of Economic Power Base Structure: Industrial
Economic, Major Latin American Economies and Other Developing Econo-
mies, 1960 and 1976

	Agriculture as a Percentage of Gross National Product		Manufactures as a Percentage of Total Exports		Percentage of Labor Force in Agriculture	
	1960	1976	1960	1976	1960	1976
Major Industrial Economies						
United States	4	3	63	69	7	4
Soviet Union	n.a.	n.a.	32	33	42	26
Japan	15	5	89	96	33	20
West Germany	6	3	87	89	14	8
France	9	6	73	76	22	14
United Kingdom	4	4	84	83	4	3
Canada	6	4	30	47	13	8
European Southern Flank						
Portugal	25	18	55	71	44	33
Spain	21	9	12	70	42	26
Italy	15	8	73	83	31	19
Greece	23	18	9	48	56	41
Major Latin American Economies						
Argentina	17	15	4	25	20	16
Brazil	16	8	3	27	52	46
Mexico	16	10	12	52	55	45
Venezuela	6	6	0	1	35	26
Other Economies						
China (PRC)	n.a.	n.a.	n.a.	n.a.	75	68
South Africa	12	9	29	24	32	31
Israel	11	8	61	83	14	10
Poland	n.a.	n.a.	38	53	48	39
India	50	47	44	45	74	69
Australia	14	7	8	17	11	8
Iran	29	9	3	1	54	46
Average: 19 industrial countries	9	6	52	76	15	11
Average: Latin America	16	11	8.8	13.1	53.6	41

Source: World Bank, 1978; Inter-American Development Bank, 1977.

26

were manufactures in 1976, up from 4 percent 16
years earlier.

● Only 15 percent of the population in the 19 industrial countries was engaged in agriculture in
1960, and this proportion dropped to 11 percent
by 1976. In contrast, over 50 percent of population in Brazil and Mexico worked in agriculture
in 1960, and this declined only by about 5 percentage points by 1976. Thus a very large part
of the populations of these countries produced a
very small part of the national product, which
indicates serious inefficiency in these sectors.

● On all indicators, Venezuela is atypical, because
of its heavy reliance on petroleum exports as a
source of foreign exchange.

Forecasts of Economic Power Base

The major economies of Latin America now have a base
from which to maintain sustained growth on a fairly stable,
long-term basis. Their continued expansion will widen the
gap between them and the less developed economies both in
the Western hemisphere and in Africa and Asia. However, a
substantial gap will still remain between the most advanced
Latin American countries and the highly developed economies. Table 2.4 gives the expected long-term average
growth rates and forecasts the size of the world's major
economies, the major economies of Latin America, and those
of several other representative countries for 1985, 1990,
and 1995. The forecast assumes a conservative average annual growth rate of 3 percent for most of the industrialized market economies unless available information suggests
this should be otherwise. Higher growth rates are used
for the developing economies and alternative forecast
rates are given for those economies for which alternative
growth scenarios can be anticipated.

The table indicates that several shifts will occur in
the ranking of countries by economic size. The United
States will remain the world's largest economy, more than
twice the size of the Soviet Union. China, which in nearly
all respects is a developing country, will experience rapid
growth and, at the least optimistic growth rate forecast
(5.5 percent a year), will surpass Japan in size by 1995,
making it the third largest economy in the world. At more
optimistic growth rates, China will be almost equal to the
Soviet Union in economic size by that date. Japan, West
Germany, and France will retain their positions in the
second tier of countries, occupying the fourth, fifth, and
sixth positions in the world ranking. The United Kingdom
and Brazil will tie for seventh position if Brazil retains
its historical (1950-1970) growth rate of 7 percent. If

TABLE 2.4

Projected Economic Size of Selected Countries for 1985, 1990, 1995 (Dollars in 1976 U.S. billions)

Country and Rank in 1976[a]	1976 GNP[a]	Average Annual Growth 1960-1976	Average Annual Growth 1970-1976	Projected Average Annual Growth	Projected Size 1985	Projected Size 1990	Projected Size 1995
United States (1)	$1,698	4.3%	2.5%	3.0%	$2,215	$2,568	$2,977
Soviet Union (2)	708	5.2	3.9	3.5	965	1,146	1,361
Japan (3)	553	10.5	5.6	3.0	722	837	970
West Germany (4)	457	4.6	2.2	3.0	596	691	801
France (5)	347	5.4	3.9	3.0	453	525	608
China (PRC) (6)	343	6.2	6.6	5.5c	555	726	949
				6.0d	579	776	1,038
				7.0d	631	884	1,240
United Kingdom (7)	225	2.9	2.3	3.0	294	340	394
Canada (8)	174	5.6	4.8	3.5	237	282	334
				4.0	247	301	367
Italy (9)	171	5.3	2.9	3.0	223	259	300
Brazil (10)	125	8.0	10.6	6.0	211	283	378
				7.0	230	322	452
				8.0	250	367	539
Spain (11)	104	7.3	5.4	6.0	176	235	315
Poland (12)	98	4.3	6.5	5.0	152	194	248
Netherlands (14)	85	5.3	3.4	3.0	118	144	149
Australia (15)	83	5.4	3.5	4.0	119	164	175
Mexico (18)	68	7.3	5.5	6.5	125	175	225
				7.0	136	200	246
				8.0			294
Argentina (23)	40	4.2	3.2	4.5	59	74	92
Venezuela (29)	32	5.9	5.3	4.0	46	55	67

[a] Rank and GNP at 1976 market prices from World Bank, 1977. In addition to those listed, the following countries rank among the largest 20 economies in the world: India (13th), Sweden (16th), the German Democratic Republic (17th), Belgium (19th), Iran (20th).

[b] Growth rates from World Bank, 1978.

[c] U.S. Congress, Joint Economic Committee, 1978.

favorable circumstances permit Brazil to overcome current
problems such as high inflation, debt, and energy dependence, it may grow again at the higher rate of 8 percent.
In this case it will easily surpass the United Kingdom in
economic size, but will still not be able to move into the
group of first six nations. Few analysts expect Brazil to
register the double-digit growth rates of the early 1970s
in the future, in part because of Brazil's energy dependence. In addition, the felicitous circumstances that permitted rapid growth in the 1960s and 1970s have been
taken advantage of and are unlikely to be repeated.

The group of upper-middle-income nations will continue to be dominated by the smaller industrial economies
of Europe, both East and West. Mexico will join this
group, however, with oil income giving it the best prospects for being one of the world's most rapidly developing countries in the next decade. Australia should also
join this group. Within Latin America, Argentina, and
Venezuela are not expected to achieve spectacular growth
rates, and their economies will fall further behind though
they will remain in their relative positions as third and
fourth largest economies in the regional ranking.

Constraints on Economic Development

Absolute economic size, as measured by gross national
product, can be a misleading indicator of economic power
base, since large countries with large populations tend
to have large national products regardless of their overall levels of development and ability to sustain growth.
India, for example, ranks among the top 20 nations in
terms of economic size (it is 13th), but is among the
poorest nations in terms of per capita wealth. The previous section indicated that the major Latin American
economies have developed a base for sustained economic
growth. In the past two decades the region has experienced the highest growth rates of any world region. Some
of the countries have achieved extraordinary growth. Between 1968 and 1973 Brazil expanded at rates exceeding
10 percent each year. Recently the Dominican Republic
recorded expansion of 12 percent (IDB, 1977) as a result
of favorable world sugar prices. If the world economy
recovers momentum in the 1980s, Mexico, Brazil, and
other economies can be expected to experience very high
growth again.

In spite of the very positive prospects for Latin
American growth in the future, a number of factors can
constrain growth potential and make it difficult for the
countries to maintain very high levels of expansion over
extended periods of time. Among the constraining factors
are high population growth rates; very high levels of
foreign debt (Mexico and Brazil alone account for

25 percent of total developing country indebtedness); low
levels of domestic savings; high rates of inflation; energy
deficits; negative trade balances; low levels of education;
and inadequate supplies of skilled labor.

These factors tend to occur simultaneously in rapidly
developing economies. They influence one another and thus
compound the dampening effect on growth; they also affect
the countries' ability to make choices in allocating national wealth. Low levels of per capita income make it
hard for these countries to generate the savings and investment earnings necessary to stimulate economic expansion, and constrain the ability to purchase either imported or domestically produced goods. Countries with low
per capita incomes cannot increase their spending on education, welfare, industrial infrastructure without causing
dislocations in their economies. Low per capita incomes
mean a low domestic tax base and low government revenues.
Growth in such countries then depends heavily on international economic conditions and on foreign investment capital or international loans. The debts thus generated
further constrain growth.

For a long time we have thought that countries with
low per capita incomes--particularly those that experience
a recent rapid rise in per capita income--tend to be politically unstable (Moore, 1966; Huntington, 1968; T.
Gurr, 1970). A rapid rise in national income creates expectations and strong political pressures within the population for distribution of the benefits of new wealth.
Authoritarian governments can limit the distribution of
wealth for long periods of time, but not forever. Over
time, pressures for change--often revolutionary change--
increase. Under such conditions, historic income concentration constrains overall growth potential. Brazil's
recent focus on income distribution can be viewed as an
effort to anticipate both of these pressures. The wide
support for the revolution in Nicaragua, and the civil
conflict in El Salvador reflects, in part, the government's
failure to do so.

Unfortunately, too rapid distribution of limited income tends to slow economic growth, at least in the short
term, by decreasing available investment capital and increasing consumption spending. Capital-intensive development and rapid growth stemming from heavy government
investment are slowed when income distribution policies
are adopted.

High population growth rates in Latin America have
dampened economic growth and permitted per capita income
to rise only slowly. Between 1960 and 1977, the Latin
American population expanded at a rate of 2.8 percent a
year, compared with 2.4 percent for developing countries

as a whole, and 1 percent for the industrial countries.
In Latin American countries, per capita income grew from
$657 for 1960 to $1,065 (1976 dollars) in 1977. The long-
term trend in per capita income growth indicates that the
regional per capita gross national product will double
over the next 25 years, from $1,040 per capita in 1975 to
more than $2,000 per capita after the year 2000. In con-
trast, the developed countries' average per capita income
is projected to increase from $6,200 to $14,302, an increase of 230 percent.

Because population growth has absorbed a large portion of the increase in regional per capita product, the
gap in standard of living between Latin America and the
developed countries widened over the last 15 years and
will continue to widen in the future, despite the very
rapid growth of individual countries within the region.
This is demonstrated in Table 2.5, which projects per
capita income growth for the major industrial economies,
for the four largest Latin American economies, and for
other selected countries of the world for 1985, 1990, and
1995. During this period per capita GNP should more than
double for the rapidly growing developing countries. However, it will change substantially less in other developing countries. The point to note, however, is that despite
the marked change in the rankings of the countries in
terms of total GNP, the countries in both groups will
continue to rank in approximately the same order in terms
of relative per capita income.

Also important to consider is that those countries
with high overall growth rates and low population growth
rates will experience the greatest real gain in wealth
per capita. For example, if historical growth rates
(7 percent) continue, per capita wealth in Spain, an
economy approximately the size of Brazil's, will improve
by only 179 percent. Mexico's per capita wealth will
grow by a similar amount at its historical growth rate
of 6.5 percent per year, and by 230 percent at the more
optimistic growth rate of 8 percent. In other developing
countries, such as India and the People's Republic of
China, rapid population growth will have even greater
dampening effects on real wealth. Even at the optimistic
growth rate of 8 percent a year (in which China's per
capita income will increase by 200 to 267 percent in constant value), China will remain among the poorer nations
of the world as measured by per capita wealth.

In sum, although the gap between the per capita
wealth of the industrial countries and that of the
middle-income developing countries will decrease over
time, it will remain significant well beyond the present
century. Per capita income is important in determining
the real expansion potential of an economy, its ability

TABLE 2.5
Forecast of per Capita Gross National Product for Selected Countries,
1985, 1990, 1995 (1976 U.S. $)

Country	Per Capita Income 1976	Projected Average Annual Growth, per Capita Income[a]	Projected Income per Capita 1985	1990	1995
United States	$7,890	2.2	$9,597	$10,700	$11,930
Soviet Union	2,760	2.6	3,477	3,953	4,495'
Japan	4,910	1.6	5,664	6,132	6,638
West Germany	7,380	2.8	9,462	10,863	12,472
France	6,550	2.2	7,967	8,883	9,904
China (PRC)	410	3.8	538	691	883
		4.3	599	739	912
		5.3	653	844	1,094
United Kingdom	4,020	2.8	5,154	5,917	6,794
Canada	7,510	2.1	9,054	10,046	11,146
		2.6	9,462	10,757	12,230
Italy	3,050	2.2	3,710	4,136	4,612
Brazil	1,140	3.1	1,501	1,748	2,036
		4.1	1,637	2,001	2,446
		5.1	1,784	2,287	2,933
Spain	2,920	5.0	4,530	5,781	7,379
Poland	2,860	4.1	4,106	5,020	6,137
Netherlands	6,650	2.1	8,018	8,896	9,870
Australia	6,100	2.5	7,618	8,619	9,752
Mexico	1,090	3.0	1,422	1,649	1,911
		3.5	1,486	1,764	2,096
		4.5	1,620	2,019	2,516
Argentina	1,550	3.2	2,058	2,409	2,820
Venezuela	2,540	1.0	2,778	2,920	3,069

Source: World Bank, 1978 and author's calculations.

[a]Calculated as projected GNP growth rates (Table 2.4) minus population growth rates.

32

to engage in capital intensive undertakings such as building sophisticated military capabilities, and the political
pressures which the population can place on government.
Therefore, in evaluating the economic power base of the
developing and nearly-developed countries, one must consider both overall economic size as measured by gross national product and availability of income as measured by
per capita wealth.

In terms of overall economic size, the large Latin
American nations most resemble the advanced developing
nations of the southern flank of Europe and the industrial
economies of Eastern Europe today (see Table 2.4). However, per capita income in all of these countries is
higher than it is in Latin America (average $2,500 as
compared with $1,200 for the major Latin American coun-
tries). All of the middle-income European countries have
population growth rates approximating the average for the
industrialized developed countries (1 percent a year) and
economic growth rates approximating 5 percent. Real wealth
will increase in these southern flank countries at a much
faster pace than in the Latin American countries over the
next 25 years. As the table indicates, per capita GNP in
Spain and Poland, for example, will approximate that of
France and Germany by 1995. In contrast, per capita
wealth in Mexico, Brazil, or Argentina will not by the
same date have reached that of Spain or Poland today.
Overcoming the dual gaps in gross national wealth and in
per capita national wealth will have to be a major goal
for Latin American political leaders in decades to come.

LATIN AMERICA'S ECONOMIC LINKAGES TO THE
INTERNATIONAL COMMUNITY

Latin America's relations with the United States and
the world outside the hemisphere are directly influenced
by the nature of economic interactions. The Latin American countries are important sources of raw materials for
the industrial economies of the world and important markets for the products of those economies. It is in the
national interest of both the industrial economies and
the Latin American nations to expand commercial relations
with traditional and new trading partners, and to keep
open the maritime routes that carry their trade.

The economic interests in Latin America are defined
in terms of (1) levels of trade, (2) levels of investment and loan exposure, and (3) dependence on critical
raw material supplies including petroleum and other industrial raw materials necessary to the performance of
the industrial economies. In each of these areas, Latin
America is heavily dependent on the United States and
other developed economies. Participation by developed

nations in the Latin American economies is much more critical to the Latin Americans. Despite their increasing
role in the world economy and their position as the most
developed of the developing regions, Latin American economies, even the major ones, continue to play a relatively
minor role in the global economy. Only in their overin-
debtedness do they have important leverage over the developed world economy.

Trade Relations

For most of the period after World War II, the United
States dominated the economic relationships of the Western
Hemisphere. For nearly a decade, however, this situation
has been changing. With the re-emergence of the European
economies, the emergence of Japan as a global economic
power, and the expansion of individual economies within
the region, Latin America's network of economic linkages
is rapidly diversifying. U.S. dominance of the trade
equation is being reduced as the Latin Americans begin to
trade more equally with the other major economic regions
of the world. Table 2.6 shows that trade relations with
the developed countries are beginning to look more like
the pre-World War II period than the postwar pattern of
U.S. dominance. Nevertheless, although the U.S. share of
the Latin American market is declining, the overall value
of U.S. trade and investment in Latin America continues to
increase, paralleling the different countries' own growth.

Continued economic growth is the principal concern
of the governments in the region and it is defined as an
integral element of their national security doctrines.
Recent rapid growth in Latin America stemmed largely from
the adoption of a new economic model emphasizing greater
trade and integration into the global economy. This new
model has replaced the closed-economy, import-substitution
model that guided development through the mid-1960s. The
new model emphasizes trade, access to foreign markets,
and acquisition of foreign exchange to purchase the capital goods and technology necessary for continued growth.
These emphases have, in recent years, caused contention
between the Latin American countries and the developed
countries. The latter are seeking to defend their own
domestic economies from competition from abroad and are
beginning to evidence concern over the developing economies' high levels of foreign debt and demands for technology transfer as conditions for multinational investments.

Over the next two decades, Latin American governments
will have to concentrate their attention on the international factors that will affect their growth. The countries still lack domestic savings and investment capital,
so sustained long-range growth requires investment by
both foreign private sources and international financial

TABLE 2.6
Percentage Distribution of Latin American Imports and Exports, 1913, 1948, 1976, and 1980

Import Source/ Export Market	Exports				Imports			
	1913	1948	1976	1980	1913	1948	1976	1980
Western Hemisphere	36.1	48.8	53.6	53.9	32.0	65.5	41.1	50.9
United States	29.7	39.2b	35.8	34.7	25.5c	52.8d	27.3	29.3
Latin America	6.2	9.3	16.7	17.8	6.1	10.9	12.8	19.5
Canada	0.2	1.3	1.1	1.4	0.4	1.8	1.9	2.1
Europe	50.9	27.8	29.8	21.6	59.8	14.5	20.7	16.2
United Kingdom	20.7	13.1	3.6	3.0	24.8	7.7	3.1	3.0
Other Europea	30.2	35.0	26.1	18.6	14.7	6.8	17.6	13.2
All others	13.0	23.4	16.6	24.4	8.2	20.0	38.1e	32.9
Total	100.0	100.0	100.0	100.0	100.0	100.0	100.0	100.0

Source: Pan American Union (1952); International Monetary Fund, 1978, 1981.

aConsists of Belgium, France, Germany, Italy, Netherlands, and Sweden.

bUruguay and Bolivia were responsible for greatest share of increase. Venezuela, Haiti, Colombia, El Salvador, and Guatemala made above-average gains.

cPrincipally from Cuba, Argentina, Brazil, and Mexico.

dPrincipally Cuba, Venezuela, Brazil, and Mexico.

ePrincipally oil-producing countries.

institutions. Latin America also must expand its exports
of traditional and, especially, nontraditional products.
In pursuing markets for their products, the Latin Americans seek increased access to their traditional markets
in the United States and Western Europe and expanded access to new markets in Japan, Canada, Asia, Africa, and
the centrally planned economies.

While the Latin Americans are in the process of diversifying their trading partners and the products in
which they trade, the overall trade equation in the region remains the traditional one in which the Latin American countries, like other developing areas, provide raw
materials (food and fuels) to industrial markets and the
developed countries provide manufactures, technology, and
equipment to the developing countries.

In seeking to expand their market shares in the industrial world, Latin American nations fight an uphill
battle. The industrial countries account for nearly
80 percent of total world trade. They represent the
largest and wealthiest markets, and primarily trade with
each other. In Latin America, only Brazil, Argentina,
and Mexico export substantial amounts of manufactured
goods. While Latin American countries depend heavily on
exports to the developed markets for their foreign exchange, the Latin American market represents an opportunity, not a necessity, for the developed countries.

The industrial economies of the Organization for Economic Cooperation and Development (OECD)[1] are the major
markets for and suppliers to Latin America. OECD countries absorbed about three-quarters of Latin America's
exports during the 1962-1976 period and supplied about
the same proportion of its imports. Table 2.7 gives the
comparative market shares for the period. It indicates
that the OECD market, particularly the European Economic
Community and the United States, has declined in importance both as a source and market for Latin American
trade. This is due principally to two factors: (1) the
increasing cost of petroleum imports from the Middle East
and Africa, and therefore greater share of import dollars
spent on petroleum and (2) greater intraregional trade.
Both these factors tend to increase the relative prepon-
derance of the "rest of the world" category in the market
share distribution. At the same time, however, the value
of Latin American trade with the OECD countries has risen
steadily and dramatically.

The OECD countries trade mainly with each other and
rely to a small extent on Latin American trade in their
overall international commerce. Table 2.8 indicates that
in 1970, 77 percent of exports and 76 percent of imports

36

TABLE 2.7
Latin American Trade With the OECD and Other World Areas, 1962-1965, 1973-1976, and
1977-1980 (Market shares in percentages)

Trade With:	Exports			Imports		
	1962-1965	1973-1976	1977-1980	1962-1965	1973-1976	1977-1980
United States	35.0	35.5	34.2	41.8	33.4	27.5
Japan	3.6	4.5	5.6	3.8	7.3	6.2
European Economic Community (EEC)	29.1	21.3	23.2	26.1	20.9	17.2
Total OECD	76.9	71.6	68.7	80.5	70.1	57.3
Rest of world	23.1	28.3	31.3	19.5	29.9	42.7

Source: Inter-American Development Bank, 1978.

TABLE 2.8
Industrialized Countries' Trade with World Regions, 1970, 1975,
and 1981 (Percentage market shares)

	All Industrial Countries[a]					
	1970		1975		1981	
	Exports	Imports	Exports	Imports	Exports	Imports
United States	12.9	13.7	9.5	11.8	11.1	11.5
Japan	3.3	4.1	3.2	4.0	3.3	5.5
European Community	51.1	48.1	37.0	36.4	36.9	33.4
Other industrial[b]	-	-	15.5	13.9	13.6	13.2
Developing countries	19.5	20.5	24.6	29.5	29.8	32.2
Latin America	5.5	5.6	6.3	5.6	6.6	6.1
Africa	3.9	5.1	5.7	5.9	5.8	6.2
Middle East	2.2	4.0	6.8	11.9	7.8	12.8
Asia	5.6	4.4	5.6	4.4	6.7	5.7
USSR and East Europe	3.5	3.1	4.2	2.7	2.8	2.6
Other	2.3	1.4	1.7	3.2	5.4	1.6

	United States					
	1970		1975		1981	
	Exports	Imports	Exports	Imports	Exports	Imports
United States	-	-	-	-	-	-
Japan	10.7	14.7	8.8	11.7	9.3	14.6
European Community	32.1	27.7	21.6	16.9	22.4	15.9
Other industrial[b]	-	-	26.7	26.4	23.7	21.8
Developing countries	28.8	26.3	38.1	42.1	40.6	44.1
Latin America	13.2	12.0	15.8	16.3	17.9	14.9
Africa	2.2	2.0	3.9	6.3	3.7	10.1
Middle East	2.3	0.9	9.0	9.4	7.3	9.4
Asia	8.5	8.5	8.2	8.9	9.8	10.9
USSR and East Europe	0.8	0.6	2.3	2.4	7.6	0.3
Other	2.6	2.9	2.5	1.7	4.3	2.1

Table 2.8 (con't.)

TABLE 2.8 (cont'd)

| | Japan | | | | | |
| | 1970 | | 1975 | | 1981 | |
	Exports	Imports	Exports	Imports	Exports	Imports
United States	31.1	29.5	20.2	20.1	27.2	17.7
Japan	-	-	-	-	-	-
European Community	14.9	10.4	10.8	6.1	13.2	6.0
Other industrial[b]	-	-	8.6	14.1	6.0	10.9
Developing countries	40.0	39.8	47.7	55.9	-	61.9
Latin America	5.1	7.1	7.6	3.9	6.5	4.5
Africa	5.6	4.0	4.4	4.1	4.9	3.2
Middle East	2.8	11.9	10.1	28.9	11.4	28.2
Asia	23.5	15.4	23.6	20.8	22.8	24.6
USSR and East Europe	5.4	4.7	4.8	3.0	2.8	1.7
Other	3.0	1.4	9.9	-	5.2	3.2

| | European Economic Community | | | | | |
| | 1970 | | 1975 | | 1981 | |
	Exports	Imports	Exports	Imports	Exports	Imports
United States	8.0	10.2	5.5	8.2	6.6	8.4
Japan	1.3	1.8	0.9	2.1	1.0	2.7
European Community	66.1	61.4	49.9	49.4	50.2	47.5
Other industrial[b]	-	-	13.9	11.3	12.5	11.8
Developing countries	15.2	17.6	24.1	25.5	25.2	25.4
Latin America	3.4	3.8	3.5	3.0	3.1	3.2
Africa	4.7	6.5	7.4	6.9	7.8	6.4
Middle East	2.3	4.1	5.7	10.6	7.5	10.2
Asia	2.5	2.1	2.9	2.7	3.4	3.4
USSR and East Europe	4.4	3.8	4.3	2.9	2.6	3.3
Other	2.1	1.1	6.0	2.4	5.3	3.1

Source: International Monetary Fund.

Notes on following page.

TABLE 2.8 (cont'd)

[a]Industrialized countries are defined by the IMF as Australia,
Austria, Belgium, Canada, Denmark, Finland, France, the Federal Republic of Germany, Iceland, Ireland, Italy, Japan, the Netherlands,
New Zealand, Norway, Spain, Sweden, Switzerland, the United Kingdom,
and the United States.

[b]Figures for Industrial Economies in 1970 include data for both the
European Community and Other Industrial countries.

of the OECD countries were traded among themselves. In
1975, these figures fell to 70 percent and 69 percent, and
by 1980, 67 percent of OECD exports and 64 percent of imports were traded within the OECD. The greatest shift in
market shares occurred in trade with the Middle East, as
a result of the increased cost of petroleum and increased
import purchasing power of the OPEC countries. Of all
the OECD members, Japan has the most trade with the developing world (40 to 50 percent of its foreign trade)--a
result of its lack of raw materials, which constitute the
principal exports of developing countries, including those
in Latin America. Japan's major trading partners in the
developing world are in the Middle East, where Iran has
been the primary petroleum supplier, and the Far East,
its own political sphere of influence and an area rich in
resources for which transportation costs for Japan are
low. Latin America's share of the Japanese market is
still quite small, though the level of trade in both directions is growing. The balance of trade still heavily
favors Japan.

European OECD countries trade mostly with one another
(over 60 percent of all trade) and although their trade
with the developing regions has increased, it is oriented
toward the Middle East and Africa, Europe's traditional
sources of raw materials. Latin America's share of the
European market has declined over the period examined in
the table from 3.8 percent to 2.8 percent of OECD Europe's
imports. The Western European economies would not seem
to offer great opportunity for expansion to the Latin
Americans in general.

Latin America continues to enjoy its greatest market
share with the United States. Over time, this share has
increased, despite the redistribution of trade that occurred with the OPEC price increase. Mexico's proximity
to the United States heavily influences the level of Latin
American trade with the United States, as Mexico is responsible for approximately 60 percent of all Latin American exports to the United States.

If Latin America plays a relatively small role in the
developed economies' trade equations, the latter are extremely important in the Latin American equation. The
distribution of trading partners for the Latin American
nations is presented in Table 2.9, which breaks the region into six subregions. Venezuela, which is included
in the Caribbean along with the island republics, accounts
for 40 percent of the trade of the subregion. West coast
South America includes all the countries from Colombia to
Chile. The South Atlantic region includes Argentina,
Paraguay, and Uruguay, but Argentina accounts for 90 percent of the trade represented by the subregion. Except
for the South Atlantic countries, Brazil, and, to a lesser

TABLE 2.9
Distribution of Latin American Trade by World Region, 1970, 1975, and 1980
(Market prices in U.S. $ millions, percentages in parentheses)

	Mexico					
	1970		1975		1980	
	Exports	Imports	Exports	Imports	Exports	Imports
Total	$1,205	$2,461	$2,859	$6,580	$15,348	$19,516
United States	847 (70.5)	1,567 (64.0)	1,667 (58.0)	4,112 (62.5)	9,688 (63.1)	12,814 (65.7)
Latin America	126 (10.5)	90 (4.0)	448 (16.0)	519 (8.0)	1,358 (8.8)	7,198 (4.1)
East Europe and Soviet Union	4 —	6 —	10 —	23 (.3)	61 (.4)	200 (1.0)
Japan	69 (6.0)	86 (3.5)	109 (4.0)	298 (4.5)	563 (3.7)	1,039 (5.3)
Africa	1 —	2 —	4 —	49 (.7)	30 (.2)	26 (.1)
West Europe and Canada	144 (12.0)	699 (27.0)	367 (13.0)	1,484 (22.5)	2,276 (14.8)	3,946 (20.2)
Other	14 (1.0)	41 (1.5)	254 (9.0)	95 (1.5)	1,372 (8.9)	693 (3.6)

TABLE 2.9 (cont'd)

| | Central America | | | | | |
| | 1970 | | 1975 | | 1980 | |
	Exports	Imports	Exports	Imports	Exports	Imports
Total	$1,200	$1,586	$2,259	$3,740	$5,934.3	$9,321.1
United States	447 (37.0)	576 (36.0)	921 (36.0)	1,238 (38.0)	2,073.5 (34.9)	2,829.9 (30.4)
Latin America	311 (26.0)	465 (29.0)	731 (28.5)	1,316 (35.0)	1,460.6 (24.6)	2,839.3 (30.5)
East Europe and Soviet Union	10 (1.0)	4 –	6 (.3)	18 (.5)	13.8 –	17.9 –
Japan	79 (7.0)	147 (9.0)	132 (5.0)	270 (7.0)	187.1 (3.2)	773.1 (8.3)
Africa	2 –	1 –	18 (.7)	2 –	4.8 –	3.8 –
West Europe and Canada	295 (24.5)	334 (21.0)	713 (28.0)	664 (18.0)	1,823.6 (30.7)	1,673.6 (18.0)
Other	56 (4.5)	59 (4.0)	38 (1.5)	232 (6.5)	370.9 (6.3)	1,183.5 (12.7)

43

Caribbean

	1970		1975		1980	
	Exports	Imports	Exports	Imports	Exports	Imports
Total	$5,387	$4,750	$18,250	$15,775	$32,566.9	$35,752.4
United States	2,260 (42.0)	1,734 (36.5)	8,569 (47.0)	4,266 (28.0)	12,715.4 (39.0)	8,364.6 (23.4)
Latin America	1,443 (27.0)	872 (18.5)	4,717 (26.0)	2,899 (18.0)	8,805.2 (27.0)	8,943.4 (25.0)
East Europe and Soviet Union	2 (–)	22 (.5)	42 (.2)	30 (–)	75.9 (.2)	58.2 (.2)
Japan	47 (1.0)	236 (5.0)	59 (.3)	677 (4.0)	741.4 (2.3)	1,429.4 (4.0)
Africa	45 (1.0)	210 (4.5)	329 (2.0)	1,334 (8.5)	197.4 (.6)	1,254.5 (3.5)
West Europe and Canada	1,471 (27.0)	1,334 (28.0)	3,709 (20.0)	3,295 (20.5)	8,751.7 (26.9)	7,222.5 (20.2)
Other	119 (2.0)	342 (7.0)	828 (4.5)	3,274 (21.0)	1,279.6 (3.9)	8,468.4 (23.7)

TABLE 2.9 (cont'd)

West Coast South America

	1970		1975		1980	
	Exports	Imports	Exports	Imports	Exports	Imports
Total	$3,416	$3,401	$5,862	$7,361	$15,564.5	$17,263.1
United States	914 (27.0)	1,086 (36.0)	1,562 (27.0)	2,573 (35.0)	4,089.2 (26.3)	5,859.7 (33.9)
Latin America	379 (11.0)	647 (21.0)	1,458 (25.0)	1,496 (20.0)	3,337.7 (21.4)	3,408.8 (20.2)
East Europe and Soviet Union	67 (2.0)	29 (1.0)	306 (5.0)	80 (1.0)	331.5 (2.1)	194.8 (1.1)
Japan	356 (10.5)	201 (6.5)	391 (7.0)	646 (9.0)	1,353.0 (8.7)	1,863.3 (10.8)
Africa	13 —	4 —	10 —	19 —	58.8 (.4)	375.2 (2.2)
West Europe and Canada	1,641 (48.0)	1,032 (34.0)	1,979 (33.5)	2,261 (31.0)	4,920.9 (31.6)	4,607.6 (26.7)
Other	46 (1.5)	42 (1.5)	156 (2.5)	284 (4.0)	1,453.7 (9.3)	884.7 (5.1)

South Atlantic

	1970		1975		1980	
	Exports	Imports	Exports	Imports	Exports	Imports
Total	$2,069	$1,986	$3,483	$4,646	$9,386.3	$13,380.4
United States	198 (9.5)	465 (23.5)	238 (7.0)	720 (15.5)	799.4 (8.5)	2,813.5 (21.0)
Latin America	429 (21.0)	477 (24.0)	1,075 (31.0)	1,161 (25.0)	2,738.4 (29.2)	2,977.9 (22.3)
East Europe and Soviet Union	102 (5.0)	29 (1.5)	352 (10.0)	109 (2.0)	1,514.5 (16.1)	106.5 (.8)
Japan	112 (5.5)	89 (4.5)	144 (4.0)	515 (11.0)	264.1 (2.8)	1,205.5 (9.0)
Africa	18 (1.0)	21 (1.0)	185 (5.0)	221 (5.0)	98.9 (1.1)	299.9 (2.2)
West Europe and Canada	1,051 (50.5)	805 (40.5)	1,136 (37.5)	1,529 (33.0)	3,051.8 (32.5)	4,803.9 (35.9)
Other	159 (7.5)	100 (15.0)	363 (10.5)	393 (8.5)	919.2 (9.8)	1,173.2 (8.8)

TABLE 2.9 (cont'd)

	Brazil					
	1970		1975		1980	
	Exports	Imports	Exports	Imports	Exports	Imports
Total	$2,739	$2,845	$8,670	$13,592	$18,361	$25,410
United States	676 (24.6)	918 (32.2)	1,337 (15.4)	3,386 (24.9)	3,636 (19.8)	4,690 (18.5)
Latin America	321 (11.7)	554 (19.4)	1,369 (15.7)	865 (6.4)	2,604 (14.2)	3,258 (12.8)
East Europe and Soviet Union	142 (15.2)	59 (2.0)	762 (8.8)	224 (1.6)	1,114 (6.1)	281 (1.1)
Japan	145 (5.2)	178 (6.2)	671 (7.7)	1,256 (9.2)	1,429 (7.8)	1,236 (4.9)
Africa	59 (2.1)	84 (2.9)	399 (4.6)	535 (3.9)	586 (3.2)	697 (2.7)
West Europe and Canada	1,290 (47.0)	1,088 (38.2)	3,378 (38.9)	4,486 (33.0)	6,846 (37.2)	5,609 (22.1)
Other	101 (3.7)	181 (6.3)	659 (7.6)	2,838 (20.8)	2,146 (11.7)	9,639 (37.9)

Source: International Monetary Fund, 1976 and 1981.

extent, west coast South America, the United States is
the principal trading partner of all the subregions. It
clearly dominates the trade pattern for Mexico with 70 percent of Mexico's exports and 64 percent of its imports in
1970. In 1976 these figures shifted as the United States
received 58 percent of Mexico's exports and provided
62 percent of its imports in 1975. U.S. oil purchased
from Mexico caused these figures to rise again in 1980,
when the United States accounted for 65 percent of Mexico's exports and provided 65.7 percent of its imports.
Intraregional trade agreements such as the Central American Common Market (CACM), the Caribbean Common Market
(CARICOM), and the Latin American Free Trade Association
(LAFTA), have resulted in substantial shares of Central
American, Caribbean, and west coast South American trade
circulating within the region. Brazil's and Argentina's
trade with "Latin America" consists primarily of trade
with each other.

Despite increasing diversification of trading partners, the U.S. and European markets, by virtue of their
very size, continue to dominate the trade patterns in
Latin America. The trade profile for Brazil, one of Latin
America's most aggressive traders, has diversified substantially, with Europe accounting for the largest share
of both imports and exports, and the U.S. share declining
sharply. Brazil's trade with the Middle East (included
in "Other") is up, but the balance is heavily in favor of
the oil-producing countries. Japan is a growing market,
as are Africa and the East European bloc, but they are
very small factors in the overall equation that links
Brazil to the developed Western economies. The United
States has nearly four times the market share of its nearest rivals, Germany (within the EEC) and Japan. After a
period of decline from the early 1960s through 1972, the
U.S. market share in the region began to improve in the
mid-1970s chiefly because the cost of U.S. goods relative
to European goods declined following the sharp decline of
the dollar in 1978.

While the OECD economies are the main trading partners
for Latin America, Latin America provided less than 5 percent of OECD imports by value in 1977, down from over
8 percent in the early 1960s. Latin America received
5.3 percent of all OECD exports in 1976, down from 6.5 percent 12 years earlier.

In recent years about 80 percent of OECD imports from
Latin America were primary commodities, particularly food
and fuels. Although OECD manufactures imports nearly
tripled in value since the beginning of the 1970s, imports
from Latin America did not rise commensurately. Latin
American manufactures exports still consist primarily of
textiles, clothing, wood, leather, and footwear, all of

which encounter increasing protectionist resistance in
the industrial countries' markets. The longer term picture is somewhat more promising. OECD imports of manufactured items from Latin America did increase substantially between 1961 and 1976, rising from 9.3 percent of
total OECD imports to 19.8 percent.

Summary

The bulk of Latin American trade occurs with the industrial economies of Europe and the United States. Maritime commerce is vital for both the Latin American countries
and the industrial economies. For the latter, the North
Atlantic and northern Pacific sea-lanes and the petroleum
supply line from the Persian Gulf around the Cape of Good
Hope are most important. Of the Latin American nations,
only Brazil depends critically on Middle Eastern or African petroleum imports and therefore on long maritime supply lines. All of Latin America depends on extended maritime links to major markets in the industrial economies.

LATIN AMERICA AND CRITICAL RAW MATERIAL SUPPLIES

Critical Materials Dependence: The Problem

The risk of absolute worldwide shortage of most essential materials except, perhaps, petroleum is slight
during this century and beyond (see Table 2.10). Nevertheless, dependence on imported materials necessary to
national economic well-being is of concern to both developed and developing countries. Because of their more
diversified and sophisticated economies, the developed
countries are more vulnerable to disruptions in raw material supplies than are the developing countries, which
tend to be the suppliers of critical raw materials.

Concern over raw material supplies focuses on the
following issues:

- Rising prices that accompany diminishing reserves,
  plus greater demand from the developed countries
  themselves;

- Potential for cartelization of selected materials,
  including copper, tin, and bauxite;

- Potential for political instability in critical
  supplier states, plus limited alternate sources
  of supply; and

- Increasing tendency for processing of raw materials to occur in the developing countries

TABLE 2.10
World Reserves and Resources of Critical Raw Materials

	World Mine Production 1977[a]	Known Reserves	Sources	Known Resources	Adequacy
Columbium	20,525	22 million	Brazil* Thailand Nigeria Canada USSR	32 million	More than adequate
Mica (sheet)	43,601	Very large	India* Brazil Malagasy West Africa Market economies Centrally planned economies (CPE's)	Very large	More than adequate
Strontium	25,850	Very large	Mexico* Spain United Kingdom CPE's Other	Very large	More than adequate
Manganese	26,400[b]	6 million	South Africa* CPE's Australia Gabon Brazil	2 million 3 million	More than adequate

TABLE 2.10 (cont'd)

	World Mine Production 1977[a]	Known Reserves	Sources	Known Resources	Adequacy
Cobalt	32,200[c]	1.6 million	Zaire* CPE's New Caledonia Zambia Philippines	5 million	
Tantalum	880[d]	130,000	Canada Zaire* Nigeria Thailand Brazil Malaysia Australia	n.a.	Adequate
Chromium	925[b]	2.7 million	Canada CPE's South Africa Europe	92 million	
Bauxite	81,000[b]	24.5 million	Guinea Australia Jamaica Brazil Guyana Market economies Morocco	35.40 billion	Adequate because of substitutes

Bismuth	9,480[d]	Australia CPE's Bolivia Peru Japan Canada Mexico	184,000	184,000 — Adequate
Platinum Group	6,400[e]	South Africa* USSR Canada	562,000	1.1-1.8 — 509 times demand
Tin	228,000[f]	Indonesia China Thailand Bolivia Australia Brazil	10.2 million	More than adequate
Mercury	240,500[g]	Spain CPE's United States Algeria Italy Mexico	5.2 million	Unknown — Adequate
Nickel	800,300[b]	Various market economies New Caledonia Canada, CPE's	60 million	143 million — Adequate

TABLE 2.10 (cont'd)

	World Mine Production 1977[a]	Known Reserves	Sources	Known Resources	Adequacy
Zinc	6,803[b]	175,000	Various market economies Canada Australia Central America Peru, Mexico	2 billion	Adequate
Tellurium	n.a.[d]	100,000	United States Rest of world		Adequate byproduct of other ???????
Selenium	2,860[d]	372,000	United States Peru Canada Chile Other	n.a.	Adequate
Antimony	73,270[b]	4.7 million	China Bolivia USSR South Africa Mexico	5.6 million	

Mineral					
Tungsten	94,640[d]	4 million	China (69%), Canada, North Korea, Brazil, Bolivia, Burma, Thailand, Australia	More than 3 times reserves in U.S. alone	Adequate
Cadmium	19,800[c]	760,000	Canada, Various market economies, CPE's, United States, Japan, Mexico	23 million	Adequate
Gold	38.49[h]	1,215	South Africa, USSR, United States	1.9 million	Adequate
Gypsum	79,300[f]	2 million		Large	
Vanadium	64,300	21.4 million	South Africa*, USSR, Australia, Chile, Other market economies	62 million short tons	More than adequate

TABLE 2.10 (cont'd)

	World Mine Production 1977[a]	Known Reserves	Sources	Known Resources	Adequacy
Iron Ore	840	254,700 million long tons +102.6 million recoverable short tons	USSR Australia Brazil Canada Others Venezuela	800 billion crudence +260 short tons iron	
Titanium	9,400	72,400	United States Japan CPE's USSR* Brazil India Australia	130 million	Adequate

Source: U.S. Department of Interior, Bureau of Mines, 1976, 1978.

[a]1,000's of pounds unless otherwise noted. [b]1,000's of short tons. [c]Short tons, metal content.

[d]1,000's of pounds, metal content. [e]1,000's of troy ounces. [f]Metric tons.

[g]76-pound flasks. [h]Million troy ounces. [i]1,000 pounds contained metal.

[j]Millions of long tons.

*Principal source.

themselves with resultant injury to the developed
countries' processing sectors.

The security implications of these concerns are two-
fold: They are economic, in that changes in patterns of
price, supply, and level of prior processing can have at
least temporary destabilizing effects on importing industrial economies; They are also defense-related, that is,
in the event of an absolute cut-off of supplies, the industrial countries have limited stockpiles which, when
depleted, would force production shutdowns and weaken the
ability to resist threat.

Proposed solutions to problems of raw materials dependency include the following:

- Conservation through diminished consumption, increased efficiency in extraction, and recycling;

- Increased domestic production and standby production potential, chiefly by raising domestic price
  levels; and

- Diversification and improved reliability of
  sources of supply.

Potentially only the United States and the Soviet
Union could become resource-independent by practicing the
first two options. The Europeans and Japanese, aware of
their inability to be self-sufficient, have adopted policies of diversification of supply sources. The policies
entail diversification of purchases and stimulation of
increased production in a variety of supply areas. The
latter policy is fully in keeping with the developing
countries' efforts to develop domestic resources and to
cultivate new and diverse markets.

The sources of raw material imports are different
for each of the major consuming areas. The United States
depends largely on Canada and Latin America (particularly
Mexico) for its mineral imports, while Western Europe
looks more toward Africa for its nonfuel raw materials.
Japan's largest nonpetroleum raw materials suppliers are
the United States, Australia, and Canada. Historical
and former colonial ties and geographic proximity account
in large part for these different supply orientations.
Table 2.10 indicates that worldwide availability of reserves for most, but not all, of the critical industrial
raw materials is such that the traditional consumer-
supplier relationships will remain largely intact, paralleling linkages between historical spheres of political
influence, geographic proximity, and transportation
costs.

56

Levels of Dependence on Imported Raw Materials

The United States and its allies in Western Europe and Japan are the world's largest consumers of raw material resources, but their resource dependency varies considerably. The United States is both a consumer and important supplier of some resources. In many areas the United States has the potential capacity for self-sufficiency. In contrast, the Western European countries and Japan are self-sufficient in virtually no raw materials. Table 2.11 indicates these countries' degree of import dependency on selected industrial raw materials. The European community is 70 to 100 percent dependent on imports from nonmember countries for most raw materials. Of the "critical" raw materials, the community can supply itself with a large part of what it needs of only two products, aluminum and iron ores, and even in these cases self-sufficiency is not economically feasible. The community imports nearly all of its chromium ore, nickel, phosphates, manganese, and tungsten and more than 90 percent of its copper and tin. Japan imports more than 90 percent of its total nonfuel raw material needs; more than half of Japan's imports are raw materials. Virtually all of Japan's oil and two-thirds of its coal consumption are imported. Japan is the world's largest importer of iron ore; Japan has virtually no iron ore (International Economic Studies Institute [IESI], 1976).

Because of the importance of raw materials, it is necessary to examine the sources of supply for critical material imports and determine the extent to which they affect the evaluation of U.S. and allied national interests in Latin America.

U.S. Critical Materials Suppliers. A recent study evaluated the degree of possible U.S. policy concern associated with selected raw material imports, based on an assessment of available reserves, potential for cartelization, lack of ready substitutes, high import dependence, and high dollar volume of imports. Table 2.12 summarizes the study's findings.

Compared with other industrial countries or regions, the United States is relatively self-sufficient in raw materials. This country imports approximately 15 percent of what it consumes in critical nonfuel materials as compared with 75 percent and 90 percent for OECD Europe and Japan (IESI, 1976).

Table 2.13 lists 28 raw materials for which the United States depends on imports for an important share of domestic consumption, and indicates the degree of import dependence and source of major supplies. The rising

TABLE 2.11
Dependence on Selected Imported Industrial Raw Materials,
1975 (Imports as a percentage of consumption)

	United States	European Community	Japan
Aluminum (ore and metal)	84	75	100
Chromium	91	98	98
Cobalt	98	98	98
Copper	(*)	98	90
Iron (ore and metal)	29	55	99
Lead	11	85	73
Manganese	98	99	88
Natural rubber	100	100	100
Nickel	72	100	100
Phosphates	(*)	100	100
Tin	84	93	97
Tungsten	55	100	100
Zinc	61	70	53

Source: U.S. Office of the President (1977).

*Net exporter.

58

TABLE 2.12
Degree of Policy Concern With Industrial Raw Material
Imports and Nature of Policy Problems

Major Concern	Moderate Concern	Lesser Concern
Bauxite/Aluminum (2,4,5,6)	Asbestos (1)	Antimony (2,5)
Chromium (2,3,4,5)	Cobalt (2,4,5)	Arsenic (5)
Copper (4,6)	Fluorspar (2,5)	Columbium (2,5)
Platinum Group (2,3,4,5,6)	Manganese (2,3,5,6)	Gold
Petroleum (2,4,5,6)	Mercury (4,5)	Iron Ore (6)
	Tantalum (2,3,5)	Lead
	Tin (2,5,6)	Nickel (2,5,6)
	Tungsten (4)	Selenium (5)
	Natural Rubber (2,4,5,6)	Silver
		Strontium (2,5)
		Titanium (5)
		Zinc (1,2,5,6)

Source: International Economic Studies Institute (1976).

Key: 1. Limited world resources
      2. Limited U.S. reserves
      3. Lack of ready substitutes
      4. Vulnerability to producer action (cartelization)
      5. High import/consumption ratio
      6. High dollar volume imports

TABLE 2.13
U.S. Import Dependence on Critical Raw Materials and
Source of Major Suppliers, 1973-1976 (Figures in parentheses are exporting country's share of total U.S.
imports)

	Net Import[a] Reliance (%)	Major Suppliers
Columbium	100	Brazil (83), Thailand (10), Nigeria (3), Malaysia (2), other (2)
Mica	100	India (73), Brazil (20), Canada (5), other (2)
Strontium	100	Mexico (85), Spain (15)
Manganese	98	Ore: Brazil (37), Gabon (31), Australia (14), Republic of South Africa (10), other (8)
		Ferromanganese: France (35), Republic of South Africa (32), Japan (14), other (19)
Cobalt[b]	98	Zaire (47), Belgium-Luxemborg (24), Norway (7), Finland (6)
Tantalum	94	Thailand (43), Canada (17), Australia (6), Brazil (4), other (30)
Chromium[b]	90	Chromite: Republic of South Africa (30), USSR (24), Philippines (18), Turkey (14), other (14)
		Ferrochromium: Republic of South Africa (34), Rhodesia (24), Japan (16), other (26)
Asbestos	85	Canada (96), Republic of South Africa (3), other (17)

60

TABLE 2.13 (cont'd)

	Net Import[a] Reliance (%)	Major Suppliers
Bauxite/ Alumina	91	Bauxite: Jamaica (48), Surinam (18), Guinea (13), other (21) Alumina: Australia (64), Jamaica (23), Surinam (11), other (2)
Fluorspar	81	Mexico (73), Spain (8), Italy (4), South Africa (3), other (12)
Bismuth	80	Peru (20), Japan (19), United Kingdom (18), Mexico (13), other (30)
Platinum Group Metals	88	South Africa (33), USSR (29), United Kingdom (23), other (15)
Tin	85	Malaysia (50), Thailand (14), Bolivia (14), Indonesia (8), other (14)
Mercury	73	Spain (27), Algeria (27), Mexico (20), Yugoslavia (19), other (7)
Nickel	71	Canada (60), Norway (7), New Caledonia (7), Dominican Republic (7), other (19)
Zinc	60	Canada (57), Mexico (15), Honduras (10), other (8)
Tellurium	-	Canada (56), Peru (32), other (12)
Selenium	58	Canada (68), Japan (11), Mexico (5), Yugoslavia (4), other (12)

TABLE 2.13 (cont'd)

	Net Import[a] Reliance (%)	Major Suppliers
Antimony	50	Metal: People's Republic of China (18), Mexico (16), Belgium-Luxembourg (13), United Kingdom (10), other (43) Ores and Concentrate: South Africa (44), Bolivia (20), Mexico (15), other (21) Oxide: South Africa (41), United Kingdom (22), France (14), People's Republic of China (8), other (37)
Tungsten	56	Canada (23), Bolivia (17), Peru (12), Thailand (11), other (37)
Cadmium	49	Metal: Canada (29), Australia (16), Belgium-Luxembourg (15), Peru (5), other (22)
Gold	60	Canada (44), Switzerland (22)[e], USSR (12), other (22)
Gypsum	35	Canada (75), Mexico (18), Jamaica (4), Dominican Republic (2), other (1)
Vanadium	38	South Africa (56), Chile (27), USSR (9), other (8)
Barite	38	Peru (31), Ireland (24), Mexico (15), other (30)
Silver	38	Canada (33), Mexico (30), Peru (13), United Kingdom (9), other (15)
Iron Ore	33	Canada (47), Venezuela (28), Brazil (12), Liberia (6), other (7)
Titanium	28[c]	Japan (52), USSR (37), United Kingdom (11)

62

TABLE 2.13 (cont'd)

	Net Import[a] Reliance (%)	Major Suppliers
Petroleum	38[f]	Crude:[g] Nigeria (18), Saudi Arabia (18), Canada (17), Venezuela (8), other (39)
		Products:[h] Venezuela (23), Netherlands Antilles (18), Virgin Islands (16), Canada (11), other (11)

Source: U.S. Bureau of Mines, Mineral Commodity Summaries, 1978.

[a]Average, 1973-1977. Net Import Reliance = imports - exports + adjustments for government and industry stocks changes.

[b]Considered a strategic import.

[c]Value for 1975. Source: Bureau of Mines, Mineral and Materials Monthly, July 1976.

[d]Imports from Norway are nickel-copper matte of Canadian origin.

[e]Swiss exports are mostly of South African origin.

[f]Import reliance has steadily increased from 35 percent in 1973 to 43 percent in 1977.

[g]Imports of crude in 1976 were 31 percent above 1973-1976 average.

[h]Product imports in 1976 were nearly 16 percent below 1973-1976 average, but 1977 imports increased by 7 percent over 1976 level.

cost of petroleum imports has been a principal source of
U.S. balance of payments problems since the beginning of
the oil crisis in 1973. In 1977 the United States paid
$44.5 billion for imported petroleum and petroleum prod-
ucts, about 30 percent of the total value of its imports
that year.

In 1977 the United States imported industrial raw
materials at a cost of $545 million (less than 1 percent
of total imports). The United States imported approximately 15 percent of its nonfuel industrial raw material
requirements, with Canada providing approximately 50 percent of U.S. needs (IESI, 1976). Canada was also the
United States' principal supplier of asbestos, nickel,
zinc, tellurium, selenium, tungsten, gold, gypsum, silver,
and iron ore (see Table 2.13). The overland transportation routes for shipment of most of these commodities are
secure, given the close politico-military relations between the two countries. Continued supply is assured
given the close economic interdependence between the
Canadian and U.S. economies.

The United States is Canada's chief trading partner,
receiving 70 percent of Canada's exports and providing
70 percent of its imports. In turn, 22 percent of U.S.
exports go to Canada and 20 percent of its imports come
from Canada. Some Canadian exports to the United States
are shipped through the Panama Canal and the security of
this trade is influenced in part by the security of that
waterway.

Mexico is the United States' second most important
supplier of raw materials in the hemisphere. Mexico is
the main supplier of fluorspar, strontium, and cadmium,
and is an important source of silver, zinc, gypsum, antimony, mercury, bismuth, selenium, barium, rhenium, and
lead.

With the advent of Mexican petroleum production and
exports, Mexico will become even more important to the
United States. It is expected that Mexico could supply
up to 2.5 million barrels per day, 30 percent of the U.S.
petroleum imports, by the mid-1980s. In addition, if
the proposed natural gas pipeline is constructed, Mexico
could supply the United States with up to 2 billion cubic
feet of natural gas per day in the 1980s and beyond. As
in the case of Canada, the supply line for these critical
imports is secure from external threat. Political decisions within Mexico and the United States determine
availability.

Venezuela is the hemisphere's third most important
supplier of raw materials to the United States; during the
1973-1976 period shown on the table Venezuela provided

28 percent of U.S. iron ore imports, 23 percent of petroleum products (28.7 percent in 1977), and 8 percent of
crude petroleum (4.6 percent in 1977). Venezuela's importance as a supplier of petroleum and products may decline
in the future as Mexican oil becomes available and as
Alaskan crude is distributed more widely throughout the
United States.

The critical raw materials considered to have major
policy concern for the industrial nations are bauxite,
chromium, copper, platinum group metals, and petroleum
(see Table 2.12). In addition to importing a significant
amount of petroleum from Venezuela, the United States relies heavily on Jamaica for bauxite/alumina and receives
about 26 percent of its copper imports (on which the
United States has a still low but rising import reliance)
from Peru and Chile. Thus Latin America is a very important source of supply of three of the five critical materials for which the United States has major policy concern.

In contrast, chromium and platinum group metals are
supplied to the industrial nations principally by South
Africa and the Soviet Union. Continued supply of these
two strategic commodities is of vital concern to the
United States and its allies because of (1) limited reserves in the Western industrial world, (2) the lack of
ready substitutes in industrial applications, and (3) vulnerability to producer political action because of the
concentrated source of supply.

Security Considerations. As just noted, concern over
raw materials supplies focuses on price stability and
availability or vulnerability to cutoff of supplies. Decisions to raise prices of raw materials would have tem-
porarily destabilizing impacts on the industrial economies, but, as the OPEC-determined oil price increases
have demonstrated, increases can be absorbed over time.
Because of their heavy dependence on imports, European
and Japanese economies are more seriously affected by
price increases than is the United States. However, the
developing world's economies have been the hardest hit of
all by the OPEC price increases. Within Latin America,
Brazil is the only major oil-importing country, and its
economy suffered a severe setback as a result of increased
petroleum import costs. The spin-offs of higher oil
prices have also affected the other countries.

The main threats to continued supply of raw materials
stem from (1) politically motivated decisions to embargo
trade with certain countries; (2) domestic political instability, which can and has caused cutoffs of mine production (as in the case of African copper and cobalt), or
interruption of internal lines of transportation to ports;

and (3) international conflict in which long sea-lines of
communication expose merchant shipping to enemy interdiction or restrict access to ports. Again, Europe and Japan
are more vulnerable than is the United States to threats
of supply disruption, and both Europe and Japan have
undertaken diversification of supply partners and creation
of stockpiles of critical materials (IESI, 1976).

International conflict that would result in a debili-
tating cutoff of supplies of critical materials almost of
necessity presumes conflict involving the superpowers.
Only the superpowers have the naval capacity to sustain
an interdiction effort over an extended period of time.

Politically motivated decisions to embargo shipments
of critical materials to selected countries would be effective against the industrial powers in the cases of
only a few materials (Table 2.10). Embargoes would have
to be coordinated among several producers including, in
the case of the most important strategic materials such
as chromium and platinum, the Soviet Union. It is generally accepted that the economic interests of materials-
exporting nations would argue against prolonged embargoes
of shipments to the Western allies, the traditional and
major markets for primary commodities. The loss of these
markets would have disastrous domestic effects in the em-
bargoing countries. For this reason an embargo would not
be expected to last long. Recent efforts to form cartels
for materials other than petroleum are instructive. Cartels have been unsuccessful because some producers have
been unwilling to withhold their commodities from the market in anticipation of higher prices (see Krasner, 1974).
The marketplace has served to extract a compromise between
exporters' demand for higher prices and importers' rejec-
tions of those prices. The importing nations have successfully found sellers at their own price levels.

Domestic political instability is a particular threat
to supplies originating in Southern Africa, if racial and
political tension continue to increase in that region.
This possibility is of particular concern to the industrial powers since, in several cases, Africa is the free
world's prime supplier of critical materials (especially
gold, platinum, chromium, and cobalt). The other major
supplier for chromium, platinum, cobalt, and many other
materials is the Soviet Union. The Soviets have ample reserves of these commodities and, assuming they were not
partners to the conflict, could supply the needs of the
West for an extended period of time.

The potential for domestic political instability in
the Middle East oil-producing countries is even more
threatening to the world economy. This possibility with

66

respect to an Arab-Israeli conflict has been amply demonstrated in the Iranian revolution that ousted the pro-Western Shah, and threatened in the Iran-Iraq war that began in 1980. The impact of prolonged reduced output on world economies--particularly on the European and Japanese economies, which receive a significant percentage of their total consumption from Iran and Iraq--is yet to be seen. Only Saudi Arabia currently has the additional pumping capacity to entirely fill the gap.

The Latin American countries are not likely to engage in embargo tactics or to experience the political instability that would shut off supplies at the source. Not only do they lack sufficient control of world supply to engage in an embargo, but also their immediate development goals do not permit them to forgo the inflow of capital and foreign exchange needed for development investment that would result from embargo activities. Moreover, their political disposition favors the Western allied community and would not lead them to impose sanctions on the allies, particularly sanctions that would cause them serious economic hardships. Only in a few countries, none of which is an important supplier of critical materials, can scenarios of political instability be envisaged that would result in a serious decrease in overall exports.

Long merchant sea-lanes could be threatened in the case of open conflict between the United States and the Soviet Union. U.S. allies would be threatened more than would the United States because of the latter's lower import reliance and the proximity of its major suppliers to critical materials (Mexico, Canada, and Venezuela). U.S. crude petroleum supplies from Africa and the Middle East could be threatened by Soviet action in the Indian Ocean, along the African coast off South Africa, or through the Atlantic narrows. In such a contingency U.S. policymakers would have to determine whether Venezuelan, Mexican, Alaskan, and Indonesian supplies could be guaranteed and whether they would be sufficient to meet U.S. and at least a part of Allied needs.

LINKAGES THROUGH INVESTMENT AND LENDING

Increasing interdependence between the developed and developing economies is measured in terms of trade flows on the one hand and financial flows--private and official investment--on the other. The influx of external financial resources to the developing countries has been a prime factor in their recent development progress, providing investment capital and foreign exchange that would otherwise not have been available in the developing world. Financial flows to the developing countries have had a significant impact on the developed economies. Credit

and investment are frequently linked to purchases of
equipment, machinery, food, technology, and management
services in the lending country. In turn, the developing
country receives technology and industrial managerial and
marketing support along with private investment. The
process thus is one of mutual benefit.

The developed countries now provide direct assistance
primarily to the poorest, or low-income (per capita income
up to $400), countries. Financial flows to the middle-
and higher-income countries consist of export credits,
private investment, and bank loans. These accounted for
two-thirds of total net flows of external resources to the
non-oil-producing countries in the period 1975-1977. The
volume and direction of financial flows provides an indication of the developed world's degree of involvement in
developing economies, as well as an assessment of those
economies thought to be the most dynamic. The available
evidence clearly demonstrates the importance of Latin
America, especially, Brazil and Mexico, in the view of
private banks and investors.

Export Credits

Export credits are a classic mechanism for financing
exports, and one of the least expensive modes of financing available to developing countries. Export credits
include loans from official export credit agencies and
private export credit with official guarantees such as
supplier of buyer credits. Between 1970 and 1980, officially supported export credits from industrial countries
grew at about 5.3 percent per year (OECD, 1982), from 2.7
billion to 14.7 billion. Most export credits are private
credits. France, Germany, the United States, and the
United Kingdom provide the majority of export credit financing. Eight countries received more than one-half of
the export credits allocated to the non-oil-producing developing countries between 1975 and 1977. These were, in
order of magnitude of credits provided, Brazil, Indonesia,
Korea, Mexico, Greece, Yugoslavia, Taiwan, and the Philippines (OECD, 1978).

Private Investment

Direct private foreign investment in the developing
countries increased at the rate of 13 percent a year between 1970 and 1976. Latin America has accounted for
40 percent of net direct investment flows in recent years.
Of the nine countries that received over half of total direct investment in 1976, six were in Latin America and the
Caribbean. In order of magnitude of investment, they were
Brazil, Bermuda, Bahamas, Argentina, Netherlands Antilles,
and Peru. Of the $76 billion book value of foreign pri-
vate direct investment in the developing countries at the

end of 1976, Mexico, Bermuda, Panama, Brazil, Venezuela,
and Argentina figured among the 16 countries accounting
for two-thirds of total investment stock. Brazil, Mexico,
and Argentina together accounted for 21 percent of all
private overseas direct investment stock in the developing
world in 1976 (OECD, 1978: Table E.1).

Table 2.14 provides data on U.S. direct private investment abroad for 1966, 1970, 1977, and 1980. The bulk
of U.S. direct investment abroad was located in the developed countries (68 percent in 1966 and 73 percent in
1977 and 1980). Canada was the largest single recipient.
Latin America, however, accounted for more than 70 percent of U.S. investment in the developing countries in
1966 and 72 percent in 1980. Within Latin America, Venezuela was the most important country for U.S. investment
in 1966 and 1970, followed by Mexico. After the nationalization of U.S. petroleum interests in Venezuela in
1976, Brazil moved into first place, with nearly twice
the level of investment that went to Mexico, and Venezuela
dropped to fourth behind Argentina.

International Bank Lending

One of the most salient changes in international economic relations over the past 15 years has been the expansion of private bank lending to the developing countries.
In the 1950s, direct investment by private corporations
was the principal means of transferring working capital
from the developed world to the developing world. In the
1960s official lending, both bi-lateral and multi-lateral,
and direct development assistance became the predominant
mechanisms for moving funds from the wealthy to the developing countries. Latin America was the major region
of focus for U.S. development assistance projects, and
countries such as Brazil, Chile, and Colombia received
42 percent of all U.S. assistance to the area. By the
late 1960s most Latin American countries had achieved an
overall level of development that no longer permitted them
to qualify for concessional assistance. However, having
established their creditworthiness and with clear indications of very bright long-term growth prospects, countries
in the region became increasingly attractive to international private capital. In the 1970s private bank lending
to the developing world expanded geometrically. The
causes of the rapid expansion were (1) the easy availability of funds because of the global economic expansion
of the 1960s and, beginning in 1973, a rapid increase in
volume of petrodollars and (2) low, even negative, interest rates.

By 1982 private banks held over $700 billion in out-
standing debt to the developing world and Eastern Europe
(Time, January 10, 1983). Brazil and Mexico held the

TABLE 2.14
United States Direct Investment Abroad, 1966-1977 (U.S. $ millions)

	1966	Percentage	1970	Percentage	1977	Percentage	1980	Percentage
All Areas	$51,792	100.0	$75,480	100.0	$148,782	100.0	$213,468	100.0
Developed Countries	35,290	68.0	51,819	68.6	108,047	72.6	157,084	73.6
Canada	15,713	30.3	21,015	27.8	35,398	23.8	44,640	20.9
Europe	16,390	31.6	25,255	33.5	60,591	40.7	95,686	44.8
Other[a]	3,187	11.9	5,549	7.3	12,058	8.1	16,758	7.9
Developing Countries	13,866	26.7	19,192	25.4	33,706	22.6	52,684	24.7
Latin America	9,752	18.8	11,110	14.7	27,739	18.6	38,275	17.9
Argentina	758	1.5	1,022	1.3	1,505	1.0	2,446	1.1
Brazil	882	1.7	1,526	2.0	5,956	4.0	7,546	3.5
Mexico	1,329	2.5	1,912	2.5	3,175	2.1	5,940	2.8
Venezuela	2,136	4.1	2,241	3.0	1,779	1.2	1,897	.9
Other Western Hemisphere[b]	1,157	2.2	1,858	2.5	9,009	6.1	12,311	5.8
Africa	1,344	2.5	2,427	3.2	2,783	1.9	6,051	2.8
Middle East	1,462	2.8	1,545	2.0	-3,083	--	2,281	1.1
Asia and Pacific	1,308	2.5	2,260	3.0	6,267	4.2	8,397	3.9
Other	2,635	5.0	4,469	5.9	7,029	4.7	3,701	1.7

Source: U.S. Department of Commerce, 1977, 1978, 1981.

[a] Japan, Australia, South Africa, and New Zealand.

[b] Offshore financial operations in Bahamas, Bermuda, etc.

[c] Panama is one of the largest recipients with Brazil, Argentina, Mexico, and Venezuela.

largest and second largest debts in the developing world,
each standing at 60 billion dollars (nearly 90 billion by
year end). Chile, with a 19 billion dollar debt but small
population base, had the highest debt per capita in the
world. Even oil-producing Venezuela became a major international debtor.

The size of the Latin American debt, especially that
of the super-debtors, Brazil and Mexico, was already a
source of concern in the mid-1970s (see OECD, 1978). In
1978-1979, the OPEC countries introduced a second series
of steep price increases that resulted in an increasingly
onerous burden for oil-importing countries. Some less
developed countries saw over half their foreign exchange
going to pay for oil imports. In 1979, a new chairman of
the U.S. Federal Reserve Bank, Paul A. Volcker, was tasked
to bring U.S. inflation under control. The clampdown on
expansion of the U.S. monetary system resulted in a steep
rise in interest rates that translated into slowed demand
in the developed world and much more onerous terms of borrowing for the developing world. Less developed country
growth slowed dramatically after 1980. Whereas expansion
had been 5 to 6 percent per year in the 1970s, it slowed
to 2.5 percent by 1981 and less than 2 percent in 1982.
By the early 1980s, the combination of prolonged inflation
and global recession and sharp drop in commodity prices
caused debt and debt service to skyrocket until even the
most economically active countries no longer could meet
payment on their debts. The second half of 1982 was a
period of crisis in international financial markets that
will not likely be resolved until the last half of the
decade.

Table 2.15 shows the evolution of the Latin American
and developing country debt over time and underscores dramatically the shift from official to private bank lending.
In the first years after the OPEC price increase of 1973,
lending to the rapidly growing developing countries, including both OPEC and industrializing oil-importing countries in Latin America, expanded dramatically. Loans
tended to be publicly guaranteed and had a maturity of
longer than one year. In 1973, 60 percent of Latin America's debt was private bank debt, a sign of the region's
earlier graduation from official assistance. By 1980,
77.9 percent of the total debt of Latin American countries
was held privately. This figure was only 58.5 for all developing countries. In 1973, bank debt accounted for 39
percent of the public debt in Latin America, but by 1977,
this figure had risen to 55 percent (Ffrench-Davis, 1982).
The bulk of private lending at that time represented syndi-
cated Eurodollar loans--recycled petrodollars. After 1977,
interest rates, which had remained remarkably stable over
the decade, particularly in light of steadily rising inflation, began to rise, making further lending more costly.

TABLE 2.15
Evolution of Latin American and Developing Countries' Debt, 1973-1980

	1973	1977	1980	Annual growth rate 1973-1977	Annual growth rate 1977-1980
Public debt (billions)					
Latin America	27.0	71.6	123.6	27.6	20.0
All developing countries	79.4	180.7	306.8	22.8	19.3
Total debt[a] (U.S. billions)					
Latin America	42.8	104.2	205.4	24.9	25.4
All developing countries	108.4	238.4	441.4	21.8	22.8
Public debt as share of total debt					
Latin America	63.1	68.7	60.2		
All developing countries	73.2	75.8	69.5		
Bank debt as share of total debt					
Latin America	60.0	70.0	77.9		
All developing countries	39.7	49.1	58.5		

Source: Ffrench-Davis, 1982.

[a]Total debt includes public debt (publicly guaranteed liabilities with maturity of more than one year), nonguaranteed debt, and bank loans with a maturity of one year or less.

This trend was enhanced by the 1979 change in U.S. monetary policy. Maturities became shorter and the amortization rates climbed steeply, bunching sharply in the first years of the 1980s. For example, the amortization rate on the commercial debt was approximately 12-13 percent in 1973, but averaged 42 percent in 1978-1980 and 46 percent in 1981 (Ffrench-Davis). World Bank data show that in 1980 over one-fourth of the total debt had to be paid annually as compared with only 10 percent in the 1960s. Table 2.15 underscores the dramatic shift in structure of the debt from long-term financing to very short-term financing. In 1980, fully 40 percent of Latin America's debt was in nonguaranteed short-term loans, whose terms of borrowing were much less favorable than those for public debt.

By year-end 1981, the International Monetary Fund (IMF) could report that 32 countries were in arrears on their debts as compared with only 15 in 1975. Poland defaulted on $2.5 billion in payments on its $27 billion debt in March of 1981, sending the first chills through the private banking system. The Polish default, coupled with continuing high interest rates and bleak growth forecasts, raised the cost of borrowing even more. In spring 1982, Argentina entered into a financial crisis. The timing of the crisis was determined by the country's extraordinary commitments during the Falkland Islands War, but Argentina's problems had been building over several years as a result of the country's economic policy and performance. Mexico, the largest Third World debtor at the time, announced its inability to pay its debt in August 1982. Brazil, which had been successfully rolling over its own financial obligations for the two years previous, suddenly found bankers to be overly cautious and funds unavailable. It too was unable to meet principal payments in December 1982 and January 1983.

United States commercial banks are the principal holders of the Latin American debt, with about 30 percent of the total. In contrast, U.S. bank exposure in Eastern Europe, the "other" trouble area for private banks, is small compared to that of European banks. U.S. banks held only 10 percent of the Polish debt, while European banks, especially West Germen banks, held the bulk of the $80 billion East European debt. The structure of trade is the most important factor influencing who lends in what region. European banks lend to East European countries because European firms sell their goods to the Eastern European countries. The United States holds over 30 percent of the import market in Latin America, more in countries like Mexico (65 percent), or in Central America (40 percent), and consequently U.S. banks hold a proportionately larger share of those countries' debt. Table 2.16 shows the total debt of the major Latin American countries for

TABLE 2.16
Latin American Foreign Debt Indicators
(U.S. $ billions)

	External Debt			Percentage of 1982 Debt Owed to U.S. Banks	Total Debt Service as Percent of Exports		
	1980[a]	1981[b]	1982[b]		1980	1982	1983
Argentina	$12.2	$35.6	$43.0	35%	19.9%	31%	154%
Bolivia	2.9	3.8*	3.1	--	26.2	65	118
Brazil	51.5	61.4	87.0	37	36.1	67	117
Chile	5.1	12.6	17.2	52	23.5	46	104
Colombia	6.7	8.5	10.3	55	11.2	19	95
Costa Rica	2.4	3.8	--	13	16.7	43	--
Dominican Republic	1.7	2.1	--	24	12.8	25	--
Ecuador	3.7	5.6	6.6	47	14.4	53	102
Honduras	1.6	2.0	--	37.5	10.2	22	--
Jamaica	1.7	2.0*	--	10	13.1	27	--

TABLE 2.16 con't.

	External Debt			Percentage of 1982 Debt Owed to U.S. Banks	Total Debt Serivce as Percent of Exports		
	1980[a]	1981[b]	1982[b]		1980	1982	1983
Mexico	$39.0	$73.0	$80.1	39%	33.2%	40%	126%
Peru	8.4	8.8	11.5	44	32.7	45	79
Venezuela	11.1	26.0	29.5	37	14.8	28	101

Source: Inter-American Development Bank, 1982: Table 55 (1980 data); deVries, 1983; Time, January 10, 1983.

[a]Public debt does not include short-term debt with less than one year maturity.

[b]Gross public debt includes short-term debt.

debt service ratio, or payments due on the debt as a percent of exports (which provide dollar earnings to pay off
the debt). A comparison of the level of external debt in
1980 and 1983 shows that some countries like Brazil, Colombia, and Peru were more cautious in expanding their indebtedness than others. Brazil's debt expanded by 60 percent, as did Colombia's and Peru's. In contrast, Venezuela's debt and Argentina's almost trebled between 1980
and 1982; Chile's debt multiplied 240 percent; Mexico's
by 100 percent.

The very high debt service ratios mean that the Latin
American countries will have to reduce their imports
sharply to meet commitments to the international financial
system. This in turn will cause dramatic slowdowns in
their own industrial growth and a concomitant reduction in
demand for manufactured goods in the industrial countries
(the United States sells 40 percent of its total exports
to developing countries; OECD countries as a whole sell
30 percent of their exports to the Third World). One U.S.
bank has estimated that a halving of new lending to the
non-oil developing countries would cost approximately 1.5
percentage points in growth in those countries, and .5
percentage point in the industrial countries. It is
widely recognized in both developed and developing world
capitals that the key to the 1980s debt crisis is renewed
industrial country growth, which in turn would fuel developing country growth and bring about a slow evolution toward the more bouyant economic scenarios that characterized the late 1960s and earlier 1970s.

NOTE

1. This discussion of OECD-Latin American trade is
based on Inter-American Development Bank, 1978.

76

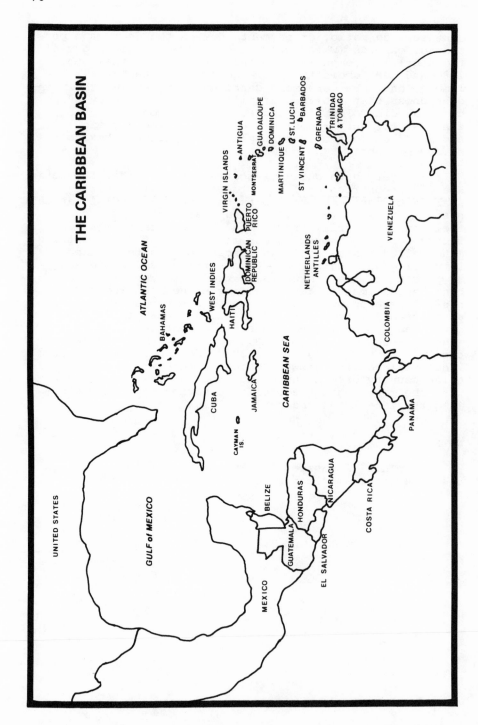

THE CARIBBEAN BASIN

3
The Caribbean Basin:
Focus of Immediate Concerns

The Caribbean basin[1]--Central America to Panama, Colombia, Venezuela, and the West Indian island states that
rim the eastern and northern Caribbean sea--is the principal focus of U.S. political and security interest in
the Western Hemisphere. U.S. interest in the region derives from four sources:

1. The area constitutes the presumably "vulnerable"
    southern flank of the United States over which
    this country has felt obliged to extend its in-
    fluence since the early nineteenth century and
    especially since the decision to build the Panama
    Canal.

2. The region is the poorest and most politically
    unstable in the hemisphere, with a high potential
    for spawning anti-U.S. regimes that might offer
    a base for the expansion of Cuban or Soviet
    activities.

3. The Caribbean is the location of military instal-
    lations necessary for defending the continental
    United States and for monitoring worldwide
    events, including Soviet military movements. The
    Caribbean is also the channel for a substantial
    share of United States trade (including crucial
    petroleum supplies), the locus of important re-
    fineries, and the source of materials necessary
    to both industrial and military capabilities.

4. Since the Cuban revolution of 1959, a potential
    direct threat to the United States exists off
    the U.S. coast. Through its alliance with Cuba,
    the USSR has the opportunity to monitor U.S.
    merchant and military shipping movements. The
    USSR also uses Cuba as a base for staging and
    refueling its own ships and aircraft. The Soviet

77

relationship limits U.S. options in dealing with Cuba.

Although the Caribbean basin is the area of greatest direct concern and traditional U.S. interest in Latin America, with the exceptions of Mexico, Venezuela, and Cuba, the region is politically unimportant in the broader world community. Only Mexico and Venezuela are significant economic powers on either a regional or world scale. Venezuela's economic power derives almost exclusively from petroleum, and Chapter 3 demonstrates that Mexico's economic power base is increasingly influenced by petroleum. Venezuela's easily accessible crude reserves are expected to last about fifteen to twenty years at current production rates. However, technology is now available and prices now make it economically feasible to develop the Orinoco heavy oil belt. Tapping the Orinoco oil, one of the world's largest reserves, will extend Venezuela's energy resource well into the next century. In comparison, other Caribbean basin countries have only a limited importance in the region. Panama is important to the United States almost exclusively because of the Panama Canal, which has a limited useful life. The United States is concerned about Cuba because of that country's links to the Soviet Union; because the Soviet Union can use Cuba as a base from which to monitor U.S. military operations on the U.S. southern flank; and because of Cuba's efforts to foster revolutions in other Western Hemisphere countries. The island nations of the Eastern Caribbean have minimal projection beyond the region and world attention has focused on the Central American countries only because of the turmoil that has embroiled the region in the last five years.

This chapter deals with the Caribbean basin as a single entity. Although this approach is realistic from the perspective of U.S. security interest, the region is far from unified either politically or economically. Several distinct subdivisions exist, including Central America; Venezuela and north coast South America; and the smaller island communities. In addition, Mexico and Cuba play important roles within the region.

Interactions among the subdivisions have traditionally been limited for a variety of reasons, including the cultural and historical backgrounds of the Commonwealth Caribbean countries,[1] the smaller countries' fear of domination or absorption by large countries, language differences that separate the Spanish-speaking, French-speaking, and English-speaking Caribbean, and economic similarities that force competition for the same markets and reduce trade within the region. Indeed close examination shows that each of the countries in the Caribbean basin has its own unique history and unique set of problems to resolve. Nevertheless, the countries of the region are also linked

in a special way by the common body of water, by common
economic problems, and by the common proximity to and dependence on the United States.

The Caribbean basin is distinctly important to the
United States because of its location at the U.S. southern flank, because it is a major shipping route to U.S.
ports and the channel of access to the Panama Canal from
the Atlantic Ocean. As a consequence, the Caribbean basin
has traditionally been the area of Latin America to draw
the most direct U.S. attention. The region was of concern when the Monroe Doctrine was announced in 1823. Central America was the focus of concern that led the United
States and Great Britain to negotiate the Clayton-Bulwer
treaty limiting each country's right to exclusive con+
of a Central American canal. By the end of the nineteenth
century, and especially in the aftermath of the Spanish
American War, Alfred Thayer Mahan's theories of the importance of sea power renewed interest in an isthmian canal
that would link the Atlantic and Pacific coasts and provide a more rapid route to newly acquired U.S. possessions
in the Philippines. The 1901 Hay-Pauncefote treaty abro-
gated Clayton-Bulwer and gave the United States exclusive
freedom to build a canal. Once the canal was built, U.S.
interest in its defense led to a broadening of security
focus to include the entire Caribbean basin. The Panama
Canal served primarily a military function up to and
through World War II. The whole Caribbean basin became
an important focal point of U.S. security interest immediately prior to and during World War II, as defense
planners sought to defend not only the continental United
States, but also other nations in the Western Hemisphere,
from the advances of the initially technologically superior German forces. As European powers fell before the
onslaught of the German army, the defensive positions in
the Caribbean gained importance (see Stevenson, 1976, for
an account).

The United States has intervened militarily in the
subregion on numerous occasions in defense of its perceived interests. Prior to the United States' 1934 declaration of nonintervention under the Good Neighbor Policy,
most interventions occurred in defense of private economic
interests or the security of the Panama Canal. Interventions took place in Mexico, Cuba, Panama, Haiti, the Dominican Republic, Nicaragua, Honduras, and Guatemala (Atkins, 1977). After World War II, the United States again
adopted an official policy of nonintervention in Latin
American regional politics. Numerous government changes
occurred to which the United States was an interested but
(overtly) nonparticipating observer. Cold war concerns,
however, led the United States to participate in over-
throwing the apparently leftist-leaning Arbenz government
in Guatemala in 1954, to support Cuban exiles' invasion of

Cuba in 1961, and to land troops in the Dominican Republic
in 1965. Similar concerns underlie U.S. interest in
events in Nicaragua, El Salvador, Guatemala, and Honduras
today.

With few exceptions, such as Venezuela, Mexico, Costa
Rica, Jamaica, and Barbados, the countries of the Caribbean basin are among the least politically developed in
Latin America, and this has contributed to the region's
chronic instability. Until recently, most governments in
Central America have been traditional, conservative dictatorships. Costa Rica and perhaps Panama have the most
open political systems. Honduras has only recently begun
to emulate this style. In the Caribbean, after more than
fifteen years of efforts to build democratic institutions,
a stable, democratic system seems to have emerged in the
Dominican Republic that permits transfer of power from
one party to another.

In contrast, Haiti, which shares an island with the
Dominican Republic, remains a personalist dictatorship.
After eight years experimenting with an increasingly unstable left-leaning government and increasing political
instability and economic insolvency, Jamaicans returned a
conservative leadership to office in 1980 when Edward
Seaga's Jamaica Labor Party captured 51 of the 60 seats
in the Parliament. The small island states in the West
Indies are only recently independent from European colonial rule and have little experience in self-government.
New political forces have emerged in many of those tiny
nation states that will sorely test the flexibility of
the inherited Westminster parliamentary system. Guyana
on the coast of South America and Grenada have both
adopted militant Marxist postures, threatening the political tranquility of the region.

The Caribbean basin also includes some of the least
economically developed countries in the hemisphere and
unemployment, underemployment, and poverty are widespread.
Haiti is clearly the poorest country in the region with a
per capita income of only $270 (World Bank, 1982). Per
capita income in Honduras, the hemisphere's second poorest country, is only $560. In the Eastern Caribbean is-
lands income per capita ranges from only $520 (St. Vin-
cent and the Grenadines) to $4,370 (Trinidad and Tobago),
and the tiny island states all have incomes under $1,000
per head. In most of the Caribbean countries, growth
stagnated and incomes began to decline in the 1970s as
the rising cost of energy imports began to tax their fragile economies.

As a result of their backward political and economic
conditions, all of the Caribbean basin countries have considerable potential for social and political unrest. The

lack of political and administrative experience in the
area, and the uncertainty of economic conditions, make
remedies to regional problems more difficult to find and
implement. Leftist appeals for more equitable participation in economic development are heard with sympathy among
the disadvantaged masses of the Caribbean population.
U.S. attention will increasingly be drawn to domestic crises in this region.

As already noted, with the special exception of Mexico, Venezuela, or Cuba, the Caribbean basin countries are
not politically important on a world scale. However, the
presence in Cuba of a hostile Marxist-Leninist government
poses the most serious political problem for the United
States in the hemisphere, one that has troubled U.S. administrations for more than twenty years. The United
States regards the potential establishment of additional
anti-U.S. or pro-Soviet Marxist-Leninist regimes in the
Caribbean basin as posing an intolerable threat to the region and to this country. This attitude is directly challenged by Cuba's longstanding commitment to provide fraternal support to revolutions wherever and whenever they
may occur.

The breakdown of U.S. leadership in the region that
would be symbolized by the shifting of political alle-
giances to anti-American powers would be both politically
embarrassing for the United States and would likely lead
to further political instability in the region. At the
same time, however, the United States can take confidence
in the knowledge that no external power, including the Soviet Union, could likely support several other states in
the Caribbean in the way the USSR presently supports Cuba.
This would especially be true if the United States were to
impose an economic embargo on unfriendly governments as it
has on Cuba. Since the Caribbean countries are heavily
dependent on the U.S. economy, it would not be in the
long-term economic interest of those countries to lose
either access to U.S. markets or to investments by U.S.
firms and banks. This recognition serves as a brake on
more extremist elements engaged in political struggles
in the region and complicates the political position of
the revolutionary movements in the region.

Only Venezuela and Cuba have substantial military
power in the region, and Cuba's military potential far
surpasses that of Venezuela. Mexico has explicitly
chosen not to develop a large military power base for
historical reasons and because its proximity to the United
States allows it to depend on the U.S. umbrella for military protection. Military activities throughout the region consist chiefly of coastal patrol of illegal activities (smuggling of drugs and contraband) and maintenance
of domestic stability. The latter has gained new

importance in recent years and has stimulated interest in
modernizing forces and equipment and upgrading training.

     With the United States' overwhelming economic superi-
ority, U.S. economic interests in the Caribbean basin seem
to be relatively minor. With the exception of petroleum,
the countries of the region provide no vital resources to
the United States for which substitutes are not available
elsewhere and not far from home. The Panama Canal is an
important commercial asset to the region, but adaptations
in commercial trade patterns could be made should it become obsolete or threatened. More importantly for assessing the security of U.S. economic interests, commercial
relations with the United States are essential to the economic well-being of the Caribbean basin countries and
should be maintained and strengthened over time even as
the countries seek to diversify their trading partners and
to reduce their dependence on the United States. The U.S.
market promised in the recent Caribbean Basin Initiative
offers the greatest promise to the stagnant economies of
the region in the near- and medium-term.

     None of the countries in the Caribbean basin poses a
military threat to the United States. Even in the case of
Cuba, the threat is potential and derives from Soviet support for Cuba, not directly from Cuba itself. Although
Cuba and the Soviet presence in Cuba may pose a potential
threat to the United States, the implications of exercising any attack capability would be extraordinary and are
not lost upon either country. Cuba serves to tie up U.S.
forces needed to monitor events there rather than pose a
direct threat to this country. Similarly, the Soviet
Union to date has tended to abide by agreements reached
in 1962 with the United States following the Cuban missile
crisis, and has not sought to introduce offensive weapons
into Cuba. The agreements have nevertheless been tested
on various occasions, most recently with the introduction
of Soviet MIG-23 jets into Cuba.

     Political instability and unpredictability in the
Caribbean basin pose the most serious threats to U.S. interests. Poverty, economic stagnation, and political
weakness make the region ripe for instability. While few
policymakers anticipate an active Soviet presence in the
region in the near term, manipulation of regional political and economic weaknesses have been regarded as fair
challenge to the United States in its sphere of interest.
Such provocations are intended to embarrass the United
States and to maintain regional tensions at a high and
unstable level. Unfavorable outcomes to the search for
regional stability and prosperity could result in the loss
of U.S. installations in the region and in the emergence
of anti-American governments. Such a turn of events would
make U.S. relations in the region infinitely more

difficult, complex, and costly, long before the area became host to hostile military bases. The selection of appropriate responses to political instability and to emerging ideological diversity in the Caribbean region is one
of the most serious policy challenges the United States
faces in that region.

ECONOMIC POWER BASE AND ECONOMIC LINKAGES
IN THE CARIBBEAN BASIN

The Caribbean basin represents an economic power base
about the size of a Switzerland, a Belgium, or a Mexico;
the gross regional product was approximately $125 billion
in 1980. The economic structures within the region are
nevertheless quite different from those industrialized
states. Venezuela alone accounts for over half of the
gross regional product. Petroleum is the region's most
valuable export, but this is concentrated in only two countries, Venezuela and Trinidad and Tobago. In addition,
The Bahamas, The Netherlands Antilles, Trinidad and Tobago, and Barbados all have major refineries that process
African and Middle Eastern oil for the U.S. market. Most
of the region's trade is in agricultural commodities such
as coffee, sugar, and bananas and in raw materials such
as bauxite. The United States is the region's major trading partner, receiving about 40 percent of its exports and
providing 30 percent of its imports in recent years (see
Table 3.1). Europe and other Latin American countries are
the next most important trading regions. With few exceptions, the Caribbean basin economies are weak and highly
sensitive to changes in demand in the developed countries.
Forecasts for economic growth and stability are not optimistic, and these continuing economic difficulties strongly
influence prospects for political stability in the future.

During the 1970s the Caribbean basin countries sought
to diversify their markets and suppliers to minimize their
trade dependence. Caribbean and Central American integration movements were intended to improve intraregional
trade and division of labor and to reduce dependence on
the single major market and source of investment capital
that the United States has traditionally represented.
The Venezuelan-led SELA[2] movement had a similar goal for
the entire hemisphere. Diversification of trade partners
is viewed as a crucial element in the export-led development model now adopted by most Latin American countries
(see Chapter 2). Nevertheless, in the case of the Caribbean basin economies, the United States will remain a
major market for the foreseeable future. At the same
time, development of the regional economies will serve to
guarantee a continued and expanding regional supply of
critical materials to the United States. In the event of
global conflict, the proximity of these countries to the

TABLE 3.1
Caribbean Region Trade with World Regions, 1970, 1975, and 1980
(Market prices in U.S. $ millions, market shares (in parentheses))

	Exports											
	Venezuela			Central America			Islands			Regional Total		
	1970	1975	1980	1970	1975	1980	1970	1975	1980	1970	1975	1980
Total	3,207	8,498	18,128	1,200	2,259	5,444	2,180	9,752	16,158	6,587	20,589	39,730
United States	1,215 (37.9)	3,260 (42.6)	5,571 (30.7)	447 (37)	921 (36)	2,369 (43.5)	1,045 (48)	4,949 (51)	8,459 (52.3)	2,707	9,490	16,399
Western Hemisphere	1,094 (34.1)	2,609 (30.7)	7,207 (39.8)	311 (26)	731 (28.5)	1,244 (22.9)	349 (16)	2,108 (22)	1,883 (11.7)	1,754	4,448	10,334
European Community and Canada	850 (26.5)	2,192 (25.8)	4,198 (23.1)	295 (24.5)	713 (28)	1,372 (25.2)	621 (28)	1,517 (16)	2,769 (17.1)	1,766	4,422	8,339
Japan	22 (.7)	34 (.4)	695 (3.8)	79 (7)	132 (5)	130 (2.4)	25 (1)	25 (.2)	89 (.6)	126	191	914
Africa	16 (.5)	25 (.3)	91 (.5)	2 (-)	18 (.7)	2 (-)	29 (1)	304 (3)	356 (2.2)	47	347	449
East Europe and Soviet Union	--	--	3 (-)	10 (1)	6 (.3)	7 (.1)	2 (-)	42 (.4)	62 (.7)	12	48	72
Other	10 (.3)	17 (.2)	363 (2.1)	56 (4.5)	38 (1.5)	320 (5.9)	109 (5)	811 (8.3)	2,540 (15.7)	175	866	3,223

TABLE 3.1 (cont'd)

	Venezuela			Central America			Islands			Regional Total		
	1970	1975	1980	1970	1975	1980	1970	1975	1980	1970	1975	1980
Total	1,780	4,939	9,791	1,586	3,740	6,997	2,970	10,836	16,374	6,336	19,515	33,162
United States	863 (48.5)	2,242 (45.4)	4,577 (46.7)	576 (36)	1,238 (38)	2,652 (37.9)	871 (29.3)	2,024 (18.7)	2,646 (22.3)	2,310	5,504	9,785
Western Hemisphere	80 (4.5)	351 (7.1)	1,059 (10.8)	465 (29)	1,316 (35)	1,894 (27.0)	792 (26.7)	2,548 (23.5)	2,152 (13.1)	1,337	4,215	5,105
European Community and Canada	655 (36.8)	1,827 (37.1)	2,815 (28.8)	334 (21)	664 (18)	862 (12.3)	679 (22.9)	1,468 (13.5)	3,158 (19.3)	1,668	3,959	6,835
Japan	140 (7.9)	360 (7.3)	838 (8.6)	147 (9)	270 (7)	382 (5.5)	89 (3)	317 (2.9)	794 (4.9)	376	947	2,014
Africa	5 (.3)	15 (.3)	50 (.5)	1 (-)	2 (-)	2 (-)	205 (6.9)	1,320 (12.2)	2,185 (13.3)	211	1,337	2,237
East Europe and Soviet Union	12 (.7)	25 (.5)	19 (.2)	4 (-)	18 (.5)	19 (.3)	18 (6.1)	5 (-)	33 (.2)	34	48	71
Other	23 (1.3)	114 (2.3)	433 (4.4)	59 (4)	232 (6.5)	1,186 (17)	319 (10.7)	3,160 (29.2)	4,406 (26.9)	401	3,506	6,025

(Imports)

Source: United Nations Yearbook of International Trade Statistics (various years); International Monetary Fund, Direction of Trade Statistics (various years).

United States would enhance security of ocean transport routes, and supplies could be readily diverted to meet the needs of the United States.

Principal Economic Linkages

The island economies. The island states of the Caribbean include some of the poorest countries in the hemisphere, as well as some of the better off. Of the nineteen independent states, Commonwealth countries, colonies, and territories, small size is the most salient common characteristic and the principal obstacle to growth and development. Populations range from a few thousand, as in Antigua (75,000), Dominica (83,000), or St. Kitts-Nevis (50,000) to over five million in the Dominican Republic, the largest population among the islands. Population growth rates are modest in the English-speaking Caribbean, in part because of very high rates of outmigration to U.S. territories and to the United States itself. The Dominican Republic retains a high population growth rate (3 percent) in spite of its heavy outmigration. In 1980 Gross National Products in the region ranged from $50 million in St. Kitts-Nevis and Dominica to $2.9 billion in Trinidad and Tobago and $6.2 billion in the Dominican Republic.

In 1980, per capita GNP ranged from $270 in Haiti, the poorest country in the hemisphere, to $620 in Dominica, the poorest island in the English-speaking community, to $4,370 in oil-producing Trinidad and Tobago. Montserrat, Guadeloupe, and the Netherlands Antilles are still possessions of European powers, and all have per capita incomes higher than those of the newly independent states.

Growth measured by change in per capita GNP has been low to negative in most of the region. The Bahamas, Dominica, Grenada, Jamaica, and St. Vincent all experienced net negative growth from 1970-1979 (Inter-American Development Bank, 1982). Many other countries showed barely positive growth.

The principal economic linkages of the Eastern Caribbean countries are, in order, the United States, the European Community, and neighbor economies. The principal market for all the countries is, increasingly, the United States. For example, in 1981 75 percent of Dominican Republic exports (almost exclusively sugar) went to the United States; 78 percent of Haiti's exports and 37 percent of Jamaica's went to the United States. In the Commonwealth Caribbean, a favorable arrangement with the European Community through the Lome Conventions have kept the European market open to agricultural exports from the Caribbean on a preferential basis. Nevertheless, declining production in traditional agricultural exports has been translated into failure to meet quotas in the past decade. In 1981, Barbados and Jamaica both exported about 38 percent of their total exports to the United States. Barbados sent only 8 percent of its exports to the European Community, while Jamaica sent about 20 percent of its export trade (mostly sugar) to the Community. Many of the producers of sugar, bananas, etc., in the Eastern Caribbean are meeting increasing competition from Central American producers.

Industrial imports to the Caribbean come largely from the United States and all of the countries depend heavily on Venezuela, Trinidad and Tobago, and the Netherlands Antilles for their petroleum needs. Petroleum is the principal commodity in intraregional trade.

One of the principal exports of the Caribbean island states is sugar, and sharp fluctuations in the world price for this commodity have had profound impact on the economic performance of many of the Caribbean countries. Approximately 60 percent of Caribbean basin sugar exports are destined for the United States, and the United States is the principal market for all of the countries not members of the Lome Conventions of former European colonies in Africa, Asia, and Latin America. The United States imports approximately 45 percent of its sugar requirements, about 20-25 percent of this coming from the Caribbean basin countries. A price support program for the U.S. domestic industry blocks additional imports from sugar-producing countries. The European Community, a major producer of beet sugar, receives about 30 percent of Caribbean sugar exports under prearranged quotas. Panama, El Salvador, and Honduras sell all of their sugar exports to the United States, while the U.S. takes over three-quarters of the production of the Dominican Republic, Guatemala, and Nicaragua.

In the 1970-1974 period, sugar accounted for 48 percent of the Dominican Republic's total exports, 35 percent of Barbados' exports, and 35 percent of Guyana's. By 1980, both deterioration of domestic sugar industries and diversification into other commodities had reduced these figures so that despite the fact that 1980 sugar prices were the highest in a decade, sugar represented only 23 percent of Barbados' exports, and 30 percent of the Dominican Republic's and Guyana's. In the smaller and less diversified economies, like St. Kitts', sugar continues to account for upward of 70 percent of total exports, and employs nearly 40 percent of the labor force.

The world sugar industry experienced a sharp deterioration after an unusual high in 1980. Prices that had been as high as 70¢ per pound on the international market in late 1974 (Latin America Commodities Report, 9 May

1980) fell to 7¢ per pound in 1982, while production costs remained in the range of 15-19¢ per pound. Both oversupply of cane and beet sugar and increasing competition from high fructose corn syrup sweeteners contributed to the dramatic fall in prices and both of these trends are expected to continue over the long term. The loss of hard currency export revenues over the 1981 and 1982 time frames had a profound impact on the fragile economies of the region, making their adjustment to the prolonged global recession and spiraling oil prices almost impossible.

Another factor affecting the Caribbean small-state economies is their dependence on petroleum imports. Petroleum and petroleum products imports accounted for a quarter of the Dominican Republic's imports, 15 percent of Haiti's, 16 percent of Barbados', and 32 percent of Jamaica's in 1981. Some of the smaller islands have installed hydroelectric capacity and others, like the Dominican Republic, may be able to diversify into hydroelectric and coal power electricity generation. In most cases, however, present capacity is in need of modernization and expansion before it can substitute petroleum imports.

Of $16 billion in goods imported by the United States from the Caribbean basin in 1980, $11 billion were in petroleum and petroleum products from the oil-producing and -processing countries. Venezuela is the United States' major trading partner in the region and accounts for one-third of U.S. imports from the area and nearly half of U.S. exports to the Caribbean. Because of the high value and volume of U.S. petroleum imports, Venezuela ranks eighth in order of suppliers of U.S. imports of all kinds. Trinidad and Tobago, the major source of imported petroleum products from the region, ranked twentieth among U.S. trading partners in 1977. Nevertheless, regional petroleum and petroleum products shipments to the United States represented about 15 percent of all U.S. imports of these commodities in 1981 (U.S. Department of Commerce, 1982).

Bauxite/alumina is the only other critical resource the United States derives from the Caribbean area. Jamaica, the principal supplier, has sufficient reserves to last 100 years at 1974 extraction rates (IDB, 1977). Guyana and Suriname on the coast of South America also supply the United States, but Jamaica holds a larger market share in this country. Regional bauxite/alumina production would be critical to the United States in an emergency, but in the global market it encounters increasing competition from Guinea and Australia, each of which has one-fourth of world reserves. Brazil, whose large bauxite deposits were only discovered in 1967, has nearly twice the reserves of Jamaica (U.S. Bureau of Mines, 1976) and will provide increasing competition in the present decade

if prices improve. Recently Venezuela also has discovered
a major bauxite deposit in the Ciudad Guayana region.
With one-fourth of world bauxite reserves in the Western
Hemisphere, supply of this critical resource is readily
guaranteed to the United States for a very long time, and
sea lines of transportation are relatively secure because
of proximity.

Because of their obvious dependence on one or two
export products, the Caribbean basin countries are keenly
aware of the need to diversify production. The major obstacles to these efforts have been the absence of assured
markets, lack of adequate transportation and storage infrastructure, and, until recently, the absence of real
incentives to mobilize domestic resources.

The oil shock of the 1970s, coupled with the disastrous decline in sugar incomes and dramatic shift by several import markets to higher quality banana production
in the aftermath of several destructive hurricanes in the
late 1970s have awakened both governments and entrepre-
neurs to the need to engage in a long-term economic planning. Very different countries like Barbados and Haiti
have had important successes in establishing component
assembly industries that employ large numbers of people.
Inadequate transportation facilities and small size constrain other Eastern Caribbean countries from promoting
similar industries. The Dominican Republic has had success in textile and component assembly operations in its
two duty-free industrial zones (zona franca). In 1981
and 1982, the Caribbean island leaders were among the
most enthusiastic supporters of an enlarged U.S. Caribbean economic development policy under the Caribbean Basin
Initiative.

The Central American economies. The economic basis
of the Central American countries, Panama, Costa Rica,
Honduras, El Salvador, Nicaragua, and Guatemala, is substantially larger and has greater potential than that of
the small island states. The Central American regional
product is fully half the gross product of the entire
Caribbean basin. Individual country GNPs in 1980 ranged
from $160 million in tiny and newly independent Belize,
to $7.8 billion in Guatemala, the largest economy, twice
the size of its nearest competitor, Costa Rica, whose national product was only 3.8 billion. Honduras, El Salvador, and Nicaragua are all small economies with GNPs of
less than $3 billion, and have some of the lowest per
capita incomes in the hemisphere.

The Central American countries experienced rapid
growth in the late 1960s and early 1970s, ranging from
6.5 percent (Costa Rica), 5.9 percent (El Salvador),
5.3 percent (Honduras), and 7.3 percent (Nicaragua).

Beginning in 1960 five countries in the region formed a
Central American Common Market (Panama did not join the
market*) to foster development through import substituting industrialization and intraregional trade. During
the 1960s, the market's expansion was dramatic; however,
by the late 1960s, the limits of the import substituting
industrialization model in the regional context became
apparent and growth began to slow. Because of past buoy-
ancy, the countries were nevertheless able to absorb the
first oil price increase in 1973, but heavy borrowing, a
sharp decline in the price of coffee in the 1978-1979 period, and subsequent 1979-1980 oil price increases set
the regional economies into a tailspin. Since 1977, regional instability in Nicaragua and El Salvador has further exacerbated the economic downturn by creating in-
vestor uncertainty and prompting widespread capital flight
from the region. Like the Caribbean island economies,
Central American countries trade principally with the
United States, the European Community, and their immediate neighbors in that order. Table 3.2 gives a detailed
breakdown of regional trade patterns in 1981.

As is expected, the United States is clearly the dominant export market regionwide. Of all the countries, Honduras is the most dependent on the U.S. market, Nicaragua
the least. It is interesting to note that the U.S. market
share did not decline as a result of political differences
with Nicaragua over the past several years. The United
States imports sugar, bananas, coffee, citrus fruits, and
fish from the region and provides manufactures and raw materials in return. The Central American countries supply
coffee and bananas to the European Community and this explains El Salvador's large market in the Community (34
percent of exports). El Salvador sells coffee to the
European market and Costa Rica sells bananas. In the late
1970s several of Europe's traditional Eastern Caribbean
banana suppliers failed to meet quotas because of natural
disasters (Hurricanes David and Frederick in 1979 and Allen
in 1980), and because of gradual deterioration in industry
production levels. As a result the European Community
turned to Central America, which produces a higher quality
product, and this has now earned the Central Americans a
competitive position in the European market.

El Salvador and Honduras have not traded with each
other since the 1969 soccer war, an event that weakened
the Central American Common Market. It is clear, however,
that those countries that were able to take advantage of
the regional market, Guatemala, El Salvador, and Costa
Rica, established a firm foundation of interregional trade.

*Panama has traditionally resisted inclusion in the geo-
graphic region of Central America, preferring to retain
a unique identity.

TABLE 3.2
Export and Import Market Shares of Central American Countries and
Panama, 1981 (U.S. $ millions and percentages)

	Panama		Costa Rica		Nicaragua[2]	
	Exports	Imports	Exports	Imports	Exports	Imports
Total	$316.0	$2,879.5[1]	$968.0	$1,198.0	$529.14	$730.0
United States	72.0	23.0	32.0	33.0	26.0	27.7
European Community	17.2	13.2	23.0	10.6	16.3	9.9
Latin America	17.4	13.1	34.0	40.5	11.2	53.5
Central America	--	--	28.0	17.7	9.7	27.0
Oil imports	--	--	--	19.0	--	11.4

	Honduras		El Salvador[4]		Guatemala[5]	
	Exports	Imports	Exports	Imports	Exports	Imports
Total	$846.4	$985.5	$794.0	$961.8	$392.5	$1,690.1
United States	53.0	39.0	31.0	35.0	25.0	36.4
European Community	14.8	11.3	34.0	10.3	15.0	12.8
Latin America	11.2	30.7	22.0	43.2	35.0	35.0
Central America	7.5	11.8	19.8	28.5	32.0	13.8
Oil imports	--	13.8[3]	--	10.0	--	15.8

[1]Panama's disproportionately high level of imports reflects activity in the
Colón duty-free zone.

[2]Nicaraguan exports to the United States have remained at a constant share of
total exports in spite of political differences that could have affected
trade. In 1975, the U.S. market represented 28 percent of Nicaraguan exports.
Imports from the United States have dropped substantially from 58 percent in
1975. This may result from Nicaragua's lack of foreign exchange as the same
pattern is reflected in trade with the European Community. Other major export markets for Nicaragua are Japan (10 percent) and The People's Republic
of China (17 percent). Six percent of Nicaraguan imports are from Mexico and
trade with the Comecon bloc is negligible.

[3]Honduras' principal petroleum import sources in Latin America are Venezuela
and Trinidad and Tobago. In spite of proximity, Honduras cannot refine Mexico's heavy crude oil.

[4]El Salvador's principal trading partners in the hemisphere are Guatemala and
Venezuela.

[5]Guatemala is the only Central American country with an important volume of
trade with Mexico.

92

On the import side, petroleum imports from Venezuela and
to a much lesser degree from Trinidad and Tobago make up
the bulk of large import items moving in interregional
trade. More detailed presentation of the data would show
that only Guatemala trades heavily with Mexico and Brazil
is the only other important Latin American trading partner. The Central American and the Caribbean countries do
not trade with each other.

   Venezuela. Venezuela has the wealthiest and most
diverse economy in the Caribbean basin. Its per capita
income, the highest in Latin America, is, however, modest
in comparison with incomes in developed countries. (Venezuela's per capita income is approximately equal to that
of Greece, Ireland, or the Soviet Union.) In 1980 Venezuela's Gross National Product was $60 billion, the fourth
largest of the OPEC economies, after Iran ($66 billion),
Saudi Arabia ($115 billion), and Indonesia ($69.8 billion).
Venezuela is the sixth-largest exporter of petroleum among
the OPEC countries; most of its exports go to Western
Hemisphere markets. In the past, Venezuela has been a
much more important supplier of petroleum to the U.S. market (as recently as 1974 it supplied 25 percent of U.S.
petroleum imports), but its market share has declined substantially in recent years (to 6.7 percent in 1980), as
the United States shifted to Middle Eastern, African, Mexican, and other sources.

   Venezuela's trade pattern reflects the mutual interdependence of oil exporting nations and industrial economies. Table 3.3 shows Venezuela exports its crude petroleum primarily to the United States (27.7 percent of
exports in 1980). The European Community, Canada, Japan,
and Brazil also are growing markets. In the Western
Hemisphere, the refining centers of the Netherlands Antilles are the principal recipients of Venezuelan crude
exports. Refined products are then shipped elsewhere in
the Caribbean and Central America, as well as to the
United States. Foreign exchange earned from petroleum
sales is used to purchase machinery, manufactures, and
industrial raw materials for Venezuela's expanding industrial diversification program. Venezuela's balance of
trade with the industrial countries has been decidedly unfavorable because of Venezuela's push, in the late 1970s,
to "sow the petroleum" and develop an industrial base.
Chapter 2 showed that by 1982 Venezuela had overextended
itself in this effort such that a sharp drop in oil revenues could put the country in financial distress and unable to meet payments on its debt. In addition, the country has been a net importer of foodstuffs for some time
and buys considerable grain in the United States.

   Venezuela's excessive reliance on petroleum to generate national income has been a major factor inhibiting a

more active economic role in hemisphere affairs. In 1975,
Venezuela's oil and gas industry (including refining) generated 77 percent of the central government's revenue,
96 percent of merchandise export earnings, and 29 percent
of domestic product. In contrast, agriculture, which employed about one-fifth of the Venezuelan labor force, generated only 5 percent of GNP. Extreme differences continue to exist in the standards of living in urban and
rural areas.

TABLE 3.3
Venezuelan Export and Import Market Shares, 1980

	Exports	Imports
Total (U.S. $ millions)	19,226	11,098
United States	27.7%	48.0%
Canada	9.2	4.8
European Community	12.6	20.5
Latin America and Caribbean	37.5[a]	9.5
Japan	3.5	8.0

[a]Exports to Latin America and the Caribbean are principally to the Netherlands Antilles and secondarily to
Brazil, Chile, and Colombia.

     Venezuelan development strategy, as outlined in re-
cent (1976 and 1981) development plans, places continuing
emphasis on diversification of industry, particularly
technologically advanced and capital-intensive industries
such as steel, aluminum, and petrochemicals (Kuczynski,
1977; Hayes, 1977; Inter-American Development Bank, 1982).
This program depended on both increased imports from the
developed countries and foreign private investment capital. Venezuela's links to developed economies, particularly the resource-poor economies such as Japan, with
which it can trade raw materials for capital goods, have
expanded considerably over the past decade when exports
went from 17 percent to 3.5 percent between 1970 and 1980.
More recently, the world recession has dampened demand for
petroleum and the growth in nontraditional markets, as
well as overall growth, has remained relatively stagnant
since 1980. While the development plan established targets for GDP growth averaging 7.9 percent per year for
1975-1979 (Hayes, 1977), real growth was less than 5 percent for the entire decade of 1970-1979 (World Bank,
1982). Growth dropped by 1.6 percent in 1980 and recov-
ered only slightly in 1981. Pragmatic forecasts estimate

the Venezuelan growth to range between 2 and 4 percent
through 1986.

One of the principal causes of recent economic difficulties in Venezuela has been a mounting external debt
coupled with revised OPEC targets that reduced crude oil
production from 1981 levels of 2.1 million barrels per
day(mbpd) to only 1.7mbpd. Like other oil-producing
countries, Venezuela had expanded its domestic investment
plans to take full advantage of expected continued high-
rising oil prices. Venezuela's autonomous public sector
agencies borrowed heavily in foreign commercial markets
at increasingly high interest rates in order to have investment capital at hand. By year end 1981, approximately
70 percent of Venezuela's treasury reserves were tied to
loans on behalf of the state-run autonomous agencies. The
external debt balance in December 1981 reached $9.5 bil-
lion with annual debt servicing at $2.2 billion. At year
end 1982, Venezuela, like many other Latin American countries, entered the process of restructuring its debt in
order not to default on obligations to major financial
centers in the United States and Europe.

Economic Growth Potential in the Caribbean Basin

As with other countries in the hemisphere, economic
development is the principal concern of the Caribbean
basin countries and an important force behind some of the
more dramatic political and economic policy experiments
being undertaken in the region. To date, however, success
in development has been marginal. One author writing for
the World Bank summarized the problems confronting the
English-speaking Caribbean countries:

> In the heyday of the colonial plantation, the
> size of a territory was not a significant vari-
> able; the economies of all the territories were
> based on imported slave or indentured labor,
> and secure metropolitan markets, and were large
> enough to sustain at least one plantation at an
> efficient level of output under the prevailing
> technology. The decline of the slave planta-
> tion system, technological changes calling for
> large units of production, and increased compe-
> tition from Asian and African producers of agri-
> cultural goods combined to make the small size
> of these countries a severe impediment to their
> economic and political modernization. Diminu-
> tive domestic markets have forced them to fore-
> go (sic) many of the economic advantages of
> scale; and even the few successful import-
> substituting or import-replacing activities
> have been prone to monopolistic practices.
> Modern technology requires productive and

administrative units which are simply too large
for the domestic markets of most of the Caribbean Commonwealth states. Since the capacity
to adapt this technology is limited, the choice
has usually been confined to the costly extremes
of either doing without or creating excess capacity (Chernick, 1978).

Beginning in the mid-1960s, regional integration efforts in the Commonwealth Caribbean sought to overcome
the handicaps of small size, economic fragmentation, and
extensive dependence on extraregional markets and suppliers of resources of all kinds. The Caribbean Community and Common Market (CARICOM), with its associated regional institutions, the Caribbean Development Bank (CDB),
the Caribbean Investment Corporation (CIC), and more recently, a World Bank Coordinating Body, the Caribbean
Group for Cooperation on Economic Development (CGCED) have
all directed attention to channeling capital with sound
regional development efforts. Though the record of success has been mixed, and growth has ranged between -3.7
in Jamaica, the poorest performing country, and 4.5 percent in Trinidad and Tobago, the best performing country
(World Bank, 1982), there is general consensus that without the regional integration effort most of the countries
would be in serious economic straits. The 1973 oil price
increase and subsequent stagflation in the developed
countries, along with poor domestic economic management,
produced especially severe economic dislocation in the
Caribbean states. By 1978, Guyana, Jamaica, and several
Eastern Caribbean economies were approaching economic
disaster. The less developed Eastern Caribbean countries
experienced substantial absolute decline in their standard of living over the decade (Chernick, 1978). Between
1970 and 1979, per capita Gross National Product actually
declined in real terms for most of the island economies.
Jamaica, one of the larger and most complex economies,
experienced a 1.1 percent negative growth rate for the
entire decade 1970-1980, and negative growth continued
into 1982. GNP growth averaged only 2.3 percent a year
for the Central American countries during the late 1970s.
Even Venezuela, with its substantial oil income, experienced only a 1.5 percent average per capita income improvement over the decade of the 1970s (World Bank, 1982).
The serious economic problems of dual economies, low
rates of labor absorption, unemployment, and underemployment remain to depress prospects for growth at least for
the next few years.

Forecasts of growth potential are pessimistic because
of the severity of the problems confronting these economies. Before the severe recession of 1980-1982 was recognized, average annual growth rates for the major island
economies were projected to range from 3.9 to 4.4 percent

between 1978 and 1990. Average annual growth rates for
the Central American economies were projected at 4.3 percent a year for 1976 to 1980 and 4.6 percent a year for
1986-1990. With population growth rates predicted to be
2.5 percent a year, real per capita growth for the two
periods should average closer to 2.0 percent. Such low
growth rates would result in the Caribbean basin economies falling substantially behind the larger economies of
South America and Mexico, which are expected to achieve
total growth rates ranging between 4 and 8 percent in the
1980s. The global recession will have to end, and demand
in the industrial countries improve substantially for
either the major South American economies, Mexico, or the
Caribbean basin. Venezuela's planners had projected economic growth at a rate of from 4.6 to 4.7 percent a year
between 1976 and 1990 (CACI, 1978), down from 6.0 percent
in the 1960s and 5.0 percent from 1970 to 1976 (World
Bank, 1982). More optimistic projections suggested expansion of the Venezuelan economy at a 6 to 7 percent
average over the 1980s. Growth slowed during that last
year of the 1970s, however, and GDP growth was negative
in 1980. Renewed expansion will depend on activating the
agricultural and industrial sectors. Growth is not expected to be greater than 4 percent through 1986, in part
because of continued sluggishness in the industrialized
countries which will reduce demand for Venezuelan oil
(Latin America Regional Report, 17 December 1982).

The low levels of growth projected for the Caribbean
basin countries are important to the United States for at
least two reasons. First, slower overall growth means
slower expansion of supplies of the important resources
that the United States obtains in the Caribbean region,
as well as smaller markets for U.S. exports. Second, and
more important, slower growth means continued economic
problems for the Caribbean countries. These will likely
translate into continued problems in U.S.-Caribbean trade
and other economic relations, as well as into greater political instability in the region as political leaders
look for solutions to economic problems. This second
problem is the subject of the next section.

PROSPECTS FOR STABILITY IN THE CARIBBEAN BASIN

Political science literature has well developed theories of political violence and internal war. A major authority in this literature summarizes the causal sequence
of internal war as first, the development of discontent;
second, the politicization of that discontent; and finally,
its actualization in violent action against political ob-
jects and actors. "Discontent arising from the perception
of relative deprivation (the perceived difference between
value expectations and actual position and potential) is

the basic instigating condition for participants in collective violence" (Gurr, 1970). Other scholars have argued that repression leads to aggression (R. E. Hayes,
1972). Conditions in the Caribbean and in Central America are, under these formulations, ripe for domestic violence. The political base of most incumbent regimes is
weak. Promises of rapid development and improvement in
the quality of life have been difficult to fulfill; this
failure to fulfill promises has undermined faith in existing forms of government and development models. In the
1970s massive strikes in Jamaica contributed to a sharp
decline in that nation's economy, a massive exodus of
skilled manpower, and one of the most bloody election campaigns in the nation's history. Ultimately, the voters,
tired of violence, elected a new government that promised
order and peace. Jamaica has a long tradition of elected
government that few other Caribbean basin countries enjoy.
Elections in Central America, for example, have more often
been used to perpetuate regimes in power than to offer
means for orderly change. In Central America, first Nicaragua in 1979, then Guatemala and El Salvador experienced
domestic turmoil that erupted into open violence and civil
war.

One commentator writing on the seemingly turbulent
1970s argued:

> ...with few notable exceptions, the Caribbean
> nations seem to be heading, in desperation to-
> ward an ungainly one-party statism. Partly be-
> cause the development policies of the Alliance
> for Progress did not meet their expectation,
> with the result that unemployment remains
> chronic and high while wealth remains inequi-
> tably distributed; partly because of the in-
> herent weakness of raw-material economies;
> partly because they are ever propelled by pride
> and nationalism; and for a host of other rea-
> sons, most of these countries seem to be in a
> state of political demoralization, with little
> but instability ahead. If some seem to be tak-
> ing Cuba, not Puerto Rico, for their model, it
> is less out of considered political judgment
> than out of desperation, out of a sense of not
> knowing where to turn next before the deluge.
> This makes them doubly difficult to deal with.
> (Martin, 1978)

Today, the political spectrum in the Caribbean basin
includes the established democracies of Jamaica, Barbados,
Costa Rica, and Venezuela; the new democratic experiments
in the Dominican Republic, Honduras, and Panama; right-
wing dictatorships in Central America; populist governments in Trinidad and Tobago; Marxist governments in

Grenada and Guyana; a series of new governments in the
Caribbean mini-states whose future political coloration
is as yet uncertain; and the Communist regime in Cuba.
Political stability is fairly certain in the major democratic regimes. The Dominican and Panamanian regimes
have demonstrated near-term staying power in recent elections, making the likelihood of their continued political
development and stability more optimistic. Jamaicans
have demonstrated the ability to vote out a radical regime and the system has absorbed the shock of dramatic
policy shift from Michael Manley to Edward Seaga. Elsewhere in the Commonwealth Caribbean, Westminster parliamentarism has been challenged by leftists and has sur-
vived. In Dominica and St. Lucia radical leftist
challengers were soundly defeated in open elections,
though not without sending waves of deep concern throughout the entire region. In Central America the situation
is much less certain. There entrenched conservatism,
military establishments that cannot stay out of politics,
and well organized, entrenched guerrilla forces, each unable to compromise, threaten to envelop the region in
flames. Moderate reformers have been driven from Nicaragua. Many have been assassinated in El Salvador and
Guatemala. Few of the countries can generate a consensus
on the building of a new political system.

Potential Political Leaders in the Caribbean Basin

It is always hazardous to speculate about future developments in a highly volatile and unstructured environment. However, at the present time, Cuba, Venezuela,
Mexico, and the United States seem to offer the most important alternative political and economic development
models for Caribbean basin countries. U.S. relations
with the Caribbean countries have evolved through several
phases. Two perspectives prevail in these countries' view
of their relations with the United States: first, the
United States has an overwhelming political, military,
and economic superiority while the countries have yet to
approach the standard of living and the political and
economic capabilities of the United States, and second,
these countries are considered insignificant in U.S. global policy concerns; moreover, while the United States
does regard the region as important in its own security
perspective, the region's interests receive no special
consideration from the United States.

Under these circumstances, the natural reaction in
the Caribbean basin has been to seek to reduce the imbal-
ance in relations between the United States and the other
nations in the region. During the 1970s, in particular,
this reaction was translated into vigorous efforts (1) to
establish greater independence from the United States,
(2) to be less responsive to U.S. demands, and (3) to

insist on establishing political systems that reflect the
nations' own political history and current political
needs better than the American democratic model. These
efforts were translated into diversifying trading partners, vigorously defending national economic interests
(leading to nationalization and price increases for important products), and espousing Third World interests
in North-South discussions. The United States' long domination of the region, its past actions there, and its
unique definition of its own security interests reinforce
the nationalistic desires in the region to diminish U.S.
influence in domestic political and economic processes.

In the late 1960s, with the defeat of its policy of
exporting revolution to Latin America, Cuba ceased being
politically active in the Caribbean basin. In the mid-
1970s, Cuba extended its commercial contacts throughout
the area. Cuba's economic development record appealed to
the less developed countries of the region, and its political prestige was no doubt enhanced by its excursions
into Africa and its flaunting of the United States in doing so.

The Cuban model has had considerable appeal in countries like Grenada, Guyana, and, for a time, Jamaica,
which is one of the largest and most important of the Commonwealth Caribbean countries. Similarities of economic
structure, historical experience, and racial composition--
as well as the demonstration effect of Cuba's successful
political and economic development experience--form the
bases of this appeal; so does Cuba's support for Third
World issues and an international economic order favoring
less developed countries.

Searching for a formula to break out of its own economic doldrums, in 1974 Jamaica declared itself a socialist democracy, modeled, according to one observer, after
the British Labour Party following World War II (O'Flaherty, 1978) and pursued a leadership role in Commonwealth
Caribbean affairs, as well as in international North-South
debates. Prime Minister Michael Manley strongly supported
Cuba on regional and international issues. The experiment
ended abruptly with Manley's resounding electoral defeat
in 1980 and successor Edward Seaga has sought to substitute
another political model for the Caribbean Community.

Even though Seaga may enjoy the role of principal
spokesman for the Caribbean Community, no one state en-
joys a position of political leadership in the Caribbean
basin. The English-speaking countries have much closer
ties with each other than they do with the Spanish- and
French-speaking countries. There is little interaction,
economic or political, among the three linguistic communities. Even within the English-speaking group, no single

island is a natural leader by virtue of its size or the
stature of its political leadership. Rivalry, rather
than regional solidarity, has characterized inter-island
diplomacy (O'Flaherty, 1978). Hence, the Caribbean political environment has provided a stage for leaders like
Castro, Manley, and Eric Williams of Trinidad and Tobago,
who aspire to leadership in the Third World rather than
leadership within the Caribbean region. This lack of regional leadership has hindered economic integration efforts and has contributed to the atmosphere of political
uncertainty in the area.

In contrast, in recent years Venezuela and, to a
lesser degree, Mexico have been very active in the region,
espousing regional economic cooperation, engaging in joint
economic development ventures (such as developing a baux-
ite/alumina facility in Jamaica and participating in the
regional merchant marine) and appealing to nationalist
instincts by espousing regional development policies that
exclude the United States. At the same time, Venezuela
and Mexico have defended the development of statist or
socialist political regimes and have actively helped isolate the more reactionary conservative dictatorships in
Central America. Venezuela, for example, supplied arms
to the Sandinistas in the Nicaraguan civil war. The cornerstone of Venezuelan and Mexican hemispheric policy has
been the appeal to regional national interests. This appeal has struck a responsive chord in the region and enhanced the larger countries' prestige as regional leaders. Venezuela and Mexico will probably continue as
leaders because of their own demonstrated development
success and economic power, plus their relative independence from the United States and success in attracting
U.S. participation in their own economies on their own
terms.

Venezuela is one of the most active Latin American
states in international politics. Unlike other powers in
the hemisphere, Venezuela has explicitly sponsored Latin
American integration and political liberalization since
the late 1950s. At the same time, Venezuela's most significant international action was its sponsorship, with
Saudi Arabia, of the OPEC concept in the early 1960s. It
has remained an important advocate of "Southern" positions
on international North-South questions, including oil
price increases. Venezuela's advocacy of "ideological
pluralism" as a cornerstone of its foreign policy made
Venezuela a leader in Latin American efforts to renew
diplomatic relations with Communist countries, including
Cuba, in the 1970s. Under the Carlos Andres Perez administration (1974-1978) Venezuela sponsored creation of the
Latin American Economic System (SELA), an effort to develop a regional economic entity that would specifically
exclude the United States. Perez also created the

Venezuelan Investment Fund in the Inter-American Development Bank and in 1978 announced an important joint oil facility with Mexico to supply petroleum at concessional rates to countries in the Caribbean basin.

Like Mexico, Venezuela also has been an active advocate of the New International Economic Order within the United Nations and the developing nations of the Group of 77, and has actively supported claims of other Latin American states against the United States. It strongly backed Panama in the Panama Canal treaty negotiations, has lobbied for Cuba's readmission to the Organization of American States, actively supported the Sandinistas in Nicaragua, and was one of the most vocal supporters of Argentina in the 1982 Falklands War. The consistent theme in these foreign policy initiatives has been greater Latin American independence from the United States, including ideological self-determination and economic integration, to create conditions for the exercise of Latin American influence on a world scale. On many of these issues, Venezuela has acted in concert with Mexico, the other major Caribbean power.

Since oil prices began to increase in 1973, Venezuela has had the capital to back its foreign policy with financial incentives, particularly in the Caribbean, its logical geographical sphere of influence. Venezuela has concentrated on cultivating relations with the small-country members of the English-speaking Caribbean. Venezuela was the first non-English-speaking member of the Caribbean Development Bank and remains a major source of bank funding. Venezuela's effort met with some opposition from Trinidad and Tobago, which feared Venezuela would take over some of the Caribbean markets they supplied. Indeed, Venezuela's financial generosity and strong industrial base have fostered increasingly close relations with Jamaica, the Dominican Republic, and most of the smaller East Caribbean states.

Venezuela has also been active in Central America, where it has subsidized the Central American coffee market and contributed funds to Central American development programs, particularly in Costa Rica and Honduras. It has been less active with the countries of west coast South America, though it became a member of the Andean Pact in 1973 and has provided investment funding. Venezuela trades relatively little with the Pact countries and, in general, finds its production costs higher and therefore noncompetitive in the Andean market.

It is unlikely that Venezuela will be able to continue to use its financial power to expand its political influence on the same scale as in the recent past. Domestic development goals will become increasingly important and will absorb petroleum revenues (Tugwell, 1977). As a result, Venezuela may become less active in the Andean region and further concentrate its attention in the Caribbean.

Venezuela's traditional rival in the hemisphere has been Brazil. Until 1976, Venezuelan governments have preferred to pursue national and international interests independently of Brazil (Tugwell, 1977). Venezuela strongly resented U.S. granting of special relationship status to Brazil in 1977. Brazil's expansion along its northern border in the early and mid-1970s caused particularly cold relations. Tension eased after 1978, when presidents of the two countries met and signed agreements for joint development in the Amazon.

Venezuela and Brazil are now collaborating on several ventures including the GURI hydroelectric project in eastern Venezuela. In the future, Brazil will purchase much more petroleum from Venezuela, decreasing its dependence on African and Middle Eastern oil. Trade problems and other conflicts with the developed countries could enhance Brazilian-Venezuelan solidarity on Third World issues, while trade between the two countries could prove highly beneficial, as the two economies are complementary in many ways.

UNITED STATES-CARIBBEAN RELATIONS

The Caribbean basin countries' emphasis on economic development means that economic issues, particularly trade issues, dominate their relations with the United States and extraregional powers. Nationalization of U.S. firms has occurred with minimal disruption, and U.S. firms maintain their interests in the area, increasingly selling technology and managerial and marketing experience to the countries. In many cases the firms' profitability has increased after nationalization.

Because of its proximity and size, the United States will continue to play a major economic role in the Caribbean basin. Furthermore, U.S. ability to buy elsewhere the most important raw materials the Caribbean can offer--petroleum and bauxite--means that Caribbean basin countries will be increasingly sensitive to their economic relations with the United States in the future. All proposals for diversification of production and exports in the region depend on access to the U.S. market for the new products.

The relatively independent political posture of the Caribbean basin states does not necessarily entail hostility toward the United States or create conditions for

expansion of Cuban or Soviet influence in the region.
Most observers view expansion of Soviet contacts in the
Caribbean basin as designed to embarrass the United
States, by undermining its influence in the area, rather
than to establish yet another regional outpost (Theberge,
1974; Leiken, 1982). The success of this policy is enhanced by U.S. overconcern with Soviet contacts with the
region. As far as most Caribbean states are concerned,
the Cuban experience has also demonstrated the pitfalls
of association with an extraregional external superpower.

For a variety of historical reasons, the United
States is at a disadvantage in attempting to direct the
political processes unfolding in the Caribbean basin.
U.S. interests are served by creating conditions by which
the Caribbean nations can develop their economic potential and strengthen their political systems against instability. U.S. economic interests in the region are
guaranteed by the operation of the international market
which makes the U.S. market attractive for Caribbean exporters and limits their ability to find substitutes for
this market. U.S. private investment in the area will
expand, but through joint ventures rather than through
direct ownership. As the Caribbean economies develop,
the opportunity for U.S. firms to invest there will increase. Regional powers, such as Mexico and Venezuela,
are pursuing policies in the area that parallel and serve
U.S. interests, and the United States would do well to
allow those powers to expand their influence.

CUBA: DIFFICULT NEIGHBOR

The presence in Cuba of a communist regime strongly
backed by the Soviet Union has been and will continue to
be a profound irritant to U.S. policy makers of all political stripes. The irritation stems from the inherent
incompatibility of U.S. and Cuban foreign policy goals in
the region and in the world. The Cuban perspective is
aptly summarized in the words of Cuban vice president
Carlos Rafael Rodriguez, who said, "Cuba has the duty of
carrying out, and will always carry out, a revolutionary,
proletarian internationalism" (Rodriguez, 1981).

This essential precept of Cuban foreign policy has
often been overlooked in the waxing and waning of Cuban
revolutionary activism over the past 20 years. In particular it was believed to have been forgotten in the
early 1970s, a time of unusually "correct" Cuban relations within the Western Hemisphere. More recently, analysts have been reminded again of the vigor of Cuba's
revolutionary commitment as demonstrated by its extensive
ties with revolutionary leftists throughout the Caribbean
basin.

One specialist on Cuba described Cuba as a small country with a big-country foreign policy that has consistently "reflected a clear hierarchy of objectives, in descending order: (1) survival of the revolutionary government; (2) economic development; (3) influence over governments; (4) influence over the Left; and (5) support of revolution. Although many specific Cuban policies have changed from the 1960s to the 1970s, the choices among policies have been made consistently as if they were following such an explicit hierarchy" (Dominguez, 1978).

U.S. concern over Cuban foreign policy activities responds to a reverse order of concerns; that is, it is Cuba's support of revolution, its influence over the revolutionary Left, and its influence over other governments, as well as its close relationship with the Soviet Union, that are of concern to the United States. There are a number of reasons for such concerns:

- Cuban activism in other world regions threatens U.S. interests in those regions and increases opportunities for more direct confrontation between the United States and the Soviet Union.

- Cuban activism in support of revolutionary tendencies in the hemisphere contributes to instability in a region of vital U.S. interest and directly threatens U.S. interests in democratic regimes in the region.

- Cuba provides a base of operations for Soviet fishing, naval, satellite, and communications intelligence operations and other activities that reduce U.S. freedom of movement in its southern flank region and that make defense preparedness in the region more costly.

Cuba's Extrahemispheric Activities

The record shows that Cuba has had an active extra-hemispheric foreign policy since the early days of the revolution. In the 1960s Cubans were involved in Algeria's war against Morocco, in the Congo (Brazzaville), and in the several Portuguese colonies during their wars of independence. Cuba established important foreign aid programs in São Tomé-Principe, Equatorial Guinea, and in Guinea-Bissau. In the 1970s Cuba's active role in Africa both expanded in size and number of persons, and began to coincide more directly with Soviet expansionist designs on that increasingly politically unstable continent. Cuban involvement in Angola and Somalia in the latter 1970s would not have been possible on the scale they achieved without substantial Soviet logistic support.

In the early days of Cuban involvement in Africa, Cuba's activities were generally regarded favorably by the major African countries and the regional Organization of African Unity (OAU). Cuba's support of the Popular Liberation Movement of Angola (MPLA) and its opposition to the Somalian invasion of Ethiopia, as well as its support for movements against the white regimes in Zimbabwe and in Namibia were consistent with the politics and attitudes of the majority of black African states. In the past several years, however, support for Cuba's role in Africa has dwindled. The summer 1978 meeting of Nonaligned countries in Belgrade witnessed a sharp criticism of Cuban policy in Africa and of the continuing presence of Cuban troops after colonial control or threatened invasions had ended. By the latter half of 1978, Africa and other Third World countries, as well as the United States, were criticizing Cuba's role in Africa as a proxy action for the Soviet Union.

Cuba's unquestioning pro-Soviet posture has also irritated a number of members of the Nonaligned Movement (NAM), the leadership of which Castro has long desired. As early as 1973, Col. Mu'Ammar Quadhafi, of Libya, challenged Cuba's claim to membership in the "non-aligned" movement, saying,

> In the beginning the aim of the revolution was to obtain Cuba's freedom. This freedom has no meaning if it consists of moving from the domination of one power to that of another power. ...(and) Castro is aligned. (Halperin, 1981)

Cuba's votes against United Nations resolutions condemning the Soviet Union's invasion of Afghanistan in 1979 were noted with dismay and derision within the NAM. When Castro assumed the presidency of the movement in September 1979, he brought even greater controversy to the members' debate on the movement's appropriate political posture. In 1982 strong measures were taken to preempt a self-serving effort by Castro to prolong his presidency of the movement.

Cuba's Role in Latin America

In the aftermath of its own revolutionary victory, Cuba took an active role in supporting oppositions to governments in Latin America in the early 1960s. Because of its support for revolutionary movements in the hemisphere, nearly every country but Mexico had broken diplomatic relations with Cuba by 1965. Cuba actively sought to bring about the overthrow of the Betancourt and Leoni governments in Venezuela, supporting a guerrilla movement that was not quashed until well into the decade. Relations with right-wing governments in both Nicaragua and

Guatemala were colored by those governments' support for
the Bay of Pigs invasion in 1961. Cuba provided mild
support to leftist sympathizers from both countries
throughout the 1960s and 1970s. Cuba's more famous actions promoting revolution in the hemisphere were in Che
Guevara's efforts to lead a revolution in Bolivia and to
make the Andes a second Sierra Maestra.

     In the aftermath of Guevara's defeat and death in
Bolivia, and in part because of strong Soviet pressure to
relax its revolutionary efforts, Cuba maintained a low
profile in the region.[3] In 1975 the Organization of
American States voted to lift collective economic sanctions that had been levied against Cuba in 1964 because
of its activities against neighbor governments. Relations with governments in the region improved, though
Cuba sought principally to exploit those relations that
would have greatest economic benefit to it. Thus, Cuba
established strong trade relations with Argentina, though
diplomatic contacts with the military government there
remained minimal. It cooperated with Brazil "with which
its political relations are terrible" on international
sugar issues of interest to both countries (and others in
the Caribbean) (Dominguez, 1978). It became a member and
one of the more frequent users of the Caribbean shipping
enterprise, NAMUCAR, to which Costa Rica, Jamaica, Mexico,
Nicaragua, and Trinidad and Tobago also belong. Cuba also
opened a branch of the National Bank of Cuba in Panama,
in order to take advantage of greatly expanded volume of
investment funds flowing through Panama's banks of con-
venience. Simultaneously with its expanded commercial
and government-to-government contacts in the region, Cuba
also established much closer relations with potentially
revolutionary regimes in Guyana and Jamaica and with leftist movements throughout the region. Cuba's overall policy toward its Latin American and Caribbean neighbors
changed approximately in 1978-1979, when the emphasis on
good, formal government-to-government relations was
dropped for concentration on exploiting and developing
the revolutionary potential in the region. As noted
above, Cuba had maintained good relations with revolutionary leftists in exile throughout the decade. The
surprising success of the Sandinista revolution in Nicaragua awakened Cuba (and the Soviet Union) to the possibility that revolutionary conditions might indeed exist
throughout the troubled Central American region. Cuba
had ceased its activities in support of revolution in
the 1960s when the Soviet Union insisted that the region
was not yet ripe for revolution. Suddenly, conditions
appeared right for revolutions to prosper.

     In 1978 Cuba worked closely with the Sandinista
leadership to effect a unified leadership among the three
major factions of the FSLN (Frente Sandinista de

Liberacion Nacional). At the same time, Cuba moved to
insure adequate supplies to the revolutionaries and to
facilitate the acquisition of arms and their transshipment through Panama and Costa Rica to the rebels. Cuban
advisers assisted in training FSLN personnel in Nicaragua,
in Costa Rica along the border with Nicaragua, and in Cuba
itself. Moreover, Cuban advisers operated alongside the
FSLN columns during the final thrust against Somoza beginning in mid-1979. Following the Sandinista victory in
July 1979, Cuban advisers continued to work side-by-side
with Nicaraguans in the most sensitive aspects of government, and between 3,000 and 5,000 Cubans, including 1,500
military advisers, as well as teachers and health technicians, and other specialists, were present in Nicaragua.[4]

Cuba has sought to provide similar support to other
revolutionary guerrilla organizations in Central America.
There is little question that Cubans facilitated the acquisition of weapons, ammunition, and other supplies for
the Salvadoran guerrillas during 1979 and 1980, as reported in the U.S. State Department 1981 White Paper (Department of State, 1981). More importantly, however,
Cuba provided the same leadership to the fragmented and
bickering Salvadoran left that it had given to the Sandinistas, forging unified leadership and coordinated policy
among the groups. The FMLN (Frente Farabundo Marti de
Liberacion Nacional) emerged out of a December 1979 meeting in Havana, and six months later, a unified revolutionary directorate, the DRU, was created. Cuban officials
have admitted to providing arms to the Salvadoran guerrillas from time to time, and to training Salvadorans in
military operations.

Cuba sought to exercise a similar role in Guatemala,
but with less success. Elements of the Guatemalan left
met in November 1980 in Managua to forge a unified revolutionary command (the National Revolutionary Union (UNR)
with its revolutionary directorate, the General Revolutionary Command (CGR)). Several thousand Guatemalans
have received training in Cuba. Elsewhere, Cuba has provided training to Hondurans to fight in Nicaragua and El
Salvador and supplied arms and ammunition for use by ter-
rorists within Honduras itself. A Costa Rican parliamentary commission documented extensive Cuban participation in Costa Rica in support of guerrilla movements
elsewhere in the region.

In the Caribbean islands, two countries, Grenada and
Guyana, had moved into the Cuban camp by the late 1970s,
adopting a stridently pro-Cuban and pro-Soviet rhetoric
that is quite inconsistent with the region's historical
political tendencies of Westminster parliamentarism.
Grenada and Cuba were the only two Western Hemisphere nations to vote against UN resolutions condemning the

Soviet invasion of Afghanistan (Nicaragua abstained). A
strong contingency of Cuban military advisers and trainers resides in both Guyana and Grenada, and Grenada has
been host to radical leftists from other islands in the
Caribbean.

Elsewhere in the region, Cuba has maintained close
relations with the extremist April 19 Movement (M-19) in
Colombia, providing military training to guerrilla leaders and coordinating efforts to establish greater unity
among disparate guerrilla groups. In March 1981 Colombia
suspended diplomatic relations with Cuba because of
"clear evidence of its role in training M-19 guerrillas."
Costa Rica had suspended relations earlier because of
differences with Cuba over treatment of refugees in the
Costa Rican Embassy in Havana and Costa Rica's offer of
asylum to Cubans wanting to leave their country during
the 1979 Mariel exodus. Jamaica broke relations with
Cuba following the election of Edward Seaga as Prime Minister in the fall of 1980.

Cuba's relations with Jamaica represent a special
case, both because of the intensity they achieved during
the 1970s, and concerns they evoked within the region.
Jamaica was Cuba's greatest prize in the 1970s and Jamaica's reversal in the 1980 election away from the Cuban
model represented a powerful rebuff to Castro's revolutionary ambitions in the region. Cuban relations with
Jamaica expanded dramatically during the 1970s, in part
because of a close personal relationship that developed
between Jamaican Prime Minister Michael Manley and Fidel
Castro, and the ascendency to power of more extremist
elements in the Jamaican People's National Party during
Manley's second term in office. The relationship also
developed out of the void created by the United States'
1979 cut-off of aid to Jamaica. Manley was insulted and
Castro moved quickly to soothe his feelings. During the
latter 1970s Cubans trained hundreds of Jamaican youths
in a "brigadista" program and sent large numbers of Cuban
doctors and teachers to Jamaica to work in remote vil-
lages. Later Cubans were suspected of stockpiling weapons for use by rival Jamaican gangs during the bitterly
contested 1980 elections. The newly elected Seaga government terminated Jamaica's student exchange program
with Cuba and recalled Jamaicans still in Cuba in early
1981. Though Seaga initially sought to maintain diplomatic relations with Cuba, continuing Cuban interference
in Jamaican affairs led him to break relations by year's
end and to send home the remaining Cuban diplomats, doctors, and teachers. The relationship thus swung full
circle.

Cuba's expanded political activism initiated in the
late 1970s and extending through the early 1980s caused

increased turmoil and heightened tensions throughout the
Caribbean basin, from Grenada and Guyana, and the other
fragile parliamentary democracies in the West Indies to
Colombia, Nicaragua, El Salvador, and Guatemala. Relations between the United States and Cuba cooled during
the last years of the Carter administration and became
antagonistic in the first months of the Reagan administration. By 1982, however, the overall record of Cuban
successes in the region was emerging as a negative. Grenada and Guyana were increasingly being excluded from
economic discussions of the Caribbean Community (Caricom)
countries as those countries sought to forge a common development policy for working with the multilateral banks
and the United States' new Caribbean Basin Initiative.
Grenadan Prime Minister Maurice Bishop's increasingly
strident posture drove a sharp wedge between Grenada and
its former Caribbean colleagues. While they were not
willing to expel him from membership in the community,
the members remained firm in their insistence on member
adherence to democratic principles. As noted earlier,
hotly contested elections in Dominica, St. Lucia, and
others of the small island states resulted in victories
for moderate, pro-United States parties. So far Cuban
support to the Salvadoran guerrillas has not proved effective in advancing the guerrilla position in the now
long-stalemated war. While the guerrilla forces are in
control of isolated mountainous terrain, government forces
seem able to deprive the guerrillas of further victories
in the more populous areas of the country. The people
did not rise up in support of the guerrillas either during the final offensive of January 1981, or in the elections of March 1982 when the guerrillas hoped to frighten
the people into refusing to go to the polls. In early
1982 Cuba gave public support to a Mexican proposal for
negotiations in the Salvadoran conflict, support that perhaps underscored its recognition that the war could not
be won and a compromise solution would have to be found.

Cuba's continuing presence in Nicaragua, and the
Nicaraguan revolutionary government's outspoken pro-Cuban
position, served to destroy relations between the United
States and that new government and to heighten regional
tensions in Central America. Both Honduras and Costa
Rica reacted negatively to Nicaragua's military buildup
with Cuban advisers and Soviet weaponry. In October 1982
the Panamanian Foreign Minister counseled his Cuban coun-
terpart that a continued active Cuban presence in and involvement with Central American countries would not be
desirable.

In short, in spite of its four years of aggressive
activism in support of revolutionary change in the Caribbean basin, Cuba's record of successes is limited and
outweighed by the number of countries that have broken

relations with it. The recent wave of revolutionary activism in the hemisphere evoked the same response that
Cuban activism evoked in the 1960s. Relations have soured
with all countries to which Cuba has sought to provide
clandestine support to revolutionary leftist movements.

Should Cuba choose to intervene directly in conflicts
in the Caribbean, its well-trained and proven armed forces
could make a decisive difference in the local conflicts.
However, Cuba is not likely to choose such a confronta-
tional path. Direct Cuban participation in a local conflict would certainly evoke a response from the United
States. Equally important, it would evoke protest, and
perhaps reluctant action, from other countries in the region which are quite content to call clandestinely supported guerrilla wars "domestic conflicts," but which
could not overlook a more direct military intervention.
Cuba has little to gain through involvement in the Caribbean and Central America. The region is politically unimportant and the costs of exploiting the political weaknesses in the region are high. Economically the area has
little to offer Cuba. In contrast, Cuba's relations with
the major powers in Latin America, and potentially with
the United States, are important to it, for they offer
opportunities for economic cooperation, expansion, and
diversification of trade, and acquisition of technology.
It is precisely such relations that have been most jeop-
ardized by Cuba's recent return to revolutionary activism.

Constraints of Dependence on the Soviet
Union and Economic Options

During the more constructive period of the 1970s
when Cuba focused on building good government-to-
government ties with the Latin American countries, Cuba's
relations were cordial, primarily based on pragmatic economic concerns, and, in the Caribbean, limited by the
similarities in products produced and market structures.
One observer has noted that "the gaining of foreign support for economic development has all along been the second objective of Cuban foreign policy" after guaranteeing
the survival of the revolutionary government (Dominguez,
1978).

In the 1970s Cuba's development objectives were similar to those of other Latin American and Third World countries: achieving economic development and modernization;
reducing reliance on single, primary commodity exports for
foreign exchange; and political and economic independence
from external powers. Cuba's effort to promote rapid development and diversification was severely limited by a
lack of convertible foreign exchange, by dependence on
sugar (prices for which were favorable only for brief

periods during the 1970s), and by dependence on the Soviet
Union.

After the Cuban revolution and the imposition of the
U.S. total trade embargo in 1962, Cuba became almost to-
tally dependent on the Soviet Union for its economic survival. In 1959 the United States accounted for 74 percent of Cuban exports and 65 percent of its imports. By
1961 the Soviet Union and Eastern bloc countries accounted
for 74 percent of Cuba's exports and 70 percent of its
imports. The Soviet Union's share of that trade was approximately 50 percent of imports and 40 percent of exports. The Soviet Union has provided tremendous economic
assistance to Cuba. It has absorbed the burden of Cuba's
enormous trade deficit with the Communist bloc, carrying
more than 85 percent of the cumulative deficit between
1960 and 1974 (Dominguez, 1978a). It has subsidized the
price of Cuban sugar and provided Cuba with military hardware free of charge. Along with other members of the
Eastern bloc, the USSR provided extensive credits for
Cuba's industrial development, particularly in the early
1960s. In 1972 it agreed to postpone repayment of these
credits until 1986 and to amortize the debt over approximately 50 years. Table 3.4 summarizes the extent of Soviet economic assistance to Cuba since 1960. Of total
economic assistance exceeding $8 billion (not including
military aid), nearly half has not been subject to repayment. Soviet underwriting of the Cuban economy has also
permitted Cuba to receive credits and loans in convertible currencies from capitalist countries. Cuba received
its first line of credit for $1.2 billion from Argentina
in 1973. Since then, Canada, Spain, France, the United
Kingdom, and Japan provided credits totaling an estimated
$2.6 billion by 1982. Western commercial banks hold
about $1.7 billion of that debt (Joint Economic Committee,
1982). Cuba has also received loans amounting to $519
million in the Eurocurrency market (Theriot, 1978; U.S.
Congress, Joint Economic Committee, 1982).[5]

Like other countries in Latin America, expansion and
diversification of trade were increasingly important in
Cuba's economic development strategy in the 1970s. Sugar,
Cuba's major export, continues to account for over 80 percent of its export earnings. Approximately 70 percent of
Cuba's total trade (exports and imports) is with the Soviet bloc Council for Mutual Economic Assistance (CMEA).
The Soviet Union accounts for 50 percent of Cuba's trade
with CMEA. The Soviet Union also provides Cuba with over
95 percent of its petroleum needs at a price about one-
third the OPEC price, pays about five times the world
price for Cuban sugar, and supplies a wide variety of
capital goods. Since the mid-1970s, Cuba has actively
sought manufactured goods and food grains in the West as

TABLE 3.4
Soviet Economic Assistance to Cuba, 1961-1979 (U.S. $ millions)

	1961-70	1971	1972	1973	1974	1975	1976	1977	1978	1979
Balance-of-payments aid	$2,550	$509	$631	$437	$294	$150	$150	$210	$330	$440
Trade deficit	2,160	427	535	404	259	115	115	175	295	405
Interest charges[a]	166	57	69	0	0	0	0	0	0	0
Other invisibles	224	25	28	33	35	35	35	35	35	35
Sugar preference[b]	940	56	0	97	4	580	977	1,428	2,435	2,287
Petroleum preference[c]	--	--	--	--	370	290	362	328	165	365
Nickel preference[b]	--	--	--	48	40	31	18	16	38	15
Repayable aid[d]	2,550	3,059	3,691	4,128	4,422	4,567	4,714	4,927	5,257	5,697
Total cumulative aid	$3,568	$4,133	$4,743	$5,382	$6,090	$7,099	$8,606	$10,588	$13,556	$1,666

Source: Theriot, 1978; and U.S. Congress, Joint Economic Committee, 1982.

Note: U.S. dollar values used only for illustration. Actual assistance is made in products valued at shadow prices, making it impossible to quantify accurately. Soviet assistance is not in form of hard currency.

[a] A Cuban-Soviet agreement of December 1972 exempted Cuban debt from further interest charges beginning in 1973.

[b] The sugar and nickel preferences are estimated as the difference between the values of sugar and nickel exports to the USSR and the value of these exports if sold on the world market. They are considered a grant and are not subject to repayment.

[c] The petroleum preference reflects the difference between the value of petroleum purchases from the USSR and the value of these imports at world prices. It is considered a grant and is not subject to repayment.

[d] Estimated Cuban debt to the USSR consisting of (a) an estimated $4.05 billion in aid. The USSR has agreed to postpone initial repayment of this debt until 1986.

the CMEA countries cannot satisfy all Cuba's needs in these areas.

Cuba's purchases in the industrial West are limited only by the availability of hard currency; and that, in turn, is dependent on world sugar prices. In 1975, when sugar prices were favorable, the capitalist countries supplied 45 percent of Cuba's total imports (most of which are manufactures and machinery), as compared with 30 percent in the early 1970s. In 1981 Cuba purchased approximately 22 percent of its imports from the industrial West. France, Canada, Japan, Spain, and Argentina have been the principal free world suppliers to Cuba, but Cuba also trades with most other European Community members and with Colombia, Peru, and Mexico in Latin America. Purchases in these countries rose steadily and rapidly during the 1970s, as Cuba established an economic base that required increasing inputs of capital goods and technology.

Cuba's dramatic increase in borrowing on international capital markets in the late 1970s resulted in a sharp bunching of principal and interest payments due in the early 1980s. About $1.3 billion of Cuba's $1.7 billion commercial bank debt was reported due in 1982-1983. The risky borrowing strategy of the 1970s was heavily dependent on continued high prices for sugar and low interest rates.

The global recession of the 1980s affected Cuba's access to loans from Western banks just as it did that of other developing countries (see Chapter 2). In 1981 and 1982 Cuba saw its access to new loans and credit drop dramatically as Western creditors became suspicious of Eastern bloc ability to guarantee its hard-currency debt. In August 1982 the National Bank of Cuba informed its creditors that it would seek rescheduling of approximately one-third of its principal payments on its long-term debts. Cuba sought a postponement of repayment for 10 years, with a three-year grace period. It remained committed to continue payments of interest on the debt. In presenting its case to the Western bankers, Cuba blamed the drop in the free-market price for sugar, higher interest rates, and economic pressure from the United States for its predicament.

Cuba's concession that it cannot meet payments to Western banks represents a bitter pill to swallow. Adjustment to the economic realities of 1982 will require belt-tightening in a number of areas, including both food and capital goods imports. The latter, in particular, is likely to have an important effect on Cuba's long-term growth pattern. Development of nontraditional resources

and of energy substitutes in Cuba was heavily dependent
on Western technology in the recent past.

The Soviet Role in the Caribbean

Cuba provides the Soviet Union with a base of operations for merchant marine, fishing, naval, and satellite
intelligence activities. Of these, Soviet military operations cause the most concern to the United States. The
Soviet Union's initial naval deployments to the Caribbean
in 1969 are thought to have been made in response to
Cuba's concern for a demonstration of Soviet defense commitment, as well as a reward for Cuba's support of Soviet
policy in Czechoslovakia (Theberge, 1974; Dominguez, 1978).
With the emergence of Soviet blue water naval capabilities
in the 1970s, however, Cuba also became an important element in Soviet forward naval deployment. Some have even
suggested that the Soviet Union's Caribbean presence and
Cuban facilities represent a Soviet bargaining chip for
arms limitations discussions with the United States
(Murphy, 1978).

To date, no Soviet-Cuban defense agreement has been
drawn. The Soviet Union provided Cuba with several billion dollars' worth of military hardware during the 1970s,
considerably increasing Cuba's own defense capability.
Given the USSR's relatively small presence in the Caribbean and the long USSR-Cuba logistic support line, it is
questionable whether the Soviets would, in fact, come to
Cuba's defense in a crisis. This has long been a Cuban
concern and explains, in part, Cuba's support for Soviet
policy elsewhere.

Cuba does serve as a point from which the Soviet
Union can "show the flag" in a region where it has little
influence. Cuba also provides the USSR with facilities
for closely monitoring U.S. activities, for conducting
oceanographic research and military training in an area
in which it has no previous experience, and for repairing,
outfitting, and resupplying naval and merchant vessels,
thus extending their ability to remain away from the USSR.
Hence, Cuba plays a key role in Soviet forward naval deployment and in the demonstration of Soviet capabilities
as a premier world maritime nation.

Table 3.5 shows that Soviet activities in the Caribbean, as measured by ship days, declined between 1972 and
1976 before increasing substantially in 1977 and 1978.
The majority of these ships were auxiliaries, and hydro-
graphic research and space support vessels; 100 were intelligence collectors (Department of the Navy, 1979). Soviet ships spent fewer ship days in the Caribbean between
1979 and 1981, and between August 1979 and April 1981, no
Soviet ship called at Cuban ports. In April 1981 a task

TABLE 3.5
Soviet Out-of-Area Ship Deployment (Ship days)

	Atlantic	Mediterranean	Pacific	Indian	Caribbean	Total
1969	9,600	15,400	5,900	4,100	300	35,300
1970	13,600	17,400	7,100	4,900	700	43,700
1971	14,800	18,700	6,200	4,000	700	44,400
1972	14,500	17,700	5,300	8,900	1,900	48,900
1973	13,000	20,600	6,300	8,900	1,400	50,200
1974	13,900	20,200	7,400	10,500	1,200	53,200
1975	13,200	20,000	6,800	7,100	1,100	48,200
1976	14,000	18,600	6,500	7,300	1,000	47,400
1977	15,800	16,300	7,500	6,700	1,200	47,500
1978	16,100	16,600	6,900	8,500	1,300	49,400
1979	16,900	16,600	10,400	7,600	1,100	52,600
1980	16,900	16,600	11,800	11,800	700	57,800

Source: Watson (1982).

force that included a guided missile cruiser, two guided missile frigates, and an oiler again stopped in Cuba, initiating a new period of Soviet attention to Cuba's military buildup (Valenta, 1982; Watson, 1982).

In sum, the Soviets have used their access to the Caribbean to test U.S. reaction to expansion of their naval and air power, to monitor U.S. movements, and to place themselves in a position to take advantage of opportunities to turn the political balance in the Caribbean in their favor. Because of its still limited presence in the Caribbean, as well as Cuba's extreme distance from major elements of the Soviet fleet and obvious proximity to the United States, the Soviet Union is unlikely to risk a serious challenge to the United States in the Caribbean, either directly or via a Cuban proxy. Therefore, in spite of recent concern about airfields being enhanced in Grenada and Nicaragua, the Soviet base in the Caribbean will probably not be expanded much beyond Cuba. Most Latin American nationalists do not see their interests and those of the Soviet Union (or of Cuba) as identical; nor are these nationalists eager to trade perceived U.S. domination for Soviet domination. The principal effect of the Soviet presence in the Caribbean and in Cuba has been its psychological and symbolic rather than its military and strategic impact. Nevertheless, in the still conceivable chance that war might break out between the NATO and WARSAW Pact Alliance, the Soviet position in Cuba would give it great advantage in monitoring U.S. movements and could permit the Soviets and Cubans the same opportunity to interdict U.S. shipping to support NATO that German submarines operating in the vital Florida Straits enjoyed in World War II.

Prospects for United States-Cuba Relations

Continued heavy dependence on Soviet assistance severely constrains Cuba's economic development potential and influences its political choices. Because of the extremely limited relations the United States now maintains with Cuba, the United States has almost no policy instruments short of coercion available to exercise influence over Cuban behavior. However, the coercive threat lacks credibility, is inappropriate in most situations, and is constrained by the Soviet presence in Cuba. Over time, a number of scholars have argued that the principal target of opportunity for expanding influence with Cuba appears to be the economic sphere, in which Cuba stands to gain substantially. From time to time Cuba has signaled its interest in renewing trade relations with the United States, and the Soviet Union has encouraged this. Even in periods of rapprochement such as during the first year of the Carter administration, Cuba has been unwilling to negotiate difficult issues such as compensation

of American firms for property that was nationalized.
U.S. negotiators have generally been uninterested in
agreements that fail to deal with these legal obstacles,
and little headway has been made to improve relations between the two countries.

Over the past decade, and particularly during the
relative tranquility of the early 1970s, considerable energy has been devoted to constructing arguments for and
against major U.S. initiatives to resume formal relations
with Cuba. A number of positive steps were taken during
the Gerald Ford administration (1974-1975). Secret high-
level meetings were held in Havana, and agreements were
reached on dealing with airline hijacking, among other
things. The United States also acquiesced in the 1975
OAS decision to lift corrective economic sanctions against
Cuba. However, in November 1974, Cuba sent troops to as-
sist the Popular Movement for the Liberation of Angola
(MPLA) and Secretary of State Henry Kissinger announced
that further discussion with Cuba was out of the question.

The Carter administration came into office in 1977
armed with the recommendations of the Linowitz Commission
on United States Latin American Relations, among which
were to seek improvements in relations with Cuba. Interests (sic) sections were opened in the two capitals and
discussion on issues of mutual interest commenced. Agreements on maritime boundaries and fishing rights were
signed. Greater travel between the two countries was permitted. Rapprochement was brief, however, as Cuban activities in Africa, both in Angola in late 1977 and then
in Ethiopia in January 1978, soured the atmosphere for
further discussions. In August 1979 administration officials announced the "discovery" of a Soviet brigade in
Cuba, though authorities had known that Soviet troops had
been in Cuba since the early 1960s. In the spring of
1980, seemingly in a fit of pique, Castro unleashed the
exodus of 125,000 Cubans to southern Florida. Throughout
the final two years of the Carter administration, regional
analysts watched the buildup of Cuban involvement in the
Nicaraguan government and the increasing clandestine flow
of arms into Central America. The combined set of Cuban
activities represented both an affront to the United
States and profound "lack of good faith" on Cuba's part
that could not be ignored. Though it did not recall its
Interests Section head, the Carter administration aban-
doned all intentions to pursue relations with Cuba.

The Reagan administration came into office with a
profound bias against Cuba, one that had been stirred by
campaign rhetoric in both 1976 and 1980 and in the prolonged discussion of the Panama Canal Treaty. One recom-
mendation for future administration policy stated that

> ...Cuba is not only an effective weapon for the
> Soviet Union in Africa and the Middle East, it
> is also increasingly effective as a force for
> subversion of our southern flank--the Caribbean
> and Central America. The next administration
> must understand that Havana does not want nor-
> mal relations except on its terms--terms which
> are inimical to the most basic security inter-
> ests of the United States and our friends in
> the Western hemisphere.

> ...Cuba at some point must be held liable for
> working with the Soviets on a successful policy
> of subversion and destabilization in this hemi-
> sphere. (Council for Inter-American Security,
> 1980)

In the spring of 1981, administration officials suggested
that U.S. policy toward Cuba would be designed to "keep
the Cubans worrying" (U.S. Senate, 1981). Throughout 1981
administration pronouncements seemed to suggest the possibility that even military actions could be contemplated
in dealing with the Cuba problem. By 1982, administration policy focused more intently on longer term ap-
proaches--Radio Marti, the propaganda organ designed to
bring objective information to the Cuban people, and
tightened trade and travel policies designed to reduce
Cuba's access to hard currency. The U.S. Interests Section ceased issuing visas to Cubans seeking to leave the
country, and currency and travel restrictions were
reinforced.

The policy pronouncements of administrations obscure
an important fact of the domestic American political scene
that is of profound importance in dealing with the Cuba
question: anti-Cuban sentiment is deeply rooted and
widespread in the United States and extremely emotional.
Such sentiment reflects the political frustrations of
1959-1961 when the Communist regime was first established
in this hemisphere, and it is fostered by the very strong
interest groups representing conservative interests and
the Cuban exile community in the United States. The combined political weight of these movements, together with
widespread anti-Cuban sentiment at the grassroots, caused
both President Ford and President Carter to abandon a
pragmatic approach to Cuba in their election campaigns.
President Carter also saw himself obliged to abandon his
early Cuba policy in order to achieve passage of the
Panama Canal treaties.

Wayne S. Smith, former head of the U.S. Interests
Section in Havana, has noted that U.S. perceptions of the
Cuba problem and of its solutions are distorted by sev-
eral misperceptions. The first is the belief that the

Castro regime could be "disposed" or "would disappear" if only the right "fix" could be found. In contrast, most professionals acknowledge that the Castro government is "here to stay." The second misperception is the view that Cuban actions everywhere in the world are "tests" of U.S. resolve, rather than independent policy choices motivated by Cuba's (or the Soviet Union's) own interests. Finally, Smith notes that Castro himself evokes such extremely emotional responses from both his supporters and his detractors that "dispassionate analysis between these extremes is extraordinarily rare" (Smith, 1982). In combination these idiosyncracies of U.S. public perception have precluded the implementation of a long-range policy toward Cuba by a number of U.S. administrations.

In the prevailing climate of public opinion any major bold initiative toward Cuba has very high political costs. Moreover, the benefits for taking the political risk of seeking better relations with Cuba are few. Indeed, the principal beneficiary of rapprochement would be Cuba itself. It is argued that the United States has failed to offer Cuba alternatives to its heavy dependence on the Soviet Union. Yet the United States has little to offer Cuba that could alter its dependence on the Soviet Union or its commitment to its hierarchy of foreign policy goals, including fraternal support to revolutions.

The principal obstacles to gradual engagement and rapprochement with Cuba (see Dominguez, 1978; Leogrande, 1982a, 1982b; and Smith, 1982) are precisely Cuba's heavy, but beneficial dependence on the Soviet Union. It does not pay for the military equipment that has made it the most modern armed force in the hemisphere after the United States. No possible change in U.S. policy toward Cuba could substitute for the benefits it derives from its present relationship.

Proponents of gradual engagement do not claim that Cuban policy would change if the United States modified rapprochements. Leogrande (1982) notes that

Differences (between U.S. and Cuban) values translate into sharply conflicting policies across a broad spectrum of international issues.... It would be naive to expect that even under the best of circumstances the opportunities for accord and mutual benefit will ever overshadow the occasions for conflict and competition....

The United States does not have sufficient leverage to coerce Cuba into abandoning its support for revolution; even a more constructive

policy of engagement can at best produce only
marginal Cuban restraint. Therefore, the most
effective U.S. policy is one that responds first
and foremost to the local causes of the conflicts Cuba seeks to exploit.

Opponents of engagement with Cuba tend to offer "tough-
ness" and "pressure and inducements" to gain effective
leverage over Cuba. They offer the attractive prospect
of a "finlandization" of Cuba. However, they fail to
recognize both the profound dependency on the Soviet Union, a dependency that Finland does not have, and the
paucity of policy instruments the United States might
have to exert either effective pressure or meaningful
inducements.

In the emotional atmosphere of the debate on Cuba
policy, a few analysts are increasingly attracted to a
third alternative for dealing with Cuba--a policy of
studied neglect of Cuba and Cuban issues. The policy of
studied neglect recognizes, as Leogrande noted above,
that the principal problems Cuba exploits in the hemisphere and elsewhere are problems whóse origins and solutions are independent of Cuban involvement. It also
recognizes the very low probability that Cuba's foreign
policy will change in any meaningful way, even if U.S.
policy were less pointedly antagonistic toward Cuba. The
policy also recognizes the very high domestic political
costs of engaging in any serious discussion with Cuba
unless Cuban policies are likely to change and judges
those costs too high. Finally, it acknowledges the very
small benefit that might accrue from diminished tension
between the United States and Cuba.

Over the next several years, and perhaps until many
of the questions of political direction in Central America
and the Caribbean are settled, any revision of United
States-Cuban relations is likely to be more costly than
politicians can accept. Today, relations toward Cuba
are confined within a still tolerable range. Intensified
hostilities ahd particularly direct confrontation with
Cuba are rejected by a Congress that fears provoking an
unwanted military involvement. Concessions in negotiations are resisted by the host of interests representing
hardliners, anti-Communist conservatives, Cuban exile
groups, and corporations seeking compensation for expro-
priations. If policy makers are not confronted with the
need to choose between one and another attitude toward
Cuba, U.S. relations with Cuba can continue on the present
low key for a very long time. The interests of the two
countries diverge, but conflict is minimal except in areas
where Cuba exploits problems the United States must deal
with by other means.

Studied neglect does not preclude dealing with bilateral issues such as the Mariel refugees, or cultural exchange and travel provisions, but it does not give great urgency to these issues either. Indeed, it makes explicit the ad hoc procedure that has characterized U.S. dealings with Cuba for many years. The policy worked because it created no expectations for either government or interest groups to react to.

NOTES

1. In the discussion in this chapter, the term "Caribbean basin" is used to refer to the region and set of countries bounding the Caribbean Sea, including Central America (Guatemala, Belize, Honduras, El Salvador, Nicaragua, Costa Rica, and Panama), north coast South America (only Venezuela is treated in detail), and the island republics of the Greater and Lesser Antilles. Guyana and Suriname are generally also included in the Caribbean basin but are treated only in passing in the discussion. Mexico, a power of potential major influence in the region, is treated in depth in Chapter 4. The terms Commonwealth Caribbean and East Caribbean refer to the former British, French, and Dutch colonies of the Lesser Antilles. When the term "Caribbean," as opposed to "Caribbean basin," is used, it refers to the island republics from Jamaica to Trinidad and Tobago in general.
2. Sistema Económico Latino-Americano, or Latin American Economic System.
3. Scholars regard Cuba's early activisim in Latin America to have been prompted in part by the need to obtain renewed Soviet commitment to support Cuba after the Soviets' withdrawal of missiles from Cuba in 1962, and the lukewarm economic support the Soviets offered in their 1964 trade agreement with Cuba. Cuban activism occurred at a period when Moscow and the Latin American Communist parties were "disengaging from the armed struggle" in favor of bilateral diplomatic-economic rapprochement and detente (Gonzalez, 1974).
4. The United States government and Cuba have never agreed on the number of Cuban personnel actually in Nicaragua. Castro has admitted that there are about 3,000 Cuban advisers in Nicaragua, the majority teachers, health technicians, agricultural technicians, and others. The United States maintains that in addition there are some 1,500 or more military advisers working alongside the Sandinista forces and in the government. Castro has skirted the issue, maintaining that "Cuba has not sent one soldier of its special forces or of any other forces to Nicaragua. Cuba has never sent troops to Nicaragua" (Dominguez, 1982). Cubans have been reported killed in clashes between Nicaraguan forces and counter-revolutionary forces operating along the Nicaraguan-Honduran border.

5. Dominguez (1978a) notes that "apparently Cuba cannot raise funds in the capital markets unless leaders assume that the full faith of credit of the Soviet Union stands behind Cuban borrowing."

4
Mexico: The Promise of Oil

Bruce M. Bagley

INTRODUCTION

Mexican oil and gas discoveries in the 1970s cata-
pulted Mexico into the ranks of the premier oil exporting
nations of the world almost overnight. Quite understandably, such spectacular finds during a period of global
petroleum shortages and price increases focused American
public attention on Mexico more intensely than at any
time in recent memory. However, the United States' re-
discovery of Mexico overshadows the fact that even before
the recent oil boom the bilateral relationship between
these two North American neighbors was of vital importance
to both. Indeed, the links between the United States and
Mexico constitute one of the most intense relationships
between a developed and a developing nation anywhere on
the globe and this relationship has been so for more than
a century. With oil, the interdependence of the two nations has gained new salience. But oil is not the only,
much less the most important, key to the U.S.-Mexican
bilateral relationship. Among other important elements
are:

- An essentially undefended 1,942-mile common
  border.

- The presence of millions of Mexicans and persons
  of Mexican descent in the United States and the
  likelihood that additional millions will enter
  this country over the coming decade.

- Extensive and expanding commercial trade. As
  has already been noted, Mexico is the United
  States' third largest trading partner, accounting
  for about 4 percent of total U.S. trade; the

Dr. Bruce M. Bagley is professor of Latin American Studies at The
Johns Hopkins University School of Advanced International Studies.

United States in turn is Mexico's most important
market, receiving more than 60 percent of Mexico's exports.

● Enormous U.S. investment--$5.9 billion in direct
investment and $15 billion (about 75 percent of
Mexico's total) in outstanding loans and credits--
which makes Mexico the second-ranking developing
world country in terms of U.S. financial exposure.

● Large deposits of nonpetroleum raw materials that
make Mexico the United States' second most important supplier of critical raw materials after
Canada.

● Mexico's increasingly independent foreign policy
and potential for leadership in Third World
movements.

● Mexico's potential for exercising a moderating
role in the increasingly unstable regions of
Central America and the Caribbean, despite its
traditional aloofness from regional politics.

As these examples indicate, economic issues lie at
the heart of U.S.-Mexican relations. Divergent positions
on economic issues strongly color the quality of political
relations between the two countries. The economic emphasis in U.S.-Mexican relations stems from Mexico's proximity to the United States and its long-standing dependence on U.S. markets, investment, and financing. In
contrast to most Latin American countries, Mexico has
had a relatively stable political system since its revolution (1910-1917) and, therefore, its internal political
conditions have attracted little attention in the United
States. Also because of its nearness to the United
States, Mexico has not expanded military capabilities,
nor has it been a major figure in the debate over arms
sales or military assistance in the region.

Although Mexico is one of the four major powers in
Latin America (with Brazil, Argentina, and Venezuela) and
is second only to Brazil in size, population, and economic base, Mexico has been historically the least aggressive in establishing a regional leadership role. Its
ties with neighbors in Central America have traditionally
been characterized by restraint, in part because of Central American fears of Mexican economic domination and
in part because of Mexico's own greater concern with
domestic economic and political problems. Since the
Nicaraguan revolution in 1979, however, Mexico has begun
to play a more active role in Central America and the
Caribbean. In addition, it is likely that Mexico's oil

wealth will afford it opportunities to play a greatly
expanded role in the Caribbean Basin and in the hemisphere in the 1980s.

U.S. relations with Mexico are at an important cross-
road. Mexico's petroleum wealth represents both a source
of secure energy supply for the United States for the
long term and an opportunity for rapid and diversified
development for Mexico. However, Mexico is determined to
exploit its oil wealth only at a rate and under conditions that will serve first its own national interests.
U.S. energy needs must be reconciled with Mexico's own
long-range goals and interests, particularly its desire
to establish greater self-sufficiency and independence
from the United States. U.S. interest in Mexican petroleum and Mexico's desire to reduce its economic dependence on the United States introduce unavoidable tensions
in the bilateral relationship.

Like other Latin American countries, Mexico is most
interested at present in its own economic development.
Whereas such development interests in other countries
have been overshadowed by episodic political and military
crises, in Mexico the economic issues have consistently
headed the bilateral policy agenda. Examination of the
divergent U.S.-Mexican interests provides an opportunity
to focus on themes of high priority for other nations in
the region too: trade, investment, debt, protectionism,
economic nationalism, technology transfer, and immigration. Similarly, the solutions that Mexico seeks to its
problems with its dominant partner are frequently the
solutions sought by other countries in the region. Thus,
examination of the Mexican case can help illuminate U.S.
interests in the issues that Latin American nations perceive as crucial in the inter-American relationship.

This chapter examines a number of the most important
current issues in U.S.-Mexican relations:

- The strong interdependence of U.S.-Mexican economic relations and the question of U.S.
  protectionism;

- U.S. investment in Mexico and Mexico's indebtedness to U.S. banks;

- Illegal immigration from Mexico and border
  problems;

- Potential causes, and the implications for the
  United States, of possible political instability
  in Mexico in the future; and

- U.S. access to Mexican oil and gas supplies.

U.S. relations with Mexico are profound, widereach-
ing, and likely to increase over the coming decades.
Mexico's economic potential, especially its petroleum potential, gives it special leverage in its relations with
the United States even in times of economic crisis. U.S.
interests are chiefly economic in the Mexican context,
but they have important ramifications for U.S. political
and security interests in the wider subregion of the
hemisphere. The chapter argues that U.S. interests in
the region can be most securely guaranteed by promoting
conditions that contribute to Mexico's further economic
development even if that development results in a diminution of the present U.S. economic position in Mexico or a
lower U.S. share of Mexican oil and gas exports. A
healthy Mexican economy is essential (1) to preclude the
emergence of political instability in Mexico that would
spill over into the United States and (2) to strengthen
the political and economic backbone of the broader Caribbean and Central American community of nations.

For most of the years following World War II, U.S.
foreign policy architects paid little attention to Mexico.
Economically underdeveloped, dependent on the United
States, militarily weak, and politically stable, Mexico
presented no serious challenge to U.S. economic or security interests and could easily and safely be neglected.
With the discovery of major new oil and gas reserves in
Mexico during the 1970s, however, U.S. awareness of and
interest in Mexico began to rise dramatically. Statistics
on Mexican oil potential clearly indicate why U.S. interest in Mexico has become so intense:

- In 1981 Mexico claimed 72.5 billion barrels of
  proven petroleum reserves, another 58.6 billion
  of probable reserves, and more than 250 billion
  potential reserves, ranking it among the top five
  potential oil producers in the world.

- In mid-1981, Mexico was producing 2.6 million barrels per day (bpd) and exporting 1.4 million bpd.

- By 1982 Mexico had replaced Saudi Arabia as the
  United States' most important source of imported
  oil.

- Mexico will be capable of producing up to 5 million bpd by 1985 and as many as 10 million bpd by
  1990 if it chooses.

- The United States continues to import more than
  44 percent of its petroleum needs, with approximately 5 percent coming from Mexico.

Although Mexican petroleum is obviously of growing
significance to the United States, it is not the only U.S.
interest in Mexico. Economic linkages between the two
countries are numerous and intense. Mexico's gross national product (GNP), $164 billion in 1980, ranked Mexico
as the second largest economy in Latin America (behind
Brazil's $240 billion), the 13th-largest economy in the
Western world, and the 18th-largest worldwide. In 1980
Mexico's population of 70 million was growing at a rate
of 3.3 percent a year; it is projected to reach 116 million by the year 2000 (World Bank, 1980). After Brazil,
Mexico is the largest and most significant country in
Latin America; it is rapidly emerging as a major regional
economic power and an important Third World leader.

Between 1960 and 1976, Mexico's economy grew at an
average rate of 7.3 percent annually as compared with
3.4 percent for Western industrial countries. Real growth
in 1980 was 8.3 percent. Conservative estimates for the
1980s projected Mexican economic growth at about 6.5 percent per annum. At this rate, by 1985 Mexico's GNP would
be $245 billion and by 1990, approximately $365 billion
(Central Intelligence Agency, 1981). Sheer size will increase Mexico's economic influence in the world system
and its importance to the United States.

The Mexican economy is not only growing rapidly in
size; it is also becoming increasingly industrialized.
Between 1960 and 1977, industrial sector contribution to
the Mexican GNP expanded from 29 to 36 percent, while
agriculture dropped from 16 to 10 percent. During the
same period, industry's contribution to the GNP in Brazil,
for example, expanded by only 2 percentage points, from
35 to 37 percent, while the industrial share of U.S. GNP
declined from 38 to 34 percent (World Bank, 1979). With
industrialization, Mexico has emerged as an important exporter of manufactured goods. In 1976, more than half
(52 percent) of Mexican exports were manufactures, up
from only 12 percent in 1960. The manufactures' share
of exports is twice that of other Latin American industrial nations and greater than that of the Soviet Union,
Canada, Greece, South Africa, or India (see Chapter 3,
Table 3.3). Moreover, 75 percent of Mexican manufactures
exports were destined for the developed countries, particularly the United States (World Bank, 1979).

Mexico is also an important producer of raw materials
and the United States' second most important supplier of
nonfuel raw materials, behind only Canada. Eighty-five
percent of the strontium, 73 percent of the fluorspar,
18 percent of the antimony, and significant quantities of
a variety of other raw materials of critical importance
to the U.S. economy are imported from Mexico. As in the
cases of oil and natural gas, these supplies take on

added significance because Mexico's proximity to the
United States makes them defensible in times of international crisis.

Each year Mexico supplies the United States with
millions of workers who perform low-skill tasks for relatively low wages, thus lowering U.S. labor costs. With
an aging labor force and low birth rate, the U.S. economy
is estimated to require at least 20 million extra workers
between 1980 and 2000. Sixty to 65 percent of these workers are likely to be Mexicans. Without Mexican labor,
many U.S. industries would either be forced out of business altogether or be obligated to transfer operations to
other countries.

Mexico is an important arena for U.S. investment. In
1980, U.S. direct private investment in Mexico amounted to
over $5 billion. More than 75 percent of U.S. investment
in Mexico is found in the industrial sector, giving U.S.
firms a major financial stake in Mexico's industrial economy. Indeed, U.S. multinationals operating in Mexico accounted for 50 percent of all Mexico's manufactured exports in the 1970s. By 1982 the country's public debt
reached $80 billion and U.S. commercial banks held approx-
imately 30 percent of the debt.

Mexico is the second-largest non-oil-producing recipient of international bank loans. With Brazil, it accounts for nearly one-fourth of all developing country
disbursed debt (OECD, 1978). In 1979 Mexico used more
than half of its export income to service the foreign
debt. In the mid-1970s the international financial community expressed considerable concern over Mexico's excessive indebtedness. However, oil revenues, an IMF Stabilization Plan, and Mexican President Jose Lopez Portillo's
skillful management of the economy between 1977 and 1979
restored confidence in the economy that had been badly
shaken under the previous administration (Fortune,
July 16, 1979:138-39; LAIS, Vol. I, No. 25, Nov. 16, 1979:
294-95). The U.S. financial system remains heavily exposed in Mexico and a major economic crisis there would
have severe repercussions for U.S. economic interests.
The recession and oil glut of 1981-1982, as well as the
overvaluation of the Mexican peso, raised concerns about
the Mexican economy just as the transition from Lopez
Portillo to his chosen successor, Miguel de la Madrid,
began. De la Madrid will face very difficult economic
choices when he begins his six-year term in December 1982.

While the U.S. and Mexican economies grew increasingly interdependent over the 1970s, relations between
the two nations became gradually more strained. The tensions were due in large part to Mexico's desire to re-
negotiate the terms of its relationship with the United

States to control and channel foreign investment, to gain
greater access to U.S. markets for its agricultural and
manufactured exports, and to diversify its trading partners. Mexico's growing confidence and sense of nationalism also contributed to the tension. Economic growth and
oil potential created the conditions under which Mexico
could assume a more nationalistic and independent foreign
policy toward the United States.

To continue its export-led economic expansion, Mexico
needs access to larger markets and new trading partners.
Its foreign policies have not always contributed to these
goals. In the early 1970s, the Echeverria administration
(1970-1976) broke with Mexico's traditional posture of
minimal participation in foreign affairs and adopted a
Third World-oriented policy designed to expand Mexico's
trade with the developing countries. The approach, combined with a series of reformist, welfare-oriented domestic policies, gained Mexico few new trading partners and
produced a crisis of confidence that resulted in a massive flight of capital and major devaluation (Clement and
Green, 1978).

Echeverria's successor, Jose Lopez Portillo, assumed
a more pragmatic foreign policy stance, moved to win back
international business confidence, and sought to establish more cordial relations with the United States.
Nevertheless, even during the Lopez Portillo presidency,
Mexico continued to pursue diversification of trade relationships as a main foreign policy goal. There is every
indication that Mexico will continue to pursue these foreign policy goals.

The difficulties the United States encountered during the 1977-1979 negotiations for Mexican natural gas are
one manifestation of this independence. Mexico's recent
contracts to supply oil to Canada, Germany, France, Japan,
Israel, and Spain, as well as several Caribbean Basin
countries, are another.

Mexico is particularly wary of U.S. interests in its
new-found oil wealth. The Mexicans see petroleum as an
historic, "last chance" opportunity to develop their own
economy. They have repeatedly stated that they will exploit their reserves in accord with their own national
development goals, rather than with the demands and needs
of an energy-short United States. They are willing to
sell oil and natural gas to the United States, but the
rate of production and the amount they will sell depend
on internal domestic needs and capacities rather than U.S.
or world demand. For example, with the softening of world
oil prices in 1981 and early 1982, the Lopez Portillo
government appeared likely to raise production and export
levels substantially in order to make up for lost revenues

130

(Latin American Weekly Report, February 5, 1982). The
United States might also seek to encourage higher levels
of production in Mexico by offering incentives in areas
such as trade, technology, and immigration. However,
major U.S. concessions in these areas would be difficult
to obtain in the short run because of problems of recession, unemployment, and a worsening balance of payments
in the United States.

Security issues, other than economic security, are
not at present a major item on the U.S.-Mexican agenda,
although Central American crises may make them more salient in the next few years. Mexico has enjoyed more than
50 years of relative political stability under the dominant Partido Revolucionario Institucional (PRI). Nevertheless, Mexico's long-term political stability could be
threatened by high birth rates, high rates of underemployment and unemployment (between 40 and 50 percent of the
labor force), persistent poverty in rural and urban areas,
one of the worst income-distribution patterns in Latin
America, extensive bureaucratic corruption, growing levels
of voter abstention, a weakening of PRI control over
younger elements of the population and the urban poor,
and increasing government reliance on the military. Future oil income and rapid industrialization could contribute to destabilization by increasing the pace of
urbanization and uprooting the peasant population. The
middle classes could become increasingly discontent if
the government is unable to correct the endemic problems
of waste, corruption, and economic mismanagement. Increased polarization may occur among Mexican political
and economic elites as the country experiences more dramatic challenges to its political institutions along with
rapid economic growth in the 1980s.

Mexican leaders, aware of the negative experiences
of Iran and other oil-rich countries, have attempted to
dampen rising expectations and to avoid overheating the
economy by limiting oil production and revenues to levels
consistent with the country's absorptive capacity. Between 1973 and 1977 they moved to strengthen the political
system through a process of "democratization" that gave
greater opportunities for representation to political
parties other than the PRI, and to control economic
growth through state planning. The long-term success of
these policy measures is still unclear, however.

While Mexico's prospects for stability appear reason-
ably good, the unsolved problems mentioned above indicate
that the potential for instability remains. A politically
unstable Mexico would constitute a major threat to both
the economic and security interests of the United States.
The United States must therefore be particularly sensitive
to Mexico's problems in its bilateral negotiations over

petroleum, trade, technology, immigration, and investment
during the 1980s.

The remaining sections of this chapter examine in detail the nature of U.S. interests in Mexico. The six main
issue areas important to the future development of both
countries, the improvement of U.S.-Mexican relations, and
the preservation of hemispheric stability are as follows:

- Mexican-American trade and protectionism;

- U.S. investment in Mexico and Mexican nationalism;

- The energy issues of petroleum, natural gas, and
  nuclear power;

- Mexican immigration and border issues;

- Mexican foreign policy and hemispheric security;
  and

- Constraints on Mexico's growth and political
  stability.

These issues are introduced below with a brief review of
Mexico's current position in the international economy.
Then each issue area is discussed in terms of its bi-
lateral, regional, and global implications.

MEXICO'S ROLE IN THE INTERNATIONAL ECONOMY

One of the clearest indicators of the extensive interdependence that characterizes U.S. and Mexican economic
relations is the flow of trade across the border. Tables
4.1 and 4.2 indicate the extent to which the United States
dominates Mexico's foreign trade profile. In 1977 the
United States received nearly 60 percent of Mexico's more
than $4 billion in exports. The U.S. market accounted for
85 percent of Mexico's exports to the industrial world.
Mexico's next largest export market was Brazil, with
$150 million in trade, only 6 percent of the value of
trade with the United States. The European community absorbed only 5.2 percent of Mexico's exports, with West
Germany accounting for over one-third of that market.
Venezuela, Israel, Spain, and Guatemala were other important export markets, though none accounted for more than
$100 million in trade for Mexico. Although export trade
to Japan declined sharply in 1976 and 1977, this trade
relationship is expected to grow through the 1980s as
Japan becomes a major buyer of Mexican oil. The United
States and Latin American markets have increased in importance over time, while the European market has declined
from its 1960 and 1970 positions.

TABLE 4.1
Country Markets for Mexican Exports: 1960-1980
(Percentage of total exports)

	1960	1965	1970	1971	1972	1973	1974	1975	1976	1977	1978	1979	1980
United States	59.6	54.9	59.8	60.7	66.0	58.3	56.9	57.2	60.8	65.7	64.0	69.3	78.5
Canada	0.9	0.8	0.9	1.2	1.2	1.3	2.2	1.5	1.4	1.1	0.8	0.9	1.1
Latin America	3.0	6.0	8.7	10.1	11.7	10.9	12.3	12.7	12.2	12.2	10.2	6.8	5.7
Other Western Hemisphere (Caribbean)	0.2	1.2	0.5	0.4	0.3	0.4	1.5	1.6	1.5	0.7	0.4	0.4	3.1
EEC	9.4	5.4	5.8	4.6	6.1	7.3	11.8	8.9	8.5	6.4	5.2	6.2	6.5
Other Europe	1.7	2.7	2.3	3.0	2.8	3.7	3.7	2.2	3.0	3.7	3.3	5.9	7.3
Middle East	0.1	1.9	0.1	0.1	0.1	0.3	0.4	1.9	2.2	1.8	1.8	1.5	3.4
Japan	5.8	7.1	4.8	4.3	6.6	6.5	4.8	3.7	5.1	3.1	1.7	3.3	3.7
Asia	1.1	1.3	0.5	0.4	0.8	0.7	0.8	0.9	0.4	0.5	0.3	0.5	0.4
Africa (including S. Africa)	0.3	0.3	0.1	0.1	0.1	0.1	0.2	0.1	0.1	0.3	0.2	0.1	0.1
Centrally Planned Economies	0.3	5.5	0.3	0.7	1.9	2.2	1.6	2.2	1.6	1.9	1.3	2.0	1.3
Other	17.6	12.9	16.2	14.4	2.4	8.3	3.8	7.1	3.2	2.6	10.8	3.1	-
Total %	100.0	100.0	100.0	100.0	100.0	100.0	100.0	100.0	100.0	100.0	100.0	100.0	107.4
Value (U.S. $ millions)	$764	$1,142	$1,404	$1,501	$1,695	$2,262	$2,994	$2,917	$3,469	$4,171	$5,592	$8,578	$15,340

Source: International Monetary Fund, Direction of Trade Statistics.

TABLE 4.2
Country Sources of Mexican Imports: 1960-1980
(Percentage of total imports)

	1960	1965	1970	1971	1972	1973	1974	1975	1976	1977	1978	1979	1980
United States	72.2	65.8	63.6	61.4	62.8	59.7	62.4	62.5	62.5	63.7	60.4	58.8	65.6
Canada	2.8	2.4	2.0	2.0	3.2	2.2	2.4	2.2	2.3	3.0	1.7	1.7	1.9
Latin America	1.0	2.4	3.2	4.0	3.3	5.7	5.3	6.8	4.7	5.1	4.5	5.1	3.7
Other Western Hemisphere (Caribbean)	0.2	0.2	0.5	1.0	1.1	2.0	1.3	1.1	2.1	0.5	0.4	0.5	0.2
EEC	16.8	19.6	18.7	19.4	17.6	16.7	17.6	16.6	16.3	14.7	18.5	16.4	13.8
Other Europe	3.9	4.8	6.7	6.7	5.8	6.1	4.6	4.2	4.7	5.9	4.3	4.6	4.5
Middle East	(*)	(*)	0.1	(*)	(*)	(*)	0.2	0.1	0.1	(*)	(*)	(*)	0.1
Japan	1.4	2.5	3.5	3.7	4.8	4.7	3.7	4.5	5.1	5.4	8.1	6.7	5.3
Asia	0.5	0.6	0.7	0.7	0.6	0.7	0.5	0.4	0.5	0.8	0.7	0.8	1.0
Africa	0.1	(*)	0.1	0.2	0.3	0.8	0.5	0.7	0.5	0.1	0.4	0.4	0.1
Centrally Planned Economies	0.3	0.4	0.3	0.3	0.2	0.6	0.8	0.4	0.6	0.4	0.7	0.7	1.5
Other	0.8	1.3	0.6	0.6	0.3	0.6	0.7	0.5	0.6	0.4	0.3	4.7	2.3
Total %	100.0	100.0	100.0	100.0	100.0	100.0	100.0	100.0	100.0	100.0	100.0	100.0	100.0
Value (U.S. $ millions)	$1,186	$1,599	$2,465	$2,404	$3,474	$3,813	$6,059	$6,582	$6,036	$5,486	$7,560	$11,992	$19,529

(*) represents less than 0.05 percent.

Source: International Monetary Fund, Direction of Trade Statistics.

133

The United States also dominates Mexico's imports with 60 percent of the total market share. The European community, again led by Germany, but also including the United Kingdom and France as major suppliers, provided less than one-third the U.S. share. Since the mid-1960s Japan has almost tripled its market share in Mexico and has become the third-largest supplier of imports. Nevertheless, Japan accounted for only 8 percent of all Mexico's imports in its best year, 1978. Despite increasing European and Japanese interest in selling to Mexico and Mexico's efforts to diversify sources of imports, relative market shares have remained remarkably stable over the past decade.

Mexico's trade with the European Common Market increased substantially over the decade of the 1970s although it did not approximate U.S. levels. In 1970, Mexico exported goods worth only $61 million to Europe and imported less than $500 million. By 1980, however, Mexican exports to Europe had risen to $2.1 billion while its imports had grown to almost $3.6 billion (see Table 4.1). Mexican trade linkages with Japan also expanded during the 1970s. Between 1970 and 1980 Mexican exports rose from about $69 million to about $563 million while imports grew from $86 million to $1 billion. The United States continues to be Mexico's chief trading partner, but European and Japanese imports are rapidly penetrating Mexico's markets. As new oil supply contracts with various European nations and Japan come into effect, the total volume of trade will undoubtedly expand further and the large balance-of-trade deficit that Mexico incurred with these countries during the 1970s will probably decline.

In 1981 Mexico became the United States' third-largest trading partner. During the 1970s it supplied approximately 3 percent of U.S. imports and purchased 5 percent of U.S. exports (Ronfeldt and Sereseres, 1978: 11). From 1971 to 1980 the value of Mexican exports to the United States climbed steadily from $800 million to $9.6 billion in 1980, while Mexican imports from the United States grew from $1.3 billion to $12.8 billion. Imports declined to $3.5 billion in 1977 in the wake of Mexico's 1976 economic crisis and devaluation, but rose again to $4.5 billion in 1978 and have continued to expand ever since. Between 1977 and 1978, as a result of the recovery of the Mexican economy and the expansion of oil production, the total value of U.S.-Mexican trade jumped from $9.5 billion (including tourism) to $12.7 billion. By 1981, the total bilateral trade was close to $27 billion.

Mexico's principal exports to the United States and Europe have traditionally been agricultural products and raw materials (e.g., coffee, cattle, cotton, winter

vegetables, sugar, shrimp, petroleum, zinc, and fluorspar)
and light manufactures (e.g., electronic and electrical
goods, textiles, and shoes). A product breakdown of Mexican exports is presented in Table 4.3. Mexico's imports
have typically consisted of capital goods (e.g., heavy
equipment and machinery). In the 1970s grain foodstuffs,
corn, wheat, and sorghum became increasingly significant
imports as Mexico's domestic food production failed to
keep pace with demand (see Table 4.4). The Mexican public
sector's imports expanded much faster than did those of
the private sector in the early 1970s both because the
state sector represents a large proportion of the economy
and because the Mexican government restricted the importa-
tion of luxury and consumer goods. Under the Lopez Portillo administration, this trend was reversed and the private sector now imports more than the government.

U.S.-Mexican Trade and Protectionism

    Table 4.5 indicates that throughout the 1960s and
1970s, Mexico consistently maintained a trade deficit with
all industrialized nations. Its trade deficit with the
United States alone averaged over $1 billion a year dur-
ing the 1970s. Through 1975, this deficit was largely
offset by income from U.S. tourism ($2 billion annually),
border commerce ($2 billion to $3 billion annually), and
wage remissions to Mexico by undocumented Mexicans working
in the United States ($2 billion to $4 billion annually).
In 1975, however, the Mexican trade deficit with the
United States ballooned to almost $2.5 billion as a result
of political and economic problems, particularly the
flight of $2 billion to $4 billion capital in 1975-1976,
a decline in U.S. tourism precipitated by the Jewish boycott of Mexico following the Echeverria administration's
1975 condemnation of Zionism in the United Nations, the
U.S. recession, and a fall in international commodity
prices (Ronfeldt and Sereseres, 1978).

    In response to the 1975-1976 economic crisis, the
Mexican government adopted a series of corrective measures
that were designed to restore economic equilibrium, to
restrict imports, and to spur exports. Among the most important steps were the 1976 devaluation, introduction of
new savings instruments, reorganization of the banking
system, adjustments of interest rates, and implementation
of a three-year stabilization program in accord with International Monetary Fund (IMF) guidelines, all in return
for a $1.2 billion IMF line of credit (Euromoney, 1978).
These policies were relatively successful in diminishing
the Mexican trade deficit and in stimulating GNP growth
in 1977 and 1978 (Euromoney, 1978). Despite a 133 percent
increase in oil export revenues during 1979, however, the
nation's budget deficit rose more than $6 billion, and

TABLE 4.3
Mexican Exports, 1970-1980 (Percentages of total commodity exports)

	1970	1975	1976	1977	1978	1979	1980
Food and Beverages	39.3	31.9	33.2	33.4	30.3	22.7	11.8
Fish and Fish Preparations	5.9	5.6	5.7	4.6	7.8	4.3	2.6
Fruit and Vegetables	9.3	9.0	8.2	10.7	8.9	7.6	4.2
Sugar and Honey	8.5	6.0	1.4	1.2	1.3	1.0	0.5
Coffee	6.2	6.7	10.9	11.4	6.0	6.7	2.9
Raw Materials (except fuel)	19.2	13.9	15.6	9.8	9.5	7.9	5.6
Cotton	6.9	6.1	8.4	4.4	4.6	3.6	2.1
Fertilizer and Minerals	5.2	1.7	3.6	2.9	2.5	2.0	1.6
Fuels	3.2	16.2	16.5	21.9	28.6	43.9	67.3
Crude Petroleum	(NA)	15.3	16.2	21.3	28.2	42.8	61.6
Petroleum Products	2.6	0.8	0.3	0.5	0.4	1.1	2.8
Manufactures (except machinery)	29.4	28.1	27.1	17.8	12.5	7.0	3.2
Chemicals	8.1	7.8	7.5	8.0	6.7	(NA)	(NA)
Textiles	2.3	4.0	3.7	2.8	1.7	1.9	1.0
Nonferrous Metals	7.6	5.4	4.4	1.2	1.1	1.3	1.5
Clothing	0.8	1.1	1.0	0.7	0.5	(NA)	(NA)
Machinery, Transport Equipment	10.6	9.8	7.4	5.9	9.7	6.0	4.2
Nonelectrical	4.1	4.4	4.4	2.7	3.8	1.3	0.8
Electrical	4.5	2.1	1.6	1.7	1.4	0.4	1.0
Transportation Equipment	2.0	3.2	1.4	1.5	4.5	4.3	2.4
Other	0.1	0.1	0.2	11.2	9.4	12.5	7.9
Total	100.0	100.0	100.0	100.0	100.0	100.0	100.0
Exports Value (U.S. $ millions)	$1,205	$2,861	$3,353	$4,183	$5,771	$8,768	(NA)

Source: United Nations: Yearbook of International Trade Statistics, various issues.

137

TABLE 4.4
Mexican Imports, 1970-1980
(Percentages of total commodity imports)

	1970	1975	1976	1977	1978	1979	1980
Food and Beverages	6.6	12.8	5.4	8.9	7.3	4.8	11.4
Corn	2.4	6.2	1.7	3.5	2.3	0.8	3.0
Raw Materials	8.7	6.8	8.2	9.8	9.5	5.3	4.6
Fertilizer and Minerals	1.3	1.6	1.4	1.2	1.3	(NA)	(NA)
Metalliferous Ores	2.1	2.2	1.2	1.3	1.6	1.1	1.3
Fuel	3.2	5.5	5.7	3.0	3.3	2.0	1.5
Petroleum Products	1.5	1.6	3.7	1.4	1.8	1.4	0.5
Natural Gas	1.2	2.2	1.7	1.4	7.0	0.4	0.7
Manufactures (except Machinery)	31.3	29.4	30.6	12.1	17.5	12.6	12.1
Chemicals	12.3	12.2	12.9	15.1	13.1	9.6	8.7
Iron, Steel	3.4	6.1	5.3	5.0	10.9	7.0	7.6
Metal Manufactures	2.4	1.8	1.9	1.7	1.8	1.2	1.2
Instruments (tools)	3.0	2.2	2.4	0.5	0.5	0.7	0.6
Machinery	50.2	45.4	50.0	45.3	43.6	35.3	33.0
Nonelectrical	24.0	22.0	25.0	21.4	22.0	17.1	16.0
Electrical	11.4	6.3	9.2	8.5	6.4	3.8	3.7
Transportation Equipment	14.8	17.1	15.7	15.4	15.2	14.5	13.2
Other	--	0.1	0.1	5.8	5.7	30.4	28.7
Total	100.0	100.0	100.0	100.0	100.0	100.0	100.0
Imports Value (U.S. $ millions)	$2,461	$6,570	$6,011	$5,596	$7,786.6	$11,828.8	(NA)

Source: United Nations: Yearbook of International Trade Statistics, various issues.

138

TABLE 4.5
Mexico's Balance of Trade with World Regions
(U.S. $ millions)

	1960			1970		
	Exports	Imports	Balance	Exports	Imports	Balance
Industrial countries	595.3	1,161.8	-566.5	1,036.4	2,346.4	-1,310.0
Latin America	22.7	11.5	11.2	121.9	78.5	43.4
Other Western Hemisphere	1.3	2.6	-1.3	6.8	13.0	-6.2
Asia (less Japan)	8.2	6.1	2.1	7.1	18.5	-11.4
Middle East	0.5	0.3	0.2	1.1	1.5	-0.4
Africa (less S. Africa)	0.7	0.3	0.4	1.0	0.4	0.6
Centrally planned economies	2.5	3.7	-1.2	3.8	6.3	-2.5
Totals	631.2	1,186.3	-555.1	1,148.1	2,464.6	-1,286.5

	1977			1980		
	Exports	Imports	Balance	Exports	Imports	Balance
Industrial countries	3,341.9	5,106.8	-1,764.9	12,537	17,858	-5,321
Latin America	509.8	281.4	228.4	866	765	101
Other Western Hemisphere	28.9	26.2	2.7	492	28	464
Asia (less Japan)	21.7	41.6	-19.9	154	244	-90
Middle East	73.5	0.6	72.9	513	10	503
Africa (less S. Africa)	10.8	1.6	9.2	18	11	7
Centrally planned economies	78.3	21.9	56.4	61	200	-139
Totals	4,064.9	5,480.1	-1,415.2	14,641	19,116	-4,475

Source: International Monetary Fund, Direction of Trade Statistics, various issues.

the trade deficit widened to $3 billion. In 1981 and 1982 a continuing world oil surplus produced even greater deficits.

In the mid-1970s, Mexico's continuing balance-of-trade deficit prompted increasing protectionism, implemented principally through existing tariff, quota, and licensing mechanisms. These measures were paralleled by increasing protectionism in the United States during the same period. Protectionist policies to correct employment and balance-of-payments problems on both sides of the border were possible because no general treaty or agreement regulating trade was in force. The last formal treaty, the Reciprocal Trade Agreement of 1942, had been allowed to lapse in 1950 by mutual consent, primarily because of Mexico's efforts to extend its import substituting industrialization program. A similar logic led Mexico to decline to participate in the General Agreement on Tariffs and Trade (GATT) in 1947 (Rooney, 1978), and most recently in 1980. Protectionism has now become one of the major issues in U.S.-Mexican relations and illustrates the difficulties of trying to find mutually satisfactory policies in a relationship between a major economic power and its highly interdependent developing country neighbor.

Devaluation in 1976 forced Mexican officials to alter their approach somewhat and seek a new trade policy with the United States. Thus, on December 2, 1977, the two countries signed the first bilateral trade agreement to emerge from the "Tokyo Round" of GATT negotiations. The scope of the 1977 trade agreement between the U.S. and Mexico is largely symbolic when judged in terms of the total volume of trade between the two countries. It affects a limited list of commodities involving about 2 percent ($36 million) of Mexican exports to the United States and less than 1 percent ($64 million) of U.S. exports to Mexico. Nevertheless, the agreement is significant in that it reflects a growing Mexican interest in stabilizing its trade relationship with the United States as well as a more aggressive search for trade concessions and preferences in that relationship (Rooney, 1978). Through early 1982 there were no signs that Mexico would be willing to go beyond the limited agreement, or to discuss GATT entry. However, such decisions were left to the next government, which would take office in December 1982.

Despite reductions in trade barriers, protectionism, on both sides of the border, will remain a major point of friction between the two countries for some time (Ronfeldt and Sereseres, 1978; Rooney, 1978). The Mexicans continue to protest their lack of access to U.S. markets for products such as winter vegetables, beef, shoes, and textiles. At the same time, they defend their own retention of a range of barriers to protect their own markets and industries from U.S. penetration and competition. Americans, in turn, complain about Mexican pricing policies, red tape, licensing policies, defaults on negotiated contracts, and "dumping" of products such as tomatoes,[1] cement, copper, and sulfur.

Theoretically, over the long run, both countries stand to benefit from the elimination of restrictions. The business environment would be more stable and predictable, overall trade would expand, competitive advantages could be exploited more fully (encouraging production efficiency), and prices for U.S. consumers might be lowered. For the next few years, however, the barriers to mutually acceptable accommodations are formidable. Domestic producers in many sectors in both countries would be subjected to intense competitive pressures that in some cases could force them from the market. Specific regions and communities would be particularly hard-hit and employment and balance-of-payments problems could be exacerbated significantly. In short, the political costs of reducing trade barriers are very high for any politician or administration that undertakes such policies on either side of the border. President Lopez Portillo's 1980 decision not to enter the GATT was clearly influenced by political factors.

At present, the United States would definitely profit more than Mexico from the complete elimination or substantial reduction of trade barriers, despite the regional and sectoral adjustments that the United States would inevitably have to bear. Most U.S. industries are more efficient, larger, better financed, and technologically more advanced than their Mexican counterparts (World Bank, 1979). The existence of this U.S. "edge" explains why U.S. interests have pressed Mexico to join the GATT or, alternatively, to form a North American Common Market with the United States and Canada. In either case, Mexico would be expected to provide primary products (agricultural goods, minerals, and petroleum)--products in which it has a "natural competitive advantage"--while the United States would provide high technology manufactured products.

From the Mexican point of view, such arrangements are unacceptable, for they would consign Mexico permanently to the status of a primary product exporter, deepen the country's economic dependence on the United States, and further compromise Mexico's sovereignty. For Mexico, the term "interdependence," so often invoked by U.S. authorities to describe contemporary U.S.-Mexican relations, is merely a transparent effort to "adorn" an asymmetrical relationship in which a powerful United States dominates a relatively weak and vulnerable Mexico (Rico, 1978, 1979).

In place of deepening dependency, a growing number of
Mexicans propose an "authentic national project of development" (Pellicer de Brody, 1979). Such nationalistic
assertions tend to exaggerate the extent of U.S. dominance
and to underestimate the real constraints on U.S. behavior
toward Mexico (Ronfeldt and Sereseres, 1978; Bagley,
1981). They nevertheless express deeply held beliefs and
attitudes of Mexican people in general, and of many Mexican intellectuals and policymakers in particular. These
beliefs continue to have a profound effect on U.S.-Mexican
relations on a number of levels.

Because of the widely held fear that accommodating
U.S. interests and preferences will somehow compromise
Mexican sovereignty, independence, and future options, it
is unlikely that Mexico will enter a North American Common
Market at any point in the foreseeable future. While
Mexico may join the GATT because it needs more secure access to U.S. and other developed country markets, its en-
trance will require a phase-in period of up to ten years
to moderate the impact of intensified foreign competition
on Mexican producers. In the long run, increasing coordination of trade policies would seem both desirable and inevitable. However, such coordination can come only
through piecemeal negotiations over an extended period of
time. Resistance, backsliding, misunderstandings, and
conflict are inevitable. To minimize tensions, the United
States will have to develop a much greater awareness of
Mexican economic development concerns and nationalist
sensitivities than it has demonstrated in the past. Failure to do so can only reduce trade flows, increase tensions, and prolong the process of establishing a mutually
beneficial and truly interdependent relationship between
the two countries.

U.S. INVESTMENT AND MEXICAN NATIONALISM

U.S. Investment and Financial Interests in Mexico

Mexico has traditionally been one of the prime areas
for U.S. private investment in the developing world. The
extensive U.S. presence in the Mexican economy is both a
source of contention for Mexican nationalists and a factor
drawing continuing U.S. attention to the Mexican economy.
Because of its heavy private sector investment in Mexico
and an equally high commercial bank exposure, the United
States has a vital interest in the continued growth and
stability of the Mexican economy. This interest was
clearly demonstrated during the Mexican economic crisis
of 1976, when U.S. banks were obliged to come to the res-
cue of a government that had adopted political and economic policies hostile to the United States. Since
Mexico's announcement of enormous oil reserves, U.S.

business and financial interests have become even more
deeply involved in Mexico, intensifying the symbiotic
relationship between the two economies. U.S. direct investment in Mexico rose from approximately $3.2 billion
in 1977 to over $5 billion in 1980.

Within the developing world, only Brazil, with approximately $6 billion, receives more U.S. private invest-
ment. In the 1970s, U.S.-based companies and banks accounted for nearly 72 percent of all foreign investment
in Mexico (World Bank, 1979; Ronfeldt and Sereseres, 1978;
Fagen, 1978). In comparison, the Federal Republic of
Germany accounted for about 6 percent of foreign direct
private investment and the United Kingdom for about 5 percent (World Bank, 1979). In contrast, the U.S. share of
private investment in Brazil, while larger in dollar value, accounted for only one-fourth of total foreign direct
investment in that country (Deutsche Bank, 1978).

Between 1972 and 1975, foreign investment in Mexico
represented about 5 percent of total private investment
in the Mexican economy. Foreign investment was channeled
through 4,100 separate enterprises, two-thirds of which
had 50 percent or more foreign participation. One-half
of foreign-owned enterprises and three-fourths of all foreign capital were in the manufacturing sector. The tendency for foreign concentration in manufacturing remained
nearly constant, at about 75 percent, over the decade
(World Bank, 1979).

Mexican Nationalism and Control of
Foreign Investment

Mexican authorities' attitudes toward foreign investment, particularly U.S. investment, have been ambivalent
for decades. On the one hand, they have explicitly recognized the need to permit foreign investment in order to
supplement their own domestic savings, to create jobs, and
to increase exports. On the other hand, they have been
acutely aware of the potential political challenges to
state control represented by foreign penetration. As a
result, since the late 1940s and early 1950s, the Mexican
government has directed and channeled foreign investment
into specific areas of the economy, while preventing it
from entering other areas (Weinert, 1977).

Foreign capital was essentially forced out or reduced
to minority partner status in key sectors such as oil,
utilities, communications, banking, railroads, and steel
in the 1940s. During the 1950s, this process was carried
further with the nationalization of telephones and the
last of the electrical companies (Weinert, 1977). During
the early 1970s, the Echeverria administration promulgated
a series of executive decrees that further restricted and

channeled foreign investment in the country. Electricity, banking, insurance, and related financial services as well as several sectors previously reserved for majority Mexican ownership--communication, transportation, and fishing--were completely closed to foreign investment. Moreover, new requirements were imposed for majority Mexican ownership in sectors such as glass, cellulose, fertilizers, chemicals, aluminum, and rubber (Weinert, 1977).

In February 1973, the nationalistic Echeverria administration moved even more forcefully to control foreign capital with the passage of a Law to Promote Mexican Investment and Regulate Foreign Investment. This law not only reaffirmed all previous restrictions but also required that any new companies formed, regardless of the sector, be at least 51 percent Mexican-owned. Moreover, it specifically eliminated the practice of prestanombres (whereby Mexican citizens hold shares in trust for foreigners), made the issuance of stock certificates to anonymous "bearers" illegal, and imposed criminal penalties for violations of the laws (Weinert, 1977). To implement the new law, a National Commission on Foreign Investment was authorized to reject or approve foreign investment in both new and existing enterprises. The Commission was also empowered to review any acquisitions of established companies by foreign investors. The Commission's policy has been to disapprove acquisitions that do not bring in new technology or management skills. This policy seems to have reduced appreciably the number of foreign acquisitions (Weinert, 1977).

These new regulations on foreign investment were complemented with a second Law on Technological Transfer and Use and Exploitation of Trademarks and Patent Rights, also approved in early 1973. This law introduced restrictions designed to prevent Mexicans from being charged more than their competitors in the same sector for the use of technology. The law also limited payments for trademarks to 1 percent on net sales, eliminated virtually all restrictions on Mexican exports that utilize foreign technology, and placed a ceiling on transfer payments for foreign technology and trademarks to 3 percent of net annual sales (World Bank, 1979).

The purpose of the 1973 legislation regulating foreign investment was to protect domestic industry, boost Mexican participation in joint ventures, and prevent "denationalization" of the economy. However, for foreign investors, the legislation and the entire tone of the Echeverria administration were unsettlingly antibusiness. Investors reacted by withdrawing more than $2 billion from the Mexican economy in the 18 months that followed enactment of the new legislation. This massive flight of short-term capital precipitated an economic crisis in

1975-1976 and the devaluation of the peso in September 1976 (Ronfeldt and Sereseres, 1978; Pellicer de Brody, 1979).

Ironically, the Echeverria administration's efforts to assert state authority over foreign capital had the practical effect of highlighting the tremendous importance of foreign investment to the Mexican economy. Between 1973 and 1975, Mexico's outstanding foreign debt rose precipitously from $5.6 billion to $10.6 billion as the country's worsening economic situation forced the government to borrow heavily from foreign banks, primarily in the United States (Weinert, 1977). In the wake of the 1976 devaluation, the U.S. government and the international financial community were compelled to provide massive support to the Mexican economy to avert a worsening of the crisis. The IMF provided drawing rights of $1.2 billion. A Eurocredit loan of $800 million was provided by a consortium of 64 banks, including a number of U.S. banks. The United States Treasury and Federal Reserve provided an additional $600 million in short-term drawing rights to the Bank of Mexico (Ronfeldt and Sereseres, 1978).

As of 1979, Mexico's total public sector foreign debt had risen to $30 billion, on which service payments amounted to more than $3 billion a year. In 1981, the debt passed $50 billion and in 1982 rose to $66 billion, as Mexico became the single largest developing country debtor. Private U.S. banks held between $10 billion and $12 billion of the debt in 1978 with the World Bank, U.S. Export-Import Bank, Inter-American Development Bank, and other U.S.-sponsored financial institutions also heavily involved (Ronfeldt and Sereseres, 1978; Fagen, 1978). These same institutions have continued to hold large shares in the Mexican debt.

The extent of this financial exposure has been a source of continuing concern to the United States and to the entire international financial community. By early 1979, President Lopez Portillo had managed to restore international confidence in the Mexican economy through pragmatic policies and his consistent implementation of the IMF-inspired stabilization program (Euromoney, 1978; Fortune, July 16, 1979). A critical component in this restoration of international confidence was the announcement in early 1977 of the discovery of massive new oil and natural gas reserves in the Mexican subsoil. The worldwide recession that began in 1979 and the 1981-1982 oil surplus both created serious new problems for Mexico's economic recovery. The solutions to such problems will be among the most difficult tasks confronting the new Mexican president in 1983.

ENERGY ISSUES

U.S. Interests in Mexican Oil and Natural Gas

Mexico's recent vast petroleum discoveries have fundamentally altered the traditional relationship with the United States. From the U.S. perspective, Mexico's economic and strategic significance have risen incalculably. For Mexico, oil represents an important opportunity to end its historic dependency on the United States.

As of September 1, 1981, Mexico claimed 72.5 billion barrels of proven reserves (72 percent oil; 28 percent gas) and 50 billion barrels of potential reserves (Excelsior, September 2, 1981). Whatever the exact figures ultimately prove to be, there can be little doubt that during the 1980s Mexico will become one of the major oil-producing countries of the world.

Table 4.6 ranks major oil-producing countries in terms of proven reserves as of 1979. Mexico ranked fifth in the world at that time. If estimates of its potential are even remotely accurate (i.e., 30 to 50 percent correct), it should rank with Saudi Arabia as a potential long-term petroleum supplier. Moreover, given its current low level of production and its plans to develop additional production capacity slowly (Table 4.7), its petroleum supplies should outlast those of all other producers.

Until January 1980, the Lopez Portillo administration had consistently argued that production would be maintained at the 2.25-million-bpd level through 1982, the end of its term of office. In a surprise move on January 18, 1980, however, government officials revealed that this limit would no longer hold. Output was scheduled to increase to approximately 3 million bpd by year end 1981 and to 4 million bpd in 1982 (Latin American Weekly Report, January 25, 1980). The new targets required a fundamental reassessment of the economic and industrial plans previously announced by the government, for existing projections were based on assumptions and calculations related to the 2.25-million-bpd target. By mid-year 1981, signs of policy disagreement over production targets surfaced with the surprise resignation of popular PEMEX Director Jorge Diaz-Serrano.

The decision to double oil production by 1982 can most logically be explained as the result of domestic political pressures and economic problems rather than increased U.S. or international demand. Mexico's determination to accelerate the pace of industrial growth beyond the 11 percent rate projected for 1980 was a major factor

146

TABLE 4.6
Major Oil-Producing Countries

Country	Proven Reserves (billions of barrels)	Ranking by Production	Average Production in 1978 (billions of bpd)	Percentage Changes 1978-1977
Saudi Arabia	165.7	3	8.3	-10.3
USSR	71.0	1	11.7	+ 5.9
Kuwait	66.2	10	1.8	+ 4.7
Iran	59.0	4	5.2	- 8.2
Mexico	45.8	14	1.3	+22.9
Iraq	32.1	5	2.6	+ 4.3
Abu Dabi	30.0	13	1.5	-12.8
United States	28.5	2	8.7	+ 5.5

Source: Latin America Informe Semanal, November 16, 1979, p. 294.

TABLE 4.7

Mexico: Projected Oil and Gas Production, 1978-1988

| Year | Oil Production (barrels) | | | Gas Production (cubic feet) | | | |
	Per Day (millions)	Per Year (billions)	Gas/Oil Ratio	Per Day Associated (billions)	Per Day Nonassociated (billions)	Total Per Day (billions)	Total Per Year (trillions)
1978	1.4[a]	0.511	1,200:1	1.7	0.8	2.5	0.912
1979	1.8	.657	1,200:1	2.2	.5	2.7	1.058
1980	2.2[b]	.803	1,200:1	2.6	.4	3.0	1.095
1981	2.3	.840	1,300:1	3.0	.3	3.3	1.204
1982	2.4	.876	1,400:1	3.4	.3	3.7	1.387
1983	2.5	.912	1,500:1	3.8	.3	4.1	1.496
1984	2.6	.949	1,600:1	4.2	.4	4.6	1.679
1985	2.7	.986	1,700:1	4.6	.6	5.2	1.971
1986	2.8	1.022	1,800:1	5.0	.7	5.7	2.117
1987	2.9	1.058	1,900:1	5.5	.8	6.3	2.300
1988	3.0	1.095	2,000:1	6.0	.8	6.8	2.482
Total	--	9.709	--	--	--	--	17.701

Source: Library of Congress, Congressional Research Service, 1978, p. 17.

[a]Actual

[b]PEMEX estimate

in the dramatic reversal. The desire to reduce the tremendous foreign debt and current account deficit will require a substantial re-evaluation of production and export
targets in the 1980s.

To assure access to Mexico's expanding energy supplies, in 1977 a consortium of six U.S. firms put together
a package involving (1) U.S. purchases of 2 billion cubic
feet of gas per day and (2) Export-Import Bank financial
support for the construction of a natural gas pipeline to
the U.S. border. This deal collapsed in December 1977
when James Schlesinger, then U.S. Secretary of Energy,
vetoed the package because the $2.60 per thousand cubic
feet asking price was unacceptably high.[2] The brusque
manner in which the Schlesinger veto was delivered to the
Mexican negotiators was considered so offensive that in
January 1978, the Mexicans broke off all further negotiations on the gas question (Fagen and Nau, 1978). Talks
were not resumed until after President Carter's visit to
Mexico in February 1979, more than a year later.

In the interim, Mexico's plans and priorities for its
natural gas changed substantially. The Lopez Portillo
administration took a position that, if necessary, Mexico
would use most of its production internally for domestic
industrialization and home heating, rather than concede to
the United States on this contentious issue. In the U.S.-
Mexican gas pact concluded in September 1979 the Mexicans
were willing to export only 300 million cubic feet per day
at a compromise price of $3.625 per thousand cubic feet.
The contract allowed for future increases in the amount
exported and in price levels.

Between January 1978 and September 1979, Mexico also
entered into a series of new oil supply contracts with Israel, Germany, Spain, France, Canada, and Brazil in a
pointed effort to diversify its petroleum trade away from
the United States (see Table 4.8). If the strategy were
successful, by the mid-1980s the United States' share of
Mexico's exportable surpluses of petroleum could drop from
80 percent to about 60 percent (U.S. Senate Committee on
Energy and Natural Resources, 1979). The Mexicans have
declared a target goal that no more than 50 percent of
these petroleum exports should go to any one country.

To some American observers this prospect represents
a serious problem, for it denies the United States greater
access to easily defensible petroleum supplies from neighboring Mexico. Other analysts argue that it makes little
difference who buys Mexican oil. The energy crisis is a
global problem and any additional production from Mexico,
whether or not it is consumed in the United States, will
help to relieve the world problem and may, ultimately,
help to constrain world price increases. Mexico is not a

TABLE 4.8
Partial List of Current and Future Mexican Oil Contracts

Country	Amount (bpd)	Effective Date of Contract	Duration
United States	400,000	1979	--
Japan	100,000	Under negotiation	--
France	100,000	Signed letter of intent in 1979	--
Canada	100,000	1980	--
Brazil	25,000	1980	--
Spain	25,000	1979	5 years
Israel	50,000	1979	--
Cuba/Soviet Union	70,000	Under negotiation	--

Source: Excelsior, Latin America Weekly Report, Latin America Informe Semanal, Comercio Exterior, and The Washington Post.

member of OPEC and is considered unlikely to join in the
near future, primarily because of its desire to maintain
favorable trade relations with the United States. Nevertheless, Mexico has consistently charged prices above OPEC
levels and will probably continue to do so. Given geographical proximity, however, the delivery price in the
United States for Mexican petroleum remains at or below
Middle Eastern prices.

Whether or not Mexico becomes the major supplier of
oil and gas to the United States, the two economies will
become more closely interrelated because of the development of the oil industry. First, development of Mexico's
petroleum resources will require approximately $15 billion
in investment, including at least $5 billion for the im-
port of high-technology equipment (Ronfeldt and Sereseres,
1978). Since nationalization in 1938, Mexico has not accepted direct foreign participation in the exploitation of
its hydrocarbon resources. Nevertheless, the United
States, along with Europe, Canada, and Japan, will likely
be an important supplier of investment capital, technology, and special services to Mexico. Trade between
the United States and Mexico will necessarily expand as
Mexico proceeds with its development program. Moreover,
Mexico is interested in foreign participation (up to
40 percent) in its growing petrochemical industry, already
a major area of U.S. investment.

Second, Mexico is likely to earn upward of $20 bil-
lion from oil and gas exports during Lopez Portillo's six-
year term of office. Revenues, which were roughly $1
billion in 1977, are expected to reach $8 billion to $10
billion by 1982 and to go even higher over the mid- and
late-1980s, depending on overall production levels (Pagliano, 1979). If properly managed, export revenues could
permit repayment of at least part of Mexico's monumental
foreign debt and provide for the necessary imports of
capital goods--and still leave enough to finance socio-
economic development programs. Such projects are essential to reduce Mexico's extremely high unemployment rate,
to halt the flight from the countryside to the cities,
to reduce the flow of illegals into the United States,
and to ameliorate the country's severe income distribution problems (Fagen, 1978). The rational management of
Mexico's petroleum resources and revenues is, therefore,
of fundamental importance to the resolution of critical
problems besetting Mexican society, problems that also
directly affect the United States.

Third, oil constitutes a new and powerful bargaining
chip for Mexico in its future dealings with the United
States. The precise level of Mexican petroleum production
and exports to this country is negotiable. Mexico will
undoubtedly seek to link its oil and gas exports to other

issues such as trade concessions and liberalized immigration policies. As Stanford political scientist Richard Fagen has noted:

Deals of this sort cannot be struck too openly given political forces at work on both sides of the border and the nationalistic sensitivities involved. But they "make sense" in the context of the realities of U.S.-Mexican relations and thus may be forthcoming (Fagen, 1978).

The United States is in a unique position to encourage higher levels of oil exports from Mexico. Geographical proximity and economic size make the United States Mexico's natural trading partner. By developing trade policies that complement Mexico's national development plans, particularly by lowering protectionist barriers and by increasing access to the U.S. markets for Mexican exports, the United States can maximize the likelihood that Mexico will be willing to increase the U.S. share of Mexican oil exports. The guarantee of Mexican petroleum supplies, while not necessary in purely economic terms, would have important political ramifications by reducing U.S. dependence on Middle Eastern supplies and creating the image of Western Hemispheric solidarity.

Nuclear Energy

At present, Mexico has no significant nuclear capability. It signed the nonproliferation treaty and took a leading role in negotiating the Treaty of Tlatelolco (1967) that requires parties to refrain from the development and acquisition of nuclear weapons (Treverton, 1977). Nevertheless, Mexico has a growing nuclear energy program. The prevailing view within the Mexican government is that nuclear power is as important to the country's development plans as oil itself, particularly because demand for electricity is growing geometrically and will soon outstrip the capacity of hydroelectric, coal-fired, thermoelectric, and geothermic stations (Latin American Weekly Report, November 16, 1979). By 1990, Mexico hopes to have two commercial reactors in operation, generating 2,500 megawatts of electricity, or about 1.5 percent of total domestic consumption. By the end of the century, the country hopes to have enough nuclear plants to generate 20,000 megawatts of power (Washington Post, May 18, 1981).

At present, Mexico has two light-water reactors under construction in Laguna Verde, Veracruz, each of which will be capable of producing 650 megawatts of power when finished. The first is programmed to come on-stream by May 1982, some five years behind schedule. No date has been set for the second. Both reactors are being built by a

U.S. General Electric Company subsidiary, EBASCO, with
technical and engineering consulting shared by U.S. and
Mexican firms. Mexico is actively exploring alternative
technologies from Canadian and British-Dutch-West German
groups, however, and is likely to utilize non-U.S. technology in future plant construction. The Canadian CANDU
plant is especially attractive to Mexico, for the heavy
water (rather than enriched uranium) needed is not beyond
the country's present technological capability and could
be produced in Mexico. Mexico already has an enriched
uranium contract with the United States. The first shipments arrived in January 1980. Deepening technological
dependence on the United States has become a source of
intense debate and criticism in Mexico, especially after
the United States announced in 1977 that deliveries to
Mexico would be delayed while the United States met contract obligations with other countries.[3]

An alternative to the Canadian heavy-water reactors
would be natural uranium reactors. This option holds increasing appeal in Mexico because the country is potentially the world's third-largest uranium producer, after
the USSR and China. Proven reserves are currently between
8,500 and 12,000 tons. Mexico's Nuclear Energy Institute
estimates the country's probable reserves at between
500,000 and 600,000 tons. The government is now investing
$35 million a year in uranium exploration as a result of
promising discoveries in the state of Chihuahua. Recent
calculations suggest that 10 percent of the country's land
area could contain uranium.

Mexico does not currently possess the technology to
extract uranium and has not decided when to begin production. In early 1979, a Mexican team began negotiations
with URENCO, the British-Dutch-West German group, and
with British Nuclear Fuels to supply Britain and Europe
with uranium in exchange for technical assistance, including enriching of Mexican uranium abroad. Nuclear power
thus appears likely to play an important role in Mexico's
future, although it will take several decades to develop.

MEXICAN IMMIGRATION AND BORDER ISSUES

The most difficult and least understood issue affecting U.S.-Mexican relations today involves the millions of
undocumented Mexican nationals living and working in the
United States. In the opinion of William Colby, a former
director of the Central Intelligence Agency, uncontrolled
Mexican population growth and emigration to this country
is in the long run "a bigger threat to the United States
than is the Soviet Union," for by the end of the century
it could bring an additional 20 million illegal aliens
into the United States overloading this country's schools

and social services, creating ghettoes in U.S. cities, and endangering the "American Way of life" (Fagen, 1978).

Although precise data are not available, Mexican immigration into the United States is massive and growing:

- At least 5 million to 6 million Mexicans are now in the United States illegally.

- Approximately 1 million Mexicans enter the United States illegally each year.

- While most illegals return to Mexico after approximately 4 to 6 months of employment, several hundred thousand of those who come each year remain in the United States for longer periods.

- About 900,000 illegals were deported from the United States in 1981, up from 90,000 in 1967.

The basic reasons for this massive illegal migration are the huge wage differentials between the United States and Mexico and the high rates of underemployment and unemployment (approximately 40 to 50 percent of the work force) characteristic of the Mexican economy (Cornelius, 1977). Given Mexico's high population growth (at least 800,000 people are added to the work force each year) and the limited absorptive capacity of its economy, it is extremely unlikely that there soon will be any significant diminution of the flow of illegals across the border (Fagen, 1979; Cornelius, 1977).

There are a number of misunderstandings about the economic and social impact on the United States of illegal Mexican immigration that must be clarified before policy options for dealing with the situation can be explored. Major areas of misunderstanding include the following:

- How long do the illegals stay? Recent research indicates that approximately 70 percent stay for four months or less and 90 percent for less than a year before returning to Mexico.

- Do Mexican illegals take jobs away from U.S. citizens? There is no question that some American workers are hurt, but on balance it appears that Mexican immigration does not take away employment from U.S. workers. Rather, Mexican workers fill a demand not satisfied by the domestic labor force. Because of the United States' declining birth rate and aging labor force, at least 20 million additional, largely immigrant, workers will be required between 1980 and 2000 to carry out low-paid, unskilled jobs.

- Are Mexican illegals a drain on local, state, and federal programs and services? Virtually all empirical work done on the subject indicates unequivocally that migrants do not use such programs to any significant extent. Indeed, there is considerable evidence indicating that they actually help to subsidize social programs through the millions of dollars they pay in income, Social Security, sales, and other taxes.

- Do Mexican workers send dollars out of the United States? Illegals remit wages to Mexico amounting to an estimated $3 billion a year, even though 60 to 70 percent of their earnings are spent in the United States. These remittances are a more important source of foreign exchange for Mexico than the total income generated by the tourist industry.

Objectively, the benefits derived from illegal Mexican labor are substantial. Without Mexican workers, the United States would experience at least temporary labor shortages; higher labor costs would occur in agriculture, industry, and the service sector; the prices of many goods would rise; and the federal government would have to lay out huge sums to defend the border. Any unilateral effort by the United States to "close" the border to Mexican immigration would have severe repercussions for Mexico's already precarious balance-of-payments situation and thus weaken an economy in which the United States has major interests. Finally, any U.S. action to "seal" the border would threaten the stability of the Mexican political system, for it could cut off an important "escape valve" for surplus Mexican labor and increase popular discontent, especially in the Mexican countryside where unemployment already constitutes a major social problem.

Mexican authorities do not view undocumented Mexican workers in the United States as a problem. Rather, they emphasize that Mexican labor fulfills an economic function in the United States, that immigration serves as a safety valve for Mexico, and that wage remittances provide needed foreign exchange for the Mexican economy. Despite its positive functions, many Mexican officials also consider immigration a national embarrassment, for it reveals the continuing incapacity of the Mexican government to create employment opportunities and raise standards of living for large numbers of Mexican citizens.

Under these circumstances, most recent Mexican administrations have been extremely reluctant to discuss the issue at all. Whenever the United States has brought up the problem, the Mexicans have tended to focus on the mistreatment of undocumented workers in the United States and to demand that their human and civil rights be respected, even if they have crossed the border illegally. From time to time, the Mexican government has suggested the re-establishment of a contract-labor agreement (similar to the bracero program eliminated in 1964), but with little result. Recently, Lopez Portillo has attempted to link the migrant issue to trade concessions from the United States, arguing that such concessions would expand employment opportunities in Mexico and reduce pressures for migration. President Ronald Reagan has made a commitment to developing a more coherent U.S. immigration policy and, in talks with Lopez Portillo in June 1981, discussed, among other things, the creation of a pilot guest worker program that would initially affect 50,000 Mexican workers in 1982.

In light of Mexico's own internal domestic problems, no major effort to control illegal immigration is to be expected. Moreover, it is likely that Mexico will utilize its new petroleum resources to bargain, at least indirectly, for liberalization of U.S. immigration policies and greater access to U.S. markets for its exports. The United States is severely limited in its responses to such bargaining. Extreme reactions such as closing the border, as Rep. James H. Scheuer (chairman of the House Select Committee on Population) recommended in December 1978, are impractical and would provoke outrage in Mexico, inflame anti-U.S. sentiment there, and sour U.S.-Mexican relations even further (Washington Post, December 24, 1978).

There appears to be a growing awareness among U.S. policymakers, if not among the public generally, that any unilateral efforts to seal the border would be counter-productive for both the American and Mexican economies, as well as extremely costly and probably futile. "The pressures are so intense, and likely to remain so in the foreseeable future, that most Mexican illegals are not likely to be deterred, even by the most draconian restrictive measures" (Cornelius, 1977). The real question for the United States today, therefore, is not how to stop the flow of Mexican labor across the border altogether, but how to regulate and control it. Proposals presented to Congress by the Reagan administration are intended to deal with these problems of regulation and control.

The basic policy recommendations that have been advanced to deal with the Mexican immigrant problem are summarized on the following page. In one variant or another, however, each is likely to figure in policy debates and color U.S.-Mexican relations in the 1980s. Recommendations for solving the illegal migration problems include the following:

- Raise quotas for legal immigrants from Mexico from 20,000 to 50,000 a year.

- Increase the speed with which people legally entitled to live in the United States are processed through the Immigration and Naturalization Service.

- Establish a "guest" or "temporary" worker program.

- Impose sanctions, including fines, legal penalties, or both, on employers who consciously and repeatedly hire illegal workers.

- Strengthen the border patrol to increase enforcement capabilities on the frontier and in the interior.

- Grant an amnesty and renewable term temporary resident status to illegals who entered the United States prior to January 1, 1980.

- Grant permanent resident status to illegals who can demonstrate United States residency for at least ten years.

Some additional recommendations discussed but not included in the 1981 Reagan administration proposals to Congress include:

- Create a national identity card to establish worker eligibility and thereby make employer sanctions enforceable.

- Deny all public services to illegal aliens.

- Provide financial aid and technical assistance to the Mexican government to reorient its rural development strategy toward small-scale, labor-intensive industrialization.

- Grant trade concessions to Mexico to stimulate small-scale production of both agricultural and nonagricultural goods.

- Encourage birth control and family planning programs in Mexico's rural areas.

The list of additional recommendations could be extended, but the critical omission in the Reagan proposal on immigration quite clearly lies in the absence of an effective means for identifying legal workers. Without some simple and reliable system of identification, employer sanctions remain essentially unenforceable. If

there are no real costs to employers for hiring cheaper
and more docile aliens, they will continue to do so.

A second controversial area involves the "guest"
workers program. The President's Task Force on Immigration and Refugee Policy had suggested a two-year experiment permitting a proposed 50,000 Mexican workers per
year to take officially cleared jobs in the United States.
The Mexicans would have access to public schools and medical care, but not food stamps, welfare, or unemployment
benefits. The guest workers program would restrict workers to specific areas of the country with labor shortages,
fruit and vegetable cultivating areas particularly.

Organized labor, church groups, and Hispanic organizations have stated their intention to lobby against such
a program. Critics assert that guest-worker programs produce a marginalized class which has a legal status but is
denied a full place in society. The Washington Post commented in an editorial at the time of the proposal: "long
experience demonstrates that guest workers are an exploit-
able and indigestible subclass--peons." Other critics
point to the bracero program, which many observers believe
stimulated unlawful immigration. The semi-official Mexican Workers Confederation (CTM) has demanded that the
Mexican government oppose the plan, which the CTM says
will legalize the "second class status" of illegal
workers.

Many other aspects of the Reagan package--the forci-
ble detainment of Haitian refugees on the high seas, the
treatment of legal residents' family members, and so
forth--are also quite controversial. At the outset of
1982, it appears doubtful that the Reagan administration
has either the political will or the capacity to move
forcefully on the immigration issue. Domestic debate is
likely to be intense but little action can be expected
from Congress during an election year. Even beyond November 1982, it appears that the lack of a domestic consensus is likely to prevent any major new legislation for
some time.

MEXICAN FOREIGN POLICY AND HEMISPHERIC SECURITY

Growing political instability in Central America and
the Caribbean have encouraged suggestions from various
quarters that Mexico should assume a larger role in monitoring hemispheric security than it has in the past. It
is argued that, as an emerging regional power, Mexico has
a vested interest in assuring that Central American countries such as Nicaragua, El Salvador, Guatemala, and
Honduras are not engulfed in anarchy, violence, and civil
war, or taken over by "leftist extremists" supported by

Cuba and the USSR. As a petroleum-exporting country,
Mexico in theory has the economic and diplomatic tools
needed to perform such a moderating role in the region.

This section reviews briefly the past and present
foreign relations of Mexico in order to assess the likelihood that Mexico will assume an expanded role in the
Central American and Caribbean regions during the 1980s.
Special attention is paid to the changes introduced into
Mexican foreign policy by the Echeverria administration
(1970-1976), and the Lopez Portillo administration, the
term of which ended in 1982, and to the themes that can
be expected to prevail during the administration of
Miguel de la Madrid (1982-1986).

Mexico historically maintained a posture of minimal
participation in international affairs. In the first 25
years following World War II, the main aim of Mexican
foreign policy was to strengthen its "special" bilateral
relationship with the United States. In Central America
and the Caribbean, where, because of geographical proximity, Mexico might have been expected to establish a regional sphere of influence, its presence remained quite
limited. Among the reasons for Mexico's low-profile foreign policy were these:

- As a relatively poor and backward country,
  Mexico was more concerned with its own internal
  development problems than with foreign affairs.

- With more than two-thirds of all Mexico's trade
  occurring with the United States, there was
  relatively little interchange or complementarity
  between Mexico and other Latin American countries.

- Because Mexico has lived in the shadow of the
  American defense umbrella and in this century
  was not faced with any significant external
  threat, it never developed a military capability
  that would permit it to assume a major military
  role in the region. The Mexican military has
  focused its attention almost entirely on questions
  of internal security and political order (Ronfeldt,
  1978).

Despite the limited role Mexico has played in international and hemispheric relations, its foreign policy has
never mechanically reflected the wishes or interests of
its dominant neighbor to the north. In 1938 the Cardenas
administration nationalized U.S. oil companies operating
in Mexico despite serious objections from the United
States (Meyer, 1977). In 1964, Mexico refused to break
relations with Cuba or to support OAS sanctions against
the Castro regime, again despite enormous U.S. pressures

(Smith, 1970). In 1965 Mexico opposed U.S. intervention in the Dominican Republic. In each of these cases, Mexico's foreign policy behavior was more responsive to domestic problems, pressures, and demands than to external factors. At the same time, through the late 1960s, Mexico's interest in encouraging foreign investment, obtaining needed technology, and increasing its exports to U.S. markets led Mexico's leaders to adopt foreign policy positions generally in accord with U.S. interests.

With the election of Luis Echeverria Alvarez to the presidency in 1970, Mexico assumed a far more active, aggressive, Third World-oriented foreign policy than it ever had in the past. The catalyst for this change was the university protest of 1968. This protest culminated in the massacre of Tlatelolco just prior to the 1968 Olympic games in Mexico City. This event produced widespread fears of growing political instability and declining regime legitimacy among many sectors of Mexico's ruling elite. Shapira (1978) and Poitras (1974) maintain that Echeverria's new approach can be explained as a response to the deepening economic dependence and declining economic growth in the late 1960s and early 1970s. In effect, Mexico's internal political situation led the new president to seek to offset rising discontent, particularly among students and intellectuals, by adopting a more activist and radical posture in international affairs. His domestic policies--fiscal and agrarian reform and regulation of foreign capital--were also considerably more reformist than those followed by his most recent predecessors (Purcell and Purcell, 1976).

Echeverria's new foreign policy initiatives contained three basic elements: (1) support for the Charter of States' Economic Rights and Duties (or The New International Economic Order); (2) adoption of legislation regulating foreign investment and the transfer of technology; and (3) expansion of Mexico's linkages with the rest of Latin America and the Third World to promote regional unity and diversify its dependence on the United States (Shapira, 1978).

Mexico's decision to abandon its traditional emphasis on bilateral relations with the United States under Echeverria resulted in an unprecedented expansion of the nation's diplomatic ties (67 new countries were recognized), conclusion of 160 international pacts and agreements (two-thirds on commercial or economic questions), Mexico's active participation in multilateral frameworks representing developing and dependent states (the United Nations Conference on Trade and Development (UNCTAD), the U.N.'s Food and Agriculture Organization (FAO), Third World forums, and regional arenas), and closer economic ties with Europe and the Socialist bloc countries

(Grayson, 1977; Shapira, 1978). The Mexican president
himself was active in planning and implementing the new
foreign policy. His personal involvement and the radical, tercermundista tone of his policy pronouncements
were clearly geared toward increasing his popularity and
quieting leftist opposition at home. It also seems to
have reflected a sincere conviction on the part of the
president and his major economic advisers that Mexico's
continued economic expansion required a diversification
of its economic and technological dependence on the
United States. Sponsorship of a new international economic order was, in this sense, an expression of Mexico's
own economic self-interest.

During the early years of Echeverria's administration, efforts at diversification focused on the Western
industrial economies (e.g., Canada, United Kingdom, Belgium, France, Germany, Italy, and Austria). Following
the energy crisis of 1973-1974 and the subsequent recession in the Western economies, Mexico's attention shifted
increasingly toward Latin America (Brazil, Venezuela,
Ecuador, Peru, Costa Rica, and Jamaica) and the Third
World generally. This opening toward the Third World was
accompanied by adoption of increasingly outspoken policy
positions that were intended to demonstrate Mexico's
solidarity with the Third World and its goals of reordering the international economic system. In 1974, for example, Echeverria publicly condemned the repressive military governments in Chile and Brazil and called for a
return to democracy. A similar condemnation was directed
at Spain in 1975. On November 10, 1975, Mexico voted
against Israel and "Zionism" in the U.N. General Assembly.
Also in late 1975 it tilted further toward a pro-Arab
policy by permitting the Palestine Liberation Organization (PLO) to establish its first Latin American office
in Mexico City.

Mexico gained little in terms of increased trade or
investment from Echeverria's pro-Third World policies.
Indeed, trade with the United States and other industrial
countries expanded rapidly during Echeverria's term in
office. But Echeverria was able to undercut leftist domestic opposition, improve his political popularity at
home, and increase the country's prestige in Third World
forums. The price paid for these political gains was
high. As noted above, business confidence, both domestic
and foreign, declined precipitously, turning into a near-
panic flight of capital in late 1975 and in 1976. Right-
wing opposition increased significantly, creating severe
tensions within the Mexican ruling elite. The 1975 anti-
Zionist vote led the American Jewish community to declare
a boycott of Mexico during the winter holiday season of
1975; the action resulted in a 25 percent drop in tourism, one of Mexico's biggest foreign exchange earners.

Despite Echeverria's internationalism, Mexico's economic and diplomatic role in Central America and the Caribbean remained limited during his administration. Throughout the 1970s, trade between Mexico and Central America accounted for 3 percent or less of Mexico's exports and less than 1 percent of its imports (Euromoney, 1978). Though Mexico was an important economic presence in some Central American countries, its political role in the region was not key until very recently. During the mid-1970s, Mexico did play a minor role in the dispute between Guatemala and the United Kingdom over Belize. In effect, Mexico shifted from a pro-Guatemalan position to a pro-Belizean stand by withdrawing its own territorial claims over Belize, thus undercutting the validity of Guatemala's claims (Shapira, 1978). In general, however, Mexico observed a policy of noninvolvement in both the Caribbean and Central America. The August 1980 decision to collaborate with Venezuela in supplying oil to Central America and Caribbean neighbors marks the beginning of a new era.

When Jose Lopez Portillo assumed the presidency in December 1976, the chaotic economic situation obligated him to moderate the radical tone of his predecessor's foreign policy. He moved quickly to restore both foreign and domestic business confidence in the Mexican economy by providing new incentives for investment and production and by accepting IMF stabilization guidelines. The announcement of new oil reserves helped to reestablish Mexico's international creditworthiness,[4] as did the new administration's more pragmatic, middle-of-the-road approach to domestic reform.

Underlying Lopez Portillo's more moderate approach to foreign policy issues, however, is a continuing interest in diversifying Mexico's economic and diplomatic relationships away from the United States. Petroleum strengthened Mexico's bargaining position. When in 1977 and 1978 U.S.-Mexican relations cooled over the natural gas negotiations, Mexico accelerated its program of trade diversification by signing major new oil supply contracts. U.S.-Mexican relations were further strained (1) by the U.S. demands for payment of damages in the Ixtoc I oil spill in the summer of 1979 and (2) by periodic reports of abuses of the civil and human rights of illegal Mexicans along the border. The cordial discussions between Lopez Portillo and Carter in Washington, D.C., in September 1979--the gas deal for sale of 300 million cubic feet per day was signed just prior to this meeting--appeared to mark the beginning of a warming trend in U.S.-Mexican relations.

Mexico's traditional low-key approach to foreign policy was clearly reflected in the minimal role Mexico

played in Central America during the Nicaraguan civil war.
In late May 1979, a few months before the fall of Somoza,
Mexico withdrew diplomatic recognition from the Somoza
regime and urged the United States to do the same (New
York Times, May 22, 1979). Since the Carter administra-
tion had already cut off all economic and military aid to
Nicaragua in January 1979, Mexico was not taking a par-
ticularly adventurous stand.

Mexico, along with Venezuela and the Andean pact
countries, was also instrumental in quashing a 1979 U.S.
proposal in the OAS to create an Inter-American peacekeeping force to intervene in Nicaragua. In the wake of
the Sandinistas' assumptions of power in Nicaragua, Mexico
sent small amounts of emergency aid to help in the process of reconstruction.

Beginning in 1980, the Lopez Portillo administration
began to assume a more assertive role in Nicaragua and
elsewhere in the Caribbean basin. On August 3, 1980,
Mexico entered into a joint oil facility arrangement with
Venezuela in which it agreed to provide Nicaragua and
eight other Central American and Caribbean nations with
petroleum under a concessionary credit arrangement. The
number of recipient countries was later expanded to 14.

In addition, Mexico sent approximately 400 technical
advisers to aid the Sandinista regime and has provided
upward of $200 million in aid to that country (Washington
Post, May 13, 1981, p. Al). Significantly, Mexico has
entered into these relationships despite growing criticism of the Sandinistas in the United States during the
final year of the Carter administration and the more open
hostility of the Reagan administration toward the Sandinista government in Nicaragua.

Mexico's increasingly assertive foreign policy in
Central America can also be seen in El Salvador. On
August 28, 1981, after months of criticism of the United
States' support for the military-backed government of
President Jose Napoleon Duarte, Mexico issued a joint
communique with France during the United Nations Security
Council meeting, officially recognizing the leftist Salvadoran guerrillas as "a representative political force"
legitimately entitled to negotiate with the U.S.-supported
Duarte government. This action, although smoothed over in
a meeting between Presidents Reagan and Lopez Portillo in
the United States on September 17, 1981, clearly introduced a new element of stress in U.S.-Mexican relations
(Washington Post, August 29, 1981, Al7; September 18,
1981, A3).

As of 1978, Mexico's armed forces, with only 82,000
men and women, ranked only 42nd among world armed forces,

far below Mexico's position in either population or economic power base. Mexican military expenditures in 1975
were only $600 million. Although much larger than other
forces in Central America, the Mexican military is not
prepared to undertake peacekeeping roles in the region.
Furthermore, the principles of sovereignty and independence of all nations, nonintervention in the domestic affairs of other countries, peaceful resolution of conflicts, collective security, and participation in
international organizations are fundamental tenets of
Mexico's foreign policy (Grayson, 1977). Therefore,
Mexico is not likely to assume an active military role
in Central America or the Caribbean basin.

As a gesture to its domestic left and to the Third
World generally, in May 1979 Lopez Portillo warmly welcomed President Fidel Castro to Mexico for discussions
on fishing, sugar, development, oil, and trade, as well
as the upcoming (September 1979) Nonaligned conference
in Havana. The trip had symbolic importance, for it was
Castro's first trip to Latin America since he visited
Chile in 1973. There has been speculation that it marks
a renewal of the rapprochement between Cuba and the rest
of Latin America that was halted when Cuba became involved in Africa in 1976. It definitely served as a
symbolic answer to domestic critics who had accused Lopez
Portillo of being too conservative and pro-American (New
York Times, May 18, 1979). Subsequent trips by Castro to
Mexico and by Lopez Portillo to Cuba in 1980 and 1981 reaffirmed the bond between the two countries.

Economic relations between Mexico and Cuba remain
limited. The Mexicans and Cubans have discussed the possibility of an oil swap involving the Soviet Union in
which Mexico would send oil directly to Cuba while the
Soviet Union would supply Mexico's European customers,
thus cutting transportation costs for all parties. Castro
and Lopez Portillo have not reached any public accord on
this issue and no deal is now in the offing. A simpler
alternative might be for the Soviet Union to buy 70,000
barrels per day from Mexico and deliver it to Cuba without
any formal swapping arrangement in force (U.S. Senate,
1979). Mexico is currently involved in a joint venture
with Cuba to explore for petroleum on Cuba's maritime
platform (Wall Street Journal, April 17, 1981).

Mexico's friendliness to Fidel Castro and its support for the Sandinistas in Nicaragua should not be interpreted as anti-American. In keeping with the country's
revolutionary tradition, Mexican presidents have traditionally given verbal support to left-wing movements in
Latin America to dampen radical protest at home. Mexico
is certain to assume disconcerting foreign policy stances
in the future. But the U.S. and Mexican economies are

highly complementary, and the U.S. and Mexican long-term
interests are basically similar. The United States cannot count on Mexico to assume a dominant economic or political role in Central America or the Caribbean, but
Mexico's policies in those regions are likely to remain
moderate and pragmatic.

MEXICAN POLITICAL STABILITY AND CONSTRAINTS
ON MEXICO'S GROWTH

     Although the forecasts of Mexico's future economic
growth are generally optimistic, several factors could
seriously limit Mexico's continued growth. Oil cannot
solve all the country's development problems. Any severe
economic slowdown in Mexico would exacerbate domestic
discontent and increase the possibility of political disruption and instability. The major constraints on Mexico's continued growth include these:

- High population growth rates that create pressure
  for new jobs at a rate of 800,000 per year and
  increase demand for public services such as transportation, health, education, welfare, and
  housing.

- An extremely unequal income-distribution pattern
  that limits the size of the domestic market, creates social discontent, and increases mass political pressure on the state.

- A capital-intensive (rather than labor-intensive)
  growth model that relies heavily on imported technology and foreign investment.

- A large and growing foreign debt that absorbs
  more than one-half of the country's foreign exchange in debt service payments.

Population Growth

     During the 1960s and early 1970s, Mexico's rate of
population increase exceeded 3.3 percent a year, making
it one of the fastest-growing large countries in the
world. Indeed, its population expanded each year by a
greater number than the populations of the United States
and Canada together expanded, even though Mexico had
only a quarter of the base population of its two North
American neighbors. The implications of this high population growth rate are serious, for the economy must expand rapidly just to absorb the 800,000 or so new workers
entering the labor force each year. Inability to provide
sufficient employment opportunities increases the already
endemic problems of underemployment and unemployment and

spurs the flow of illegal migrants into the United States.
The need to create jobs is one of the most basic economic
problems Mexico faces over the 1980s.

In 1972 under President Echeverria, Mexico decided
to abandon its traditional pronatalist policies and to
launch a massive family-planning campaign. At his inauguration in 1976, President Lopez Portillo committed
his government to securing a population growth rate of
2.6 percent a year by the end of his term in 1982 and announced that the country would seek to achieve a 1 percent
population growth rate by the year 2000. Between 1974 and
1978 funding for population programs in Mexico jumped
from $7 million to $70 million. By the end of the 1970s,
there were indications that population growth in Mexico
had in fact already slowed dramatically, to the approximately 2.6 percent goal sought by Lopez Portillo for 1982.

If the most recent statistics are correct, the Mexican population grew by approximately 12.5 million between
1975 and 1979. By the year 2000, the population will ex-
ceed 100 million, with half under 15 years of age. Thus,
large numbers of young women are about to enter child-
bearing age over the next two decades and millions of
young adults will be entering the work force. Even if
Mexico escapes a baby "boom" during the 1980s--and escape
is by no means certain--it will nevertheless continue to
have a large labor surplus and high rates of unemployment
throughout this century. The possibility of severe social tensions is, therefore, clearly present.

Income Inequalities

Despite impressive economic growth over the past 40
years, the profile of income inequality in Mexico has
steadily worsened. The top 10 percent of income earners
in Mexico today account for 45 percent of the country's
total income, while the lowest 40 percent receive approximately 10 percent. In the United States, by comparison,
the top 10 percent receive about 28 percent of all income
while the lowest 40 percent account for 14 percent (World
Bank, 1978). This pattern of income distribution not only
results in widespread poverty and misery but also significantly limits the growth of internal demand. Along with
unemployment then, Mexico's extremely skewed income distribution constitutes a major constraint on Mexico's future growth and stability.

Capital-Intensive Versus Labor-Intensive Growth

With "petro pesos" to underwrite its development
plans, the Mexican government is currently engaged in establishing economic priorities and drawing up a specific
program of action to deal with its multiple developmental

problems. One of the major decisions that must be made
involves whether to emphasize capital- or labor-intensive
industrialization strategies. The National Industrial
Development Plan published in 1979 offered generous tax
incentives for job creation (20 percent of the annual
minimum wage for each new employee) but also emphasized
industrial plant investment and the acquisition of new
machinery and equipment. Moreover, it gave special priority to rapid development of the capital-intensive
petrochemical industry. Skeptics did not believe the
plan went far enough in the area of job creation. Nevertheless, it was undoubtedly the most complete industrial
development plan the Mexicans have yet produced. Considerably more skepticism remains about the government's
agricultural plan. Without a major push toward job creation in the rural areas, Mexico's urban employment problems will only increase, the flow of immigrants to the
United States will continue, and political tensions will
be exacerbated.

Foreign Debt

A final important constraint on Mexico's future economic growth is high foreign indebtedness. The country's
international debt grew rapidly in the 1970s, from about
$3 billion in 1970 to almost $50 billion in 1981. Service
requirements on the external debt rose to $4 billion in
1979, over half of the year's export earnings. This high
debt service ratio continues to drain capital away from
productive investment and impedes overall growth. Because of Mexico's rapidly rising petroleum export earnings, the external debt has caused relatively little concern so far among the private bankers and multinational
lenders that provide capital to Mexico, but if the debt
continues to grow, this will not remain the case.

Oil and Development

A critical aspect of Mexico's future concerns the
proper use of Mexican petroleum resources. The record of
other oil-boom nations is not encouraging. Inflation,
swollen import bills, luxury consumption, capital-
intensive industrialization, the neglect of agriculture,
regional imbalances, unsatisfied rising expectations,
and, in general, an inability to break with the most un-
attractive patterns of the past are all common in the
recent histories of nations otherwise as diverse as Venezuela and Iran (Fagen, 1978). The effective use of oil
revenues for development is the basic task facing the
Mexican ruling elite.

President Lopez Portillo himself has repeatedly emphasized that oil has given Mexico an "historical opportunity" to finance its own development, that this bonanza

must be properly managed, and that failure to do so would
lead to social "disaster" (New York Times, February 18,
1979). For this reason the Mexicans have insisted that
they will develop their new petroleum resources in accor-
dance with Mexico's own national interests rather than
with the energy needs of the United States. It also explains why they have charged OPEC-level and higher prices
for their petroleum products, although they are not members of that organization.

There are sound economic reasons for Mexico to move
cautiously toward higher levels of production. Mexico
must provide 800,000 jobs each year over the next decade
to absorb young people moving into the labor force. Oil
production and petroleum-related industries are capital-
intensive, not labor-intensive. Jobs will have to be
created elsewhere. Mexican officials must also guard
against the inflationary impact of rapid development.
The Mexican economy has a limited absorptive capacity.
A strong surge in revenues could trigger sharp price increases, perhaps before the presidential inauguration in
December 1982. Furthermore, Mexico does not have the
domestic investment capital needed to finance rapid development, either in PEMEX or in the private sector.
Even with increased petroleum income, Mexico will have
to resort to extensive foreign borrowing to carry out its
ambitious development programs. Finally, too-rapid expansion could overextend Mexican industry's capacity to
provide the necessary technology and machinery, thus
stimulating further imports and worsening the country's
already serious balance-of-payment problems.

In 1979, Mexico attained a production level of
2.25 million bpd for 1980, and planned to raise that
level to 4 million bpd by 1982. How much oil the United
States will be able to obtain from Mexico will be contingent, at least in part, on U.S. willingness to grant
trade concessions and deal with the immigration issue.
So far, protectionist sentiments and public concern over
illegal immigration have made major U.S. concessions politically difficult. The Carter administration made
none, and while the Reagan administration has begun to
negotiate on these issues, no major initiatives have yet
been implemented. In the long run, however, Mexico's
prosperity and stability and U.S. national interests in
Mexico depend on striking a mutually beneficial deal.

CONCLUSIONS

The United States has vital national economic and
political interests in Mexico. Economic interests include the following:

168

- U.S. banks hold more than $15 billion of Mexico's foreign public debt. Any major economic crisis or default would have severe repercussions for the entire U.S. financial system.

- Because Mexico is the United States' third-largest trading partner in the world, any interruption in the flow of trade across the border would have important consequences for the U.S. economy.

- Mexico has the potential to become a major exporter of petroleum to the United States and to the world.

- Mexico is an important U.S. supplier of a variety of critical raw materials.

- Sectors of U.S. industry and agriculture rely heavily on low-paid Mexican labor to remain competitive on the international market.

The United States' political interests in Mexico, which are strongly linked to these economic concerns, are equally important:

- Mexico's huge deposits of gas, oil, and several critical nonfuel raw materials combined with its geographical proximity and the defensibility of Mexican-U.S. supply lines raise Mexico to the status of a major strategic concern to the United States.

- Mexico's ability to serve as a buffer between the United States and an increasingly unstable Central America is a matter of growing importance to the United States.

- Mexican economic difficulties are closely related to U.S. border problems and immigration policies.

- The possibility that economic stagnation or poorly planned economic growth could exacerbate social and political tensions in Mexican society and precipitate political instability and breakdown is a major concern for the United States. A leftist, anti-American regime in Mexico would be undesirable and unacceptable to the United States. An authoritarian and openly repressive military regime is equally unpalatable.

If the United States is to establish a constructive relationship with Mexico over the 1980s, Mexico must remain stable and prosperous. As has been noted, the basic

tensions between the two countries today involve economic
issues such as protectionism, controls on foreign investment, transfers of technology, and the like. U.S. relations with Mexico are best served by forgoing a search
for short-term benefits and seeking instead policies that
will encourage sustained economic growth over the long
run. Hence, the negotiations over trade and Mexico's
possible membership in the General Agreement on Tariffs
and Trade (GATT) are of particular significance. A care-
fully planned mutual reduction of tariff barriers should
be of long-term benefit to both countries. In these negotiations, the United States must remain especially sensitive to Mexican nationalism and development goals and
the domestic constraints within which the Mexican president and his top policy advisers operate. Proposals of a
North American Common Market are precipitous and exacerbate Mexican fears of economic and cultural domination.
Mexicans are understandably concerned with the effects
that opening their economy to competition from United
States and other foreign firms will have on domestic producers. Establishing a stable framework for trade between
Mexico and the United States will take considerable time,
will necessarily involve important concessions to Mexico,
and will be implemented incrementally.

Although Mexico faces severe internal development
problems, it also has great promise. U.S. concessions on
access to markets will help Mexico achieve this promise.
U.S. policies are, however, only one part of an exceed-
ingly complex equation. Just as important is the capacity
of Mexico's ruling elite to carry out the long-term socio-
economic reforms. Petroleum has given Mexico an historic
opportunity to carry out the "authentic project of national development" as promised by President Lopez Portillo. The central unanswered question is whether Mexico's dominant groups have the will and capacity to design
and implement such a project. It is in the United
States' interest to encourage and facilitate the necessary reforms, even if some U.S. interests are adversely
affected in the short run.

NOTES

1. In September 1979, President Lopez Portillo, in
his third meeting with President Carter in Washington,
specifically raised the question of access to U.S. markets
for Mexican tomato exports. But protests from Florida
growers regarding Mexican "dumping" severely limited the
Carter administration's ability to respond to Mexico on
this issue. In September 1978, the Florida growers lodged
a legal suit against Mexico; the suit was withdrawn at
the request of the Carter administration but subsequently
refiled in July 1979. The growers' suit was provisionally

dismissed on October 31, 1979, by the U.S. Treasury, and a final ruling favorable to the Mexicans was handed down on March 15, 1980.

2. The price was unacceptable for at least three reasons: (1) it contained an escalator clause tied to the rising cost of No. 2 heating fuel that would have been inflationary; (2) it might have derailed the Carter administration's fragile compromise on natural gas de-regulation then under discussion in Congress; and (3) it would have prompted Canada to request an increase in the $2.16 per thousand cubic feet price for gas that it was delivering to the United States.

3. For an analysis of the origins of the "embargo" under the Carter administration and Mexican reactions to it, see Antonio Gonzales de Leon, "Las Relaciones Mexico-Estados Unidos: El Caso de la Energia Nuclear" in Foro Internacional, Vol. XIX, No. 2 (October-December 1978), pp. 326-342.

4. Though the first signs of Mexico's new oil riches began to surface in 1972, the Mexican officials played down these finds through 1976. President Echeverria, while pursuing a leadership role for Mexico in the Third World, did not want to face pressures to join OPEC or to stop selling oil to the United States, as any such ac-tions would have endangered Mexico's trading relationships with the United States.

5
Brazil: Emerging Power

Brazil is one of the most important countries emerging on the world scene today, and the Third World country most likely to become a significant political and economic global power over the next two decades. Brazil's 1981 gross national product (GNP) of about $220 billion was 8th largest in the Western world and 10th largest worldwide. Its GNP is larger than that of all of Africa, excluding South Africa (World Bank, 1978). Brazil has one of the most advanced economies in the developing world. It is the fifth largest country in the world, occupying nearly 50 percent of the South American continent. Its population, seventh largest in the world, grew at a rate exceeding 2.8 percent a year for much of the post-World War II period, and is likely to reach 200 million by the turn of the century. Brazil is by far the dominant power in Latin America.

Between 1966 and 1975 Brazil registered some of the highest growth rates in the world, up to 11.4 percent a year (1973). It averaged 8.9 percent between 1964 and 1974, as compared with 3.4 percent for the Western industrial countries. Growth continued to be buoyant until 1979 when the combined impact of the second round of oil price increases and rising interest rates slowed expansion to a standstill. Growth stood at zero in 1980 and 1981, and became negative in 1982 as the full impact of the developed world recession took effect. Brazil's recovery is assured if the world economy recovers; however, the double-digit growth rates of the early 1970s will be difficult to attain in the future. By the year 2000 Brazil should have the seventh largest economy in the world, behind only the United States, the Soviet Union, Japan, West Germany, France, and China. Brazil's economic size and diversity make it both a leader in the developing world and an aspirant to membership in the developed world.

U.S. relations with Brazil have waxed and waned over the past 35 years. Collaboration in World War II was

followed by a chilling of relations in the 1950s when
Brazilian nationalism was high. Relations warmed briefly
during the early 1960s only to cool again with the resurgence of a more radical nationalism and populism under
President João Goulart. When the United States warmly
embraced the revolutionary government of 1964, a particularly close relationship with Brazil developed, based on
U.S. collaboration in financing Brazilian development and
support for Brazil's campaign against internal subversion.
The economic miracle that accompanied this close collaboration has now progressively eroded the foundations of the
special relationship. "Successful Brazilian integration
into the world economy...weakened official ties to the
United States and a changed Brazilian leadership found a
continued junior role both unnecessary and undesirable"
(Fishlow, 1979).

U.S. relations with Brazil are at an important junc-
ture. Economic growth has given Brazil new trading partners (the European market is now more important to Brazil
than the North American market) and made available new
sources of financial assistance from among private banking
sectors in Japan, Europe, and the United States. Private
investment has made official assistance unnecessary.
Brazil increasingly deals directly with the representatives of international banks and firms, bypassing governments. It eschews a special bilateral relationship with
the United States in order to pursue its own interests
through a number of bilateral relationships, unconstrained
by the preferences of special allies.

A variety of events in the 1970s demonstrated Brazil's
new independent posture in its international relations and
indicated how Brazil's pursuit of self-interest frequently
contradicts U.S. policy preferences. In 1976 Brazil rescinded its 25-year-old mutual defense agreement with the
United States. It subsequently refused to sign the Nuclear Nonproliferation Treaty; has not given full support
to the hemispheric nuclear-free zone concept of the Tlatelolco Treaty; and in 1977 signed an agreement with West
Germany for the purchase of nuclear reactors and reprocessing technology. Brazil was an early party to claim a
200-mile territorial sea. It was frequently at odds with
the United States over access to U.S. markets for Brazilian exports, particularly textiles and leather wearing ap-
parel. In 1975 it flirted capriciously with liberation
movements in Africa, giving early recognition to the Cuban-
and Soviet-backed Popular Movement for the Liberation of
Angola (MPLA) in Angola. In the immediate aftermath of the
1973 oil crisis, Brazil courted its Arab suppliers by supporting anti-Israel resolutions in the United Nations General Assembly. More recently, it has established close relations with Iraq, one of its major oil suppliers.

Economic growth has created the objective conditions for Brazil to carry out an independent foreign policy, one in which Brazil remains committed to the West, but one which also permits it to assert its independence more seriously and with greater credibility (Fishlow, 1979). Its policies are pragmatic, self-interested, and sometimes unpredictable. Its objectives are to remove "all obstacles whatsoever that may counter [Brazil's] full economic, technological and scientific development...[since] Brazil would be, among the countries of the world, one of those that would suffer the most through affirmation of a policy of freezing of world power" (Araujo Castro, 1971).

U.S. interests in Brazil and in that country's changing role in the international community are those of a traditional ally, a major economic partner with substantial trade, enormous corporate and institutional investments, shared commitment to Western political systems, and longstanding military relations, both bilateral and through the inter-American system. As U.S. influence declines and the European and Japanese economies become stronger, and as East-West competition for the allegiance of emerging Third World countries continues, the United States is vitally interested in reinforcing its good relations with the dominant powers of the developing world. The political-military environment of the next 20 years will differ markedly from that of the first 25 to 30 years after World War II. The locus of world political-military conflict and confrontation is more likely to be in Southern Hemisphere-Third World arenas than in the Northern Hemisphere, NATO-Warsaw Pact arena. The trend is already apparent, as was demonstrated in Blechman (1977), which showed that 26 percent of U.S. use of military force short of war took place in the Third World areas. Other studies have demonstrated that a similar pattern has held for the Soviet Union (Blechman, 1977; CACI, 1977). A number of advanced developing countries like Brazil will emerge to play important roles in the political, military, and economic balance of power in the future.

Because of its already strong economic power base and its growing military capabilities, Brazil will be an important factor in U.S. global political-military thinking over the next 20 years. The United States' ability to construct a successful framework for collaboration with emerging powers like Brazil will significantly influence the future global balance of power and U.S. national security. Brazil is regarded as a "model" developing country--one that is successfully approaching political, military, and economic independence and growing in potential to influence world affairs. Establishment of a constructive and mutually satisfying relationship with Brazil could improve U.S. ability to influence Third World opinion in areas such as nuclear nonproliferation, arms

acquisition, regional conflicts, and ideological issues.
It could contribute to winning more support in the Third
World for the United States in the world balance of power.

The most important issues on Brazil's agenda for discussion with the United States are access to U.S. investment capital and markets and acquisition of technology for
Brazil's continued economic development. The national security concerns that often top the U.S. list of issues
have much less priority. Brazil in the 1980s is more con-
fident of its domestic political stability than it was in
the 1960s and has embarked on an effort to consolidate the
political system that has emerged since its 1964 revolution and to return to civilian government.

BRAZIL'S FOREIGN POLICY PERSPECTIVES

Brazil's foreign policy has traditionally been highly
pragmatic, and its new economic power permits Brazil to
pursue its own interests with even less regard to the
opinions of its traditional ally, the United States. Brazilian leaders view their country's recent rapid economic
development as providing a solid foundation for a world
role in the 1980s and 1990s. Although Brazil already is
the major power in South America, Brazil does not have
sufficient status and independence to play a major role
in the international community at large; its foreign policy objectives are linked to goals of economic development
and national political security. One scholar noted:

> The geopolitical thinking characteristic of the
> dominant military elements reinforces a widely
> held belief that the respect that Brazil can com-
> mand on the world scene depends in large part
> on its perception by the major powers as the
> dominant nation in South America. However...
> the architects of Brazilian policy are deter-
> mined to keep the development horse ahead of
> the diplomatic cart. The fundamental objective
> is first to transform Brazil into a developed
> nation in a single generation (Schneider, 1978).

When Brazil has finally mobilized its full economic
potential, it will of necessity be a world power. Hence
in 1972 Planning Minister João Paulo dos Reis Velloso emphasized that it was "in Brazil's interest to conduct foreign relations in consonance with the national development
strategy, which seeks the most rapid possible growth, modernization, and greater competitive power of the national
economy" (Schneider, 1978).

The chief motivating factors behind Brazil's initiatives abroad are economic. Brazil's leaders saw the trend

toward realignment of the developed and developing countries on North-South issues as offering a number of opportunities that Brazil could exploit in pursuit of its own
national interests, which coincide with the interests of
both developed and developing countries. As a developing
country, Brazil supports the positions of the Group of 77
nations that argues for developed world commitment to the
redistribution of economic wealth and power. Brazil's alliance with the less-developed countries on basic international economic questions provides Brazil with leverage
for dealing with the industrial powers. At the same time,
it seeks to work with the industrial powers on matters of
common interest.

As the major oil-importing country in Latin America,
Brazil has concerns over oil price and supply similar to
those of the OECD countries, and it participated in the
1976 Council for International Economic Cooperation, which
sought unsuccessfully to reconcile the interests of oil-
importing and oil-exporting countries in the wake of the
recession provoked by the 1973-1974 price hikes. As a
steel producer and exporter, Brazil would like to work
more closely with the developed-country steel producers,
but it has declined to participate in OECD steel talks so
as not to suggest that it no longer merits treatment as a
developing country. As a major borrower in the international public and private financial markets, Brazil sought
and won a permanent seat on the International Monetary
Fund board, where it hopes to influence IMF policy toward
other less-developed countries. Growing financial difficulties in the period 1979-1982 served to remind Brazilians and Brazil's advocates abroad of the fragility of the
still-developing Brazilian economic and industrial
infrastructure.

Brazil's halfway position between the developed and
the developing worlds tends to introduce ambiguity into
its international relations. Brazil has become highly
vulnerable to external policy shifts, at the same time it
has acquired flexibility to assume those positions it per-
ceives most likely to promote Brazil's own long-range
interests.

Schneider notes that Brazil's major power aspirations
have had but a minor influence on the country's foreign
policy decisions. Rather, foreign policy has been viewed
in terms of possible contribution to internal economic development. Brazil emphasizes the economic dimensions of
its world projection in part because it recognizes the
tremendous gap that continues to separate it from the developed industrial countries, and in part because it is
located in a relatively conflict-free area of the world,
where it has no large hostile neighbors and is separated
from regions of superpower conflict by the Atlantic Ocean.

Historically, Brazil has played a low profile role in continental politics. This was in part because it is sensitive to jealousies and hostilities among its Spanish-speaking neighbors, and in part because Brazil aspires to more than regional hegemony. It would prefer being included in the councils of world powers over having mere regional hegemony. At the same time, Brazil recognizes that the regional role will serve as the launching base for greater international participation.

Brazil at present has decisive influence with only a handful of small neighboring countries--Paraguay, Uruguay, and Bolivia--with which it has strong financial ties. Even in these countries, Brazil has tried to downplay its influence; for example, Brazil did not actively pursue a 1974 agreement for exchange of gas with Bolivia because of Bolivian concern over Brazil's "takeover" of Bolivian natural resources. Bolivia's own need for financing to develop the fields led it to raise the issue with Brazil again in 1982 and mutually beneficial long-term agreements were signed that will result in developing Bolivia's gas field and building a gas pipeline to São Paulo by 1985. Brazil has been diplomatically close to Chile, but found that relationship embarrassing when international public opinion turned strongly against the Pinochet government. Close association with Chile became increasingly difficult as Brazil moved progressively toward its own political opening (abertura) in the late 1970s and sought to downplay its relations with Chile. Economic ties have grown, but diplomatic relations have been given a low profile.

Brazil has determined to work more closely with Venezuela, Colombia, and Ecuador, its Amazon neighbors, through the Amazon Pact, signed in 1978. Traditionally, Brazil's relations with Peru and Argentina have been cool. In the 1970s Brazil had political differences with both countries and economic differences plus a long-standing rivalry with Argentina. In 1980, however, Brazilian and Argentine presidents exchanged visits and signed a series of ten wide-ranging agreements to promote cooperation in nuclear energy, hydroelectric power development, integration of the regional energy grid, and agricultural, scientific, and technological areas. While not all the agreements have been actively pursued in the ensuing years, they represent a dramatic break with past animosities. Historically, Brazil's relations with Mexico have been of low intensity, although this situation is changing as Brazil sees Mexico both as a source of petroleum and as an ally in industrial development. Brazil has not supported Mexico's militant "Third-Worldism," has only lukewarmly supported the Mexican-Venezuelan-sponsored Latin American Economic System, and generally has sought to remain aloof from regional political turmoil. Brazil played a statesman's role during early discussions of the Argentine-British Falkland Islands war,

leading efforts in the OAS to produce a Falklands resolution that would both defend Argentine claims to sovereignty
and also contribute to peaceful resolution of the dispute.

Despite its growing leadership position in the Western Hemisphere, Brazil's influence outside the hemisphere
remains limited. While it gives tacit support to the
Third World's call for creation of a new international
economic order, Brazil's bilateral relations with developing countries are developed on the basis of economic interests, just as are its relations with the developed nations. Brazil needs raw materials—petroleum, copper, and
coal—and continues to import basic foodstuffs in spite of
vast agricultural potential. More important, it needs
markets for its expanding manufactured exports. At the
same time, Brazil provides goods and technical assistance
for less-developed countries, and demand for these services has grown dramatically over the past ten years.
Brazil's excellent relations with Iraq are based on an
exchange of Brazilian petroleum exploration technology
for favorable prices and guaranteed supplies of Iraqi
petroleum. In 1978 Brazil concluded agreements with the
People's Republic of China for exchange of Brazilian iron
ore, pig iron, sugar, and steel products in return for
Chinese petroleum shipments in 1979 and 1980 (BOLSA, 1978).
More recently Brazil has developed a strong link to Libya,
selling weapons in exchange for oil.

Brazil's influence with the developed countries is
relatively low. Brazil depends on the industrial powers
for markets, financing, and technology, but it has no
critical resources that could be used to gain leverage
with those powers. Demand for the raw materials Brazil
does export—iron ore, aluminum, and so forth—is heavily
influenced by economic performance in the developed economies, and several major resource development projects have
been postponed in the past several years for lack of clear
markets to which to sell.

Brazil's 1975 negotiations to obtain nuclear technology from West Germany were also based on considerations
of mutual economic benefits. Germany needed a market for
its technology and uranium, which Brazil has in as yet
unknown quantities (Grabendorff, 1979). Brazil also
needed to develop alternatives to petroleum, lacked domestic know-how, and chafed at its dependence on the
United States in this area. Within several years, it was
clear that the ambitious Brazil-West German agreement
would not be carried out in full, and in 1982, much of it
was formally cancelled. Nevertheless, Brazil's international prestige was sharply enhanced by its ability to
negotiate a nuclear agreement with a major European power
over the protests of the United States (see Gall, 1976).

Brazil similarly succeeded in promoting its interests in several aspects of maritime policy, such as its relatively early (1970) declaration of a 200-mile territorial sea, its reservation of 40 percent of overseas trade for Brazilian ships, and its collaboration with European and Japanese firms to develop a major shipbuilding industry capable of producing the most sophisticated merchant and military vessels. By the 1980s Brazil had the second largest shipbuilding industry in the world. Ignoring U.S. concern over the escalation of armaments in Latin America, Brazil has purchased the sophisticated materiel it wanted in the European market. Many of its purchase agreements include licensing for production in Brazil and the eventual transfer of technology. By 1980 Brazil was the Third World's largest arms merchant with $2 billion in annual sales.

Brazil's foreign policy initiatives were striking during the Medici and Geisel administrations, 1970-1974 and 1975-1979, a period of unprecedented economic expansion. Economic difficulties were already apparent when the Figueiredo administration (1980-1985) took office in 1980 amidst signals that it would implement a lower-key, less flamboyant approach to achieve the same basic objectives. The new government's foreign minister announced that the administration would give top priority to relations with Latin America and Africa, to new efforts oriented toward industrialized nations, such as those of the European Community and the United States, and to responding to new developments in the international sphere. The thrust of Brazilian foreign policy would be maintained (Embassy of Brazil, 8 March 1979). However, domestic economic difficulties conspired to focus attention on internal issues--especially control of inflation, income distribution, increased domestic private-sector participation in economic decision making, and on agricultural development. President Figueiredo's continued commitment to political opening and return to civilian government also served to direct national attention to the domestic arena.

BRAZIL'S ROLE IN THE INTERNATIONAL ECONOMY

The expansion of Brazil's international role depends on continued economic growth. Brazil's importance in the world today is, in large part, the result of its spectacular economic growth since World War II, particularly between 1968 and 1980. Now the world's 10th-largest economy, its 1980 gross national product of $248 billion approached those of Canada ($242 billion), China ($283 billion), or Italy ($368 billion) and surpassed those of Spain ($199 billion), Poland ($140 billion), or the Netherlands ($161 billion), all middle-ranking industrial powers. Brazil's GNP is nearly double that of its nearest Latin American rival, Mexico, and quadruple that of Argentina, the third-largest Latin American economy. If Brazil continued to grow at its historical rate of approximately 7 percent a year, it would surpass both Italy and Great Britain in economic size by 1995 (see Chapter 2, Table 2.4). It should then have an economy equivalent in size to West Germany's in 1975 (CACI, 1978; Fishlow, 1978).

The structure of the Brazilian economy and the quality of its relations with both the developed and developing economies have changed dramatically during the course of its rapid development. It has diversified its exports, reduced its dependence in a variety of import areas, and expanded its economic relations to all the regions of the world. In short, it has greatly increased its ability to deal from a position of strength in its bilateral relationships. At the same time, like other developing countries, Brazil remains heavily dependent on the developed market economies both as markets for its exports and as sources of the technology, capital goods, and financial backing needed for its continued economic development. Energy dependence and an overwhelming foreign debt are serious problems for Brazil and potential constraints on future growth prospects.

This section describes Brazil's current economic relations with world regions, indicates those countries with which Brazil has the closest economic ties, and presents forecasts of Brazil's likely future growth that will make it an increasingly important world power over the next two decades. The section also reviews the factors that are likely to influence Brazil's future growth and its international relations within that time frame.

Background of Brazilian Economic Growth and Diversification

Although the foundations for growth were laid before the war, the post-World War II period was characterized by conscious planning of economic development based on import-substituting industrialization--stimulating domestic industrial development by limiting imports of products that can be produced locally. As a result, the Brazilian economy's expansion averaged 7 percent, one of the highest sustained growth rates of any country during those years; the industrial sector's average growth ranged between 8 percent and nearly 10 percent in the late 1950s and early 1960s (Syvrud, 1974). In 1962 the Brazilian economy entered a period of extreme inflation coupled with economic stagnation that extended from 1963 to 1967. The crisis resulted from the exhaustion of import-substituting industrialization strategy and the accumulated disequilibria of the rapid economic stimulation of the previous years. The regime that came to power in 1964 began to implement

a program intended to restore economic balance and return
to rapid growth. After a period of uneven adjustment,
1964-1967, the economy entered its "miracle growth" period
that lasted from 1968 through 1973, when the average
growth of 11.3 percent was curtailed by the sudden increase in oil prices and subsequent worldwide economic recession. Through 1980 the Brazilian economy demonstrated
an erratic pattern of growth averaging 6.4 percent per
year for 1975 to 1978, and accelerating to 7.3 percent
over 1979 and 1980. The full impact of increased oil
prices, global recession, and structural economic problems was felt in 1981 and 1982, however, when growth
slowed to zero.

The structure of the Brazilian economy changed dramatically in the course of its economic expansion. Between 1949 and 1975, agriculture's contribution to gross
domestic product (GDP) declined from 25 percent to 10.6
percent, while industry, growing at annual rates of 9 percent between 1950-1960 and 12.9 percent between 1967-1973,
contributed nearly 40 percent of GDP by 1975, up from only
26 percent in 1949 (Baer, 1979). The growth of industry
has permitted the substitution of domestically produced
capital and consumer goods for items formerly imported,
and a substantial diversification of Brazil's exports.

Expansion of Exports

Since 1967 Brazil's development planners have sought
to expand the number of major export products, particularly manufactured exports, and to reduce reliance on coffee and other commodities traditionally subject to sharp
price fluctuation. Table 5.1 indicates that Brazil's exports increased in value more than sixfold in the period
1964 to 1975. This expansion--facilitated in part by
sharp world price increases in Brazil's traditional commodity exports (Cline, 1976)--also stemmed from a real diversification of export products, particularly into manufactures, machinery, soybeans, and iron ore.

The impact of the diversification on Brazil's export
profile was dramatic. Coffee accounted for more than
80 percent of Brazil's export earnings as late as 1964.
By 1974, coffee accounted for only 26 percent of export
earnings. In 1975, a particularly good year for coffee
prices because of severe frosts in Brazil, the product
earned only 10 percent of total export earnings. Despite
the poor coffee performance, export earnings nevertheless
increased by 13.7 percent over the previous year. Iron
ore accounted for less than 1 percent of exports in 1964
and more than 10 percent in 1975. With 13 percent (U.S.
Bureau of Mines, 1976) of total world identified iron ore
resources and with holdings second in size only to those
of the USSR, Brazil is an increasingly important supplier

TABLE 5.1
Brazilian Exports, 1960-1980 (Percentages)

	1960	1965	1970	1975	1977	1979	1980
Food and beverages	77.8	66.5	61.8	45.8	55.6	27.7	30.1
Coffee	56.2	44.3	40.3	10.8	21.6	16.4	17.3
Sugar	4.6	3.6	4.6	12.7	3.8	3.1	8.0
Cocoa	7.4	2.6	3.9	3.4	4.4	4.2	1.8
Tobacco	1.5	3.5	1.1	1.7	1.6	2.4	1.8
Animal and vegetable oils and fats	2.5	2.9	2.5	3.1	3.7	1.5	1.1
Raw materials (except fuel)	17.9	25.0	23.3	24.2	16.5	14.3	14.3
Soybeans	-	0.5	0.9	7.9	5.8	1.5	2.5
Lumber	3.4	3.6	2.9	1.1	0.7	0.3	0.3
Cotton	3.8	6.1	5.8	1.1	0.3	1.4	1.8
Iron ore	4.2	6.5	6.5	10.6	7.5	1.0	9.7
Petroleum, petroleum products	1.0	-	0.6	2.3	1.8	0.5	1.2
Manufactures (except machinery)	2.0	6.0	9.9	15.3	13.8	4.7	5.6
Footwear/leather	-	0.3	0.9	2.5	1.4	3.1	2.4
Iron and steel	0.2	2.7	3.6	2.0	2.2	1.2	1.5
Textiles/apparel	-	1.3	1.3	4.3	4.0	0.4	0.2
Wood/cork manufactures	-	0.4	0.0	0.6	0.6	-	-
Chemicals	1.1	0.9	1.4	2.1	1.5	-	1.5
Machinery/transport equipment	0.2	7.8	3.5	10.4	12.5	18.4	18.2
Nonelectrical machinery	-	1.0	2.3	4.9	5.3	6.1	5.9
Electrical machinery	-	0.3	0.7	1.9	2.5	2.9	2.8
Transport equipment	-	0.5	0.5	3.4	3.7	9.4	9.4
Other manufactures	1.1	0.7	0.9	2.1	0.0	34.4	30.6
Totals	100.0	100.0	100.0	100.0	100.0	100.0	100.0
Export values (millions of U.S. $)	$1,269	$1,595	$2,739	$8,669	$12,120	$15,244	$20,132

Source: United Nations, various issues, and Banco Central do Brasil, 1981.

of iron ore to steel industries both in the developed and
developing worlds. It maintains long-term contracts for
iron ore exports to both Japan and China. In addition,
Brazil has large supplies of high-grade ore for its own
increasingly sophisticated steel industry. Brazil has
put together a package of $3.8 billion in U.S., Japanese,
European, and World Bank financing to develop the Carajas
mining complex in the northeast of the country (Latin
America Regional Report, 17 September 1982). The Carajas
complex had attracted attention in the 1970s but low world
prices for iron ore discouraged both U.S. and Japanese investors at the time. Brazil has sought financing to develop the iron ore, manganese, copper, bauxite, and nickel
reserves in the region so that these resources will be
ready to export when the world economy recovers, about
1985. While the prospects that all of these projects will
come on stream by mid-decade are increasingly doubtful,
Brazil's potential to become one of the world's primary
suppliers of industrial raw materials is obvious. Only
continued recession in the industrial countries constrains
the rapid development of this sector of Brazil's economy.

In 1972, Brazil became the world's second-largest
producer and exporter of soybeans. U.S. soya export controls imposed in the 1960s caused Japanese and European
consumer countries to turn to Brazil for supplies (Cline,
1976). As a result, Brazil's soya exports rose in value
from $28 million in 1966 to $2.14 billion in 1977, and
from 1.6 percent of exports to 17.7 percent. OECD forecasts in the mid-1970s indicated that world demand for
soybean products was likely to increase to such an extent
that Brazilian exports would more than triple between 1972
and 1983 (OECD, 1976). By the end of the decade, however,
competition from Argentina and Paraguay, as well as from
traditional rivals such as the United States, somewhat
dampened growth in Brazil's soybean exports.

The major accomplishment of Brazil's export expansion
program was in the area of manufactures. Between 1966 and
1977 exports of manufactured and semimanufactured products
increased from 15 percent to 32.8 percent of total exports.
In 1978, another bad year for Brazilian agriculture, manufactures accounted for approximately 50 percent of all exports by value (BOLSA, 1978) and the percentage has remained at that level since. Table 5.2 gives a more detailed breakdown of the composition of Brazil's exports of
manufactured goods from 1966 to 1980. The most significant increases occurred between 1969 and 1974. In 1975
the rate of expansion slowed because of recession and near-
saturation in the developed markets. Like many other developing countries, Brazil believed the oil price-induced
recession would be temporary and it consciously pursued a
policy of continued rapid growth, financed through increased borrowing abroad. Brazil retained growth rates

TABLE 5.2
Brazil's Exports of Manufactured Goods, 1966-1980
(U.S. $ millions)

	1966	1970	1973	1975	1977	1980
Total mfg. exports	$142	$365	$1,320	$2,376	$3,379	$11,384
(% growth)	-	(6.7%)	(49.4%)	(16.7%)	(22.9%)	
Footwear		8	94	165	174	408
Boilers, machines & mechanical apparatus & instruments	12	24	72	260	427	1,382
Processed beef	8	16	70	71	119	233
Wood veneers	4	17	33	25	25	34
Electrical machinery	5	17	84	160	281	459
Office machinery & accessories	6	28	41	108	113	227
Rolling stock & vehicles	5	15	76	317	492	73
Steel mill products	10	41	53	70	101	625
Machine tools	3	5	6	18	15	103
Cotton yarn	8	6	45	68	120	181
Vegetable & fruit juices	5	15	68	86	180	364
Cotton fabrics	2	9	53	50	69	110
Glass & glassware	-	7	12	20	21	36
Earth-moving machinery	2	8	7	20	36	75
Other	42	84	241	470	729	904

Source: Central Bank Bulletin, February 1978 and December 1981.

at about 7 percent through 1979, and the value of its exports tripled from 1973 to 1980 (Fishlow, 1982).

As noted, manufactures exports now account for over
50 percent of export earnings for Brazil. This share com-
pares with an average share of 76 percent for manufactures
exports in most developed industrial countries (World Bank,
1978) and reflects Brazil's continued importance as a producer of raw materials for the world economy. Because
Brazil's high economic growth prospects depend on the continued success of its policy to expand manufactured exports, many of Brazil's foreign policy initiatives are
aimed at overcoming protectionist barriers in the industrialized world, finding new markets in rapidly developing
countries--particularly in the larger economies of the
Middle East, Latin America, or Asia--or a combination of
these strategies. In many of these areas Brazil is directly competing with stronger, developed economies, toward which Brazil has tended to adopt a vocal "Third
World" posture. Continued friction can be expected in
the competition for markets.

Reduction of Imports

Table 5.3 shows Brazil's major imports from 1960 to
1980. The major import categories have been petroleum
(40 percent in 1980), machinery and equipment (which fell
from a high of 40 percent to 19 percent over the period),
steel, chemicals, grains (especially wheat), and fertilizers. The principal suppliers of these products have
been Iraq and Saudi Arabia for petroleum (see Table 5.6);
Argentina for grains; and the United States, Europe (especially West Germany), and Japan for capital goods. Government policy, as expressed in the Second National Development Plan, has been to reduce import dependency in a
number of areas:

● Between 1980 and 1985 Brazil should achieve self-
   sufficiency in steel and perhaps become a net
   exporter.

● Several large-scale chemical and petrochemical
   plants are under construction and, when they come
   on-stream, imports in these two categories should
   be reduced dramatically.

● Exploration and development of mineral deposits,
   particularly copper, aluminum, and zinc, should
   begin to reduce the level of imports in the coming decade.

● Production from expanding fertilizer complexes
   should increasingly satisfy domestic consumption
   requirements.

TABLE 5.3
Brazilian Imports, 1960-1980 (Percentages)

	1960	1965	1970	1975	1977	1979	1980
Food and beverages	13.6	19.9	10.8	6.2	8.9	4.5	2.4
Wheat	9.7	12.4	4.5	2.6	1.5	3.0	3.9
Raw materials (excluding oil)	4.7	4.0	2.9	2.8	3.2	2.4	2.0
Mineral fuels	19.2	20.5	12.4	26.1	31.8	37.5	44.4
Crude oil	7.7	14.3	8.5	22.9	30.0	34.7	40.8
Manufactures (excluding machinery)	26.7	33.0	38.1	33.2	30.0	32.9	30.8
Chemicals	9.5	15.9	16.6	12.8	14.7	10.6	9.9
Iron and steel	5.6	4.3	5.3	9.8	4.5	2.7	2.6
Nonferrous metals	2.8	5.1	4.9	2.9	3.9	3.7	3.6
Metal manufactures	3.0	2.1	2.6	1.5	0.2	-	-
Optical precision instruments	0.8	2.1	3.0	2.2	2.0	2.4	1.8
Machinery	35.7	22.3	35.2	31.7	26.0	20.9	19.1
Nonelectrical	18.1	13.7	20.1	20.1	14.4	12.5	10.3
Electrical	4.0	4.6	8.0	7.8	7.7	5.8	5.1
Transport equipment	13.6	4.0	7.1	3.8	3.8	2.6	3.7
Other	0.1	0.3	0.5	-	0.1	0.1	0.1
Total	100.0	100.0	100.0	100.0	100.0	100.0	100.0
Import values (U.S. $ millions)	$1,462	$1,096	$2,845	$13,573	$13,254	$15,244	$20,132

Source: Brasil, Comercio Exterior, various years.

The early 1980s saw a rapid decline in Brazilian industrial expansion as the effects of world recession, high domestic inflation, and higher interest rates in the international lending market began to be felt. Brazil's capital goods imports, necessary for continued economic expansion, began to drop as a result. Nevertheless, Brazil's capital goods imports are expected to begin to grow at an annual rate of about 20 percent once the industrial base begins to expand again. Brazil's own capital goods industry will increasingly be able to satisfy domestic demand in many areas but the country will continue to import machinery and high technology know-how from the more developed countries to broaden its industrial base.

Brazil's import quotient (imports as percent of GNP) is forecast to drop as domestic production increasingly meets demands in traditional import areas. Capital goods, investment capital, and petroleum are the three most important elements of Brazil's import dependency, and each component poses a special problem for Brazil in the unsettled economic climate of the 1980s.

Diversification of Trading Partners

Brazil's increased independence in the world has been based in large part on its ability to diversify its economic relations, thus reducing its dependence on the United States. In the 1970s world economic conditions facilitated this strategy. The rapid expansion of the European and Japanese economies (in the 1960s and 1970s) created new markets and made available to Brazil new sources of capital. Private foreign investors also have been attracted by Brazil's rapid growth.

The vastness of Brazil's raw material resources makes that country a natural complementary trading partner for resource-poor industrial countries, while the new wealth of the OPEC countries has opened additional markets for Brazilian goods and technology. These growing markets for Brazilian exports have made Brazil less sensitive to economic changes in any single market area. Nevertheless, because of a continuing demand for imported sophisticated machinery, Brazil's import suppliers will continue to be the major industrial countries of Europe, Japan, and the United States. These countries will also continue to supply investment capital to finance future development. As a consequence, one of Brazil's principal economic goals--diversification of trade partners and economic linkages--has been made very difficult.

Table 5.4 shows that the U.S. share of Brazilian exports dropped from 44 percent in 1960 to 24.7 percent in 1970 and fell as low as 15.4 percent in 1975. Data for 1982 indicate that the United States received approximately

TABLE 5.4
Country Markets for Brazilian Exports, 1960-1981
(Percentage of total)

	1960	1965	1970	1975	1976	1977	1978	1979	1980	1981
United States	44.4	31.3	24.7	15.4	18.2	17.7	22.6	19.3	17.4	17.6
Canada	1.3	2.9	1.4	2.6	1.3	1.2	1.2	1.2	1.2	1.2
Latin America and Caribbean	7.9	12.7	11.7	15.7	13.4	12.8	14.1	17.3	18.1	19.2
European Economic Community	26.7	32.3	34.9	27.9	30.4	32.1	30.3	29.8	27.1	25.4
Other Europe	9.1	10.0	11.6	10.4	12.8	11.4	5.7	7.8	8.6	6.3
Middle East and Israel	0.4	0.8	0.6	5.2	2.7	2.7	2.9	3.3	5.1	5.3
Japan	2.4	1.9	5.3	7.7	6.3	5.6	5.1	5.7	6.1	5.2
Other Asia	0.9	1.1	2.9	1.4	1.5	2.5	3.7	3.7	3.4	3.7
Africa	0.9	1.3	2.1	4.6	3.7	4.6	5.0	4.2	5.7	7.4
USSR and Eastern Europe	5.7	5.6	4.3	9.0	8.4	7.9	4.7	5.5	5.4	6.0
Other	0.3	0.1	1.5	1.1	1.3	1.5	3.4	2.2	1.9	2.7
Total value of exports (U.S. $ billions)	$2,271	$2,596	$2,739	$8,668	$10,130	$12,120	$12,659	$15,391	$20,132	$23,329

Source: International Monetary Fund, various years.

22 percent of Brazil's exports in that year. The U.S.
market ranged between 17-22 percent over the 1970s. Much
of the trade lost to the United States was reallocated to
neighboring Latin American countries, which received 18
percent of Brazil's exports in 1980 as compared with 7
percent in 1960; to the European Community, which accounted for approximately 30 percent of Brazil's exports
over most of the 1970s; and to Japan. No one market region accounts for all of export trade diverted from the
United States. Rather, Brazil has made incremental gains
in markets around the world, creating for itself a vastly
expanded base for political and economic influence, as
well as a greatly diversified set of interests in each
world region. A more detailed examination of bilateral
trade patterns within each region indicates the following:

- Responding to the overall economic dynamism in
  Latin America, Brazil greatly diversified its export market there. Whereas Argentina accounted
  for 63 percent of Brazil's exports in 1960, it
  took half that in 1980. Because of their proximity, Paraguay and Uruguay both represent growing markets for Brazil, while Mexico, Venezuela,
  and Chile each account for a major share of Brazil's Latin American exports today.

- While Germany is clearly the largest market in
  Western Europe, Brazil has significant markets in
  all West European countries. Germany receives
  about half the exports by value that the U.S. receives, and Japan about one-third. Spain and
  Italy are Brazil's fourth and fifth most important markets in the world.

- Brazil's trade is still fairly concentrated.
  The United States, Japan, and Germany are the
  recipients of nearly 60 percent of all Brazil's
  exports.

- In 1976, the Soviet Union was Brazil's seventh-
  largest export market. By 1981, Poland and the
  Soviet Union ranked ninth and tenth among Brazil's
  export markets.

- Brazil's trade with Asian countries is also expanding rapidly. In addition to Japan, Singapore,
  the Philippines, India, Indonesia, and Hong Kong
  emerged from a negligible base in 1960 to represent important markets in the 1970s. Brazil ceased
  trade with Taiwan in 1975. Its trade with the People's Republic of China increased sharply and promising trade agreements were signed in 1978.

- Iran, Iraq, Egypt, and Syria represent major markets in the Middle East that have developed since the oil price increase of 1973. In 1975 Brazil nearly ceased its trade with Israel; however, commercial relations began to improve beginning in 1980.

- In spite of rhetoric about increasing trade with black Africa, most of Brazil's export markets are in the wealthier oil-exporting countries, particularly Algeria and Nigeria. Brazil also has established a close commercial relationship with Portuguese-speaking Angola in recent years. Trade with other black African and North African countries has been very erratic, high in one year and negligible the next. South Africa, once Brazil's largest market in Africa, remains the third-largest market after Algeria and Nigeria.

Brazil's imports are much less diversified than its exports. Table 5.5 shows that the United States, Western Europe (especially Germany), and Japan are Brazil's major suppliers; together they provide nearly half of all imports. The Middle East, which includes Brazil's major petroleum suppliers, accounts for approximately one-third of Brazil's imports, up from only 1.4 percent in 1960 and 7.9 percent in 1972, the year prior to the first oil price increase. A more detailed examination of Brazil's import structure reveals continued strong links to the United States and a concentration of commercial ties to a few other countries.

The United States continues to supply Brazil with two to three times the value of goods of any other industrial trading partner, including West Germany and Japan. In 1976, Germany, Japan, and Saudi Arabia all supplied Brazil with approximately the same value of goods ($1.0-$1.2 billion). The rapidly rising cost of petroleum, and Brazil's increasing reliance on imported petroleum to maintain the momentum of its industrial expansion, shifted the import emphasis toward the oil exporting countries. By 1980 and 1981, Brazil's principal petroleum suppliers, Iraq and Saudi Arabia, together provided one-fourth of all Brazilian imports by value.

Argentina supplies more than one-third of Brazilian imports from Latin American countries. Venezuela has recently become an important supplier of petroleum to Brazil, and is now its second trading partner within Latin America. Chile has traditionally been an important trading partner, while Mexico only recently began to focus attention on the Brazilian market. Because of its size and proximity and recent dynamic growth, Brazil also represents an important market for Paraguay and Uruguay.

TABLE 5.5
Country Sources of Brazilian Imports, 1960-1981
(Percentages of total imports)

	1960	1965	1970	1975	1976	1977	1978	1979	1980	1981
United States	30.3	29.7	32.2	24.9	22.6	19.9	21.1	18.4	18.6	16.8
Canada	1.1	1.2	2.5	1.7	2.5	2.2	2.7	2.0	3.9	2.7
Latin America and Caribbean	20.4	26.4	14.0	6.3	10.2	11.9	11.0	13.1	12.5	15.0
European Economic Community	25.6	21.0	28.6	24.6	20.0	19.2	18.7	17.9	15.4	14.0
Other Europe	9.2	6.4	7.1	6.8	6.5	5.9	4.5	3.4	3.7	3.9
Middle East and Israel	3.3	5.0	5.5	19.9	25.2	27.2	27.8	31.3	27.9	30.9
Japan	2.6	3.4	6.3	9.2	7.3	7.1	4.9	6.0	4.8	5.9
Other Asia	1.3	0.5	0.6	0.6	0.5	0.6	0.7	2.2	1.8	3.6
Africa	0.4	0.3	2.9	3.9	3.6	4.5	3.5	2.8	4.7	8.9
USSR and Eastern Europe	5.6	5.9	1.9	1.5	1.5	1.5	1.3	1.1	1.0	1.9
Other	0.2	0.2	0.2	0.6	0.1	--	--	--	--	--
Total value of imports (U.S. $ billions)	$1,461	$1,097	$2,849	$13,592	$13,761	$13,193	$15,054	$19,771	$24,961	$22,995

Source: International Monetary Fund, various years.

Brazil's trade with Japan has been growing rapidly
over the past 15 to 20 years, a reflection, in part, of
aggressive Japanese marketing techniques. Brazil's purchases in other Asian countries are considerably lower in
value and volume and concentrated in the People's Republic
of China and in the industrial enclave states of Korea,
Singapore, and, more recently, Thailand. While export
trade has grown steadily since the early 1970s, Brazil has
only recently begun to make substantial purchases in Asian
countries other than Japan.

Iraq and Saudi Arabia are Brazil's two most important
suppliers of petroleum. During the 1970s Brazil became
increasingly dependent on imported petroleum. Table 5.6
identifies Brazil's principal petroleum suppliers, and it
can be seen that over time Brazil has become more and more
heavily dependent on the Arab Middle East for its
petroleum.

As noted earlier, during the 1970s Brazil forged an
especially close commercial relationship with Iraq, selling petroleum exploration technology, iron ore, military
weapons, and ultimately nuclear technology to Iraq in exchange for long-term guarantees of oil supplies. By 1979
and 1980 Iraq supplied over 40 percent of Brazil's oil imports, while Saudi Arabia's share dropped first to 30 and
then 24 percent of Brazil's supplies as Brazil began to
diversify suppliers. In 1980 Iraq drove a hard bargain
with Brazil in which it guaranteed to supply 500,000 barrels per day (bpd) of petroleum, but required that Brazil
relinquish rights in two fields where Petrobras, the Brazilian state oil company, had made important finds in 1976
and 1978.

Brazil's principal import from Africa is also petroleum. In spite of very reduced diplomatic relations,
trade with South Africa has been dynamic over the past
decade. Trade quadrupled between 1976 and 1980 and Brazil
became South Africa's principal supplier, even though the
balance of trade is heavily in favor of South Africa.
South African exports to Brazil consist mainly of phosphates which are in chronic short supply in Brazil. Brazil exports vehicle parts, tractors, machinery, timber,
and cocoa to South Africa. While South Africa has traditionally been one of Brazil's major markets in Africa,
Brazil values its prospective trade with the developing
countries of black Africa much more. The black African
market has been considered a major growth target since
the early 1970s. The market is particularly attractive
because Brazil is able to sell its manufactured goods
there, and to provide a number of technical services such
as construction engineering and petroleum exploration
(Latin America Weekly Report, 18 September 1981 and 8 May
1981).

192

TABLE 5.6
Brazil: Sources of Crude Petroleum Imports, 1976, 1979, and 1980
(U.S. $ millions, cif.)

	1976		1979		1980	
	Value	Percent	Value	Percent	Value	Percent
Middle East		31.6		43.3		
Iraq	1,197	31.6	2,632	43.3	3,779	43.6
Persian Gulf		54.7		50.1		43.1
Saudi Arabia	1,134	29.9	1,805	29.7	2,081	24.0
Kuwait	470	12.4	274	4.5	729	8.4
Iran	370	9.8	827	13.6	731	8.4
United Arab Emirates	100	2.6	140	2.3	203	2.3
South America		2.4		3.4		6.3
Venezuela	57	1.5	210	3.4	542	6.2
Peru	35	0.9	--	--	13	.1
Africa		10.4		2.8		6.7
Libya	152	4.0	25	.4	135	1.5
Gabon	100	2.6	105	1.7	299	3.4
Nigeria	81	2.1	28	.4	83	.9
Algeria	63	1.7	21	.3	81	.9
Other		.6				
USSR	13	0.3	--	--	--	--
Egypt	11	0.3	--	--	--	--

Source: Brasil, Comercio Exterior, 1976, 1981.

Beginning in 1980 Brazil began to make conscious efforts to diversify its sources of oil supplies and for the first time began to actively seek petroleum from its Latin American neighbors, especially Venezuela, from which it had bought very little in previous years, despite the proximity of the two countries. Mexico was a secondary source of supply, but one that was expected to grow over time.

Brazil's trade with the Soviet Union and the Eastern European countries increased dramatically during the 1970s, with the balance strongly favoring Brazil. Brazil has generally exported traditional primary commodities such as coffee, cocoa, soybeans and meal, and iron ore to the Soviet Union and Eastern Europe, and has purchased petroleum from the Soviet Union and coal from Poland in return. Poland has been Brazil's principal supplier of coking coal for its growing steel industry. In 1976 the Soviet Union became Brazil's seventh-largest export market, as a result of heavy purchases of soya and soya products. Nevertheless, Poland has been Brazil's principal trading partner in the Eastern Bloc. Eastern Bloc countries have long been concerned about Brazil's very positive balance of trade with them. In 1978, Brazil had an accumulated credit of $3.7 billion with the Eastern Bloc. Recently there has been a serious effort to explore new areas for product exchange because of this imbalance. Brazil has begun selling shoes in the Eastern Bloc market and will purchase some nonferrous metals, fertilizers, and chemicals in that area. The Soviet Union has indicated interest in providing turbines for Brazil's hydroelectric program.

Balance of Trade Dilemma

Over time Brazil has consistently imported more than it has exported, the result historically of Brazil's role as supplier of primary commodities--coffee, sugar, and so forth--and purchaser of more expensive industrial goods. More recently, Brazil's dependence on increasingly more expensive imported petroleum has had a sharp and deleterious effect on Brazil's balance of payments. By the mid-1970s, in the aftermath of successive oil price increases, Brazil's negative balance of trade with both the industrial economies and the oil-exporting countries in Africa and the Middle East reached difficult proportions. By 1980 the negative balance with the industrial world was more than $4.8 billion. Table 5.7 shows that the balance with the industrial countries moved from a small positive margin in 1960 ($69.7 million) to a negative margin ($-3.9 billion) in 1975, during the first oil price-induced recession. In the Middle East oil-producing region, the negative balance reached an astronomical high of $7.4 billion in 1980--nearly one-third of Brazil's

Table 5.7
Brazil's Balance of Trade With World Regions
(U.S. $ millions)

	1960			1970			1975		
	Exports	Imports	Balance	Exports	Imports	Balance	Exports	Imports	Balance
World total	$1,076.1	$1,006.4	$ +69.7	$2,147.7	$2,191.3	$ -43.6	$8,668	$13,592	$-4,924
Industrial countries							5,219	9,144	-3,925
Latin America	100.2	297.6	-196.9	321.8	342.0	-20.2	2,265	866	+1,399
Asia (less Japan)	10.2	19.2	-9.0	80.0	18.1	+61.9	188	70	+118
Middle East	4.9	49.6	-44.7	17.4	157.9	-140.5	451	2,330	-1,879
Africa	5.0	6.7	-1.7	42.4	81.3	-38.9	398	906	-508
USSR and Eastern Europe	72.1	82.1	-10.0	124.8	58.7	+66.1	653	184	+469

TABLE 5.7 (cont'd)

	1978			1979			1980		
	Exports	Imports	Balance	Exports	Imports	Balance	Exports	Imports	Balance
World total	$12,659	$15,054	$-2,395	$15,391	$19,771	$-4,380	$20,132	$24,961	$-4,829
Industrial countries	8,259	8,447	-188	9,437	9,360	-193	11,539	11,626	-87
Latin America	1,787	1,658	+129	2,641	2,584	+57	3,650	3,119	+531
Asia	468	104	+364	565	438	+127	687	459	+228
Middle East	284	4,027	-3,743	416	6,182	-5,765	757	8,176	-7,419
Africa	635	529	-106	651	572	-79	1,154	1,173	-19
USSR and Eastern Europe	600	201	+399	851	211	+1,062	1,091	250	+1,341

Source: Inter-American Development Bank, 1978; International Monetary Fund, 1981.

total exports. The petroleum import bill also explains
the Brazilian negative trade balance with Africa. For a
prolonged period in the 1960s and 1970s, Brazil also maintained a negative trade balance with its principal Latin
American trade partner, Argentina. This was due to Brazil's chronic shortfall in grain production (especially
wheat). In the late 1970s the balance shifted in Brazil's
favor. Brazil now has a very favorable trade balance with
other countries in Latin America, as it does with the Eastern European and Soviet Bloc. Because of its continuing
trade deficit with the industrial and oil-exporting nations, the latter markets as well as several new markets
in Africa and Asia will continue to be attractive and Brazil will undoubtedly seek to increase its commercial presence in these regions. However, it competes strongly with
Asian countries for exports in the developed markets and
this competition could strain relations with some African
countries in the future.

Brazil's principal concern in the future will be to
reduce its trade gap with the oil-producing and industrial
countries. The Tokyo Round of General Agreement on Tariffs and Trade (GATT) agreements sought to help Brazil's
trade with the industrial countries by lowering barriers
to Brazilian exports (especially manufactures) in the
United States and Europe, but the economic slowdown and
recession of the late 1970s and 1980s has not permitted
benefits to become apparent yet. Brazil has been pursuing a very aggressive export marketing strategy in the
Middle East and Africa, in order to overcome the wide gap
in trade there. In doing so it competes with the developed oil-importing countries. The trade balance with
these countries has important implications for Brazil's
political and economic relations with the developed countries, as well as with OPEC. Brazil's policymakers are
keenly aware of their vulnerability to political and economic pressure from the OPEC suppliers, and this awareness has prompted Brazil's efforts to distance itself
from the United States by pursuing a greater "Third World"
role.

Throughout most of the 1970s, Brazil's large foreign
reserves shielded it from the serious consequences of its
negative balance of trade. Reserves were maintained in
part by expanding the foreign debt, however, and service
and amortization payments on the debt now take an increasing share of export earnings. In January 1979 Finance Minister Mario Henrique Simonsen acknowledged a
growing crisis and announced that debt service payments
would require two-thirds of Brazil's foreign exchange
earnings in 1978. With petroleum taking 40 percent of export earnings, Brazil has little room for maneuver unless
its exports increase.

FOREIGN INVESTMENT AND LENDING TO BRAZIL

During Brazil's rapid growth in the 1960s and 1970s, Brazil's strong links to the industrial world economies, and especially the United States, were reinforced by its attractiveness to foreign capital investment and bank lending. Chapter 2 indicated that between 1975 and 1977 Brazil was the largest recipient of export credits from the developed countries to non-oil-exporting developing countries. The United States, Germany, Japan, and other EEC members provided the bulk of these credits. Brazil was also the largest developing country recipient of direct overseas private investment, with 12 percent of the total. American firms held 30.4 percent of the total foreign investment in Brazil, more than twice the level of investment by West German firms and three times the level of Japanese investment. Table 5.8 gives a breakdown of the value of different countries' foreign investment in Brazil. European and Japanese investments have been increasing sharply over the past few years, giving rise to claims by some that the United States is losing its dominant position in Brazil. But the Europeans and Japanese started from a much lower base so their percentage growth rates are high. As these rates grow, the U.S. percentage of market share must decline. At the same time, however, the total value of investment has increased for all countries.

As Chapter 2 discussed in detail, Brazil also has been one of the world's largest recipients of commercial bank loans. Brazil's foreign debt grew rapidly, from $3.7 billion in 1968 to $32 billion in 1977 and $85 billion by the end of 1982. In 1977 Brazil ranked fourth after Spain, Mexico, and Korea in net international commercial bank loans, but by 1980 it was the largest recipient of commercial bank lending and it has retained that position ever since.

The size of Brazil's international debt was already a subject of controversy in the late 1970s as the service requirements on the debt (amortization and net interest payments) rose rapidly, taking an increasing share of each year's export earnings. Brazilian authorities nevertheless argued that the burgeoning debt was not a problem so long as Brazil continued to grow. Continued growth, in turn, was dependent on the rapid expansion of Brazil's exports to world, especially developed world, markets. Given Brazil's resource base and its potential for diversified growth, the external debt caused relatively little concern among the private bankers who provided capital to Brazil. In spite of the fact that several U.S. banks were already extremely exposed in Brazil by the second half of the 1970s, leading U.S. bankers gave Brazil a "clean bill of health" in their public statements (see U.S. Senate, Committee on Banking and Finance, 1977). While none condoned

Table 5.8
Foreign Investment in Brazil, 1978 and 1981
(U.S. $ millions)

	1978			1981		
	Direct Investment	Reinvestment	Total	Direct Investment	Reinvestment	Total
Total	$8,078.1	$4,152.7	$12,230.8	$10,230.8	$4,834.1	$15,064.9
United States	2,202.5	1,487.4	3,689.9	3,401.6	1,891.5	5,293.2
West Germany	1,186.1	511.8	1,697.9	1,663.1	640.6	2,303.7
Switzerland	837.5	494.0	1,331.5	1,110.6	678.9	1,789.6
Japan	1,224.9	87.3	1,312.2	1,595.6	146.4	1,742.1
Canada	404.2	263.3	667.5	417.9	213.2	631.2
United Kingdom	378.7	227.2	605.9	532.6	465.2	997.8
France	268.2	243.4	511.6	370.1	260.8	630.9
Panama	160.0	190.0	350.0	283.0	216.8	499.8
Luxemburg	225.5	82.6	308.1	337.6	74.6	412.2
Netherlands	161.4	135.3	296.7	247.9	109.7	357.6
Sweden	149.3	97.2	246.5	270.8	136.4	407.2

Source: Brasil, Central Bank Bulletin, 1978, 1981.

a policy of continued geometric expansion of external indebtedness, it was widely believed that Brazil's mature
and sophisticated fiscal managers, the country's economic
potential, and general world economic trends would continue to support Brazil's level of indebtedness. As Chapter 2 noted, the failure of nearly all of the optimistic
assumptions about world economic expansion, and particularly the failure of the world economy to adjust to a second round of sharp petroleum price increases, undermined
these optimistic assumptions.

In 1978 Brazil's debt service payments requirements
amounted to 67 percent of the country's $12 billion ex-
ports earnings. Petroleum imports accounted for another
40 percent of the foreign exchange acquired, and only
through increasing borrowing was Brazil able to meet its
obligations and continue to import necessary capital goods
and equipment to spur its industrial expansion. By the
end of 1982, the debt required nearly 80 percent of foreign exchange generated by a sharply declining level of
exports. Energy imports took another 40 percent of dollars earned and sources of commercial bank lending were no
longer available. In the fall of 1982 Brazil's Central
Bank president made trips to both the United States and to
Europe seeking bankers' help in putting together a $14
billion package of loans necessary for Brazil to balance
its accounts at year end. The trips were by and large unsuccessful and Brazil saw itself obliged to approach the
International Monetary Fund for an Extended Fund Facility
and compensatory financing (Latin America Weekly Report,
19 November 1982). Such a step had been politically un-
thinkable in earlier governments as far back as Getulio
Vargas' in the early 1950s and Janio Quadros' or Joao Goulart's in the 1960s. With all the maneuvering, though
much of the loan package from the IMF, the World Bank, the
U.S. government, and European and U.S. commercial banks
was in place, Brazil was forced to admit that it could not
meet its debt payments due at year end. An initial mora-
torium on debt payments was declared until March 1, 1983.
Further postponements were expected.

Some have argued that the size and nature of the foreign debt give Brazil increasing leverage in the industrialized world. Because major private banks have substantial stakes in Brazil, nonpayment of the debt would
have profound international repercussions. At one level,
the argument is correct. The United States government
stepped in with unprecedented levels of direct, short-term
assistance for Brazil, as well as with vigorous lobbying
efforts in the financial crisis of 1982, in part in order
to avoid the domestic repercussions of a Brazilian default.
The Brazilian economy itself has been the most seriously
hurt by the overextended debt situation, however.

The profile of Brazil's commercial and financial relations with the developed countries underscores both the
degree of interdependence of the developed and Brazilian
economies, and the predominant position the United States
holds in these relations. The United States is still Brazil's largest single market and largest provider of investment capital--whether direct corporate investment or
commercial bank lending. While Brazil's economic relations with the United States and Germany or Japan are
critical to Brazil's own economic well-being, with the
exception of events such as the December 1982 debt crisis,
Brazil remains a relatively minor factor in the economic
activities of the advanced countries. It accounted for
only 2 percent of U.S. exports, 1.5 percent of U.S. imports, and 4 percent of total U.S. private overseas investment in 1977. While Brazil is West Germany's largest
trading partner in Latin America, trade with Brazil is
equal to less than 1 percent of all German trade, and all
German trade with all of Latin America is equal only to
its trade with Austria, one of the smaller economies in
Europe. German investment in Brazil in 1978 was equiva-
lent to half its investment in Switzerland (Grabendorff,
1979).

THE DILEMMAS OF SIZE AND EXPECTATIONS

Brazil is a continental nation and as such ranks extraordinarily high on elementary measures of power such as
gross national product, population, and geographic size.
However, these aggregate figures tend to exaggerate Brazil's relative position in the world political and economic
community and the strength of its power base. As a result,
there has been a tendency in recent years to treat Brazil
as if it were already a politically and economically developed nation. However, world economic and productive
capabilities remain concentrated overwhelmingly in the industrial countries of North America, Europe, and Japan.
As was noted in Chapter 2, a substantial gap separates
these powers from the most developed of the middle powers,
of which Brazil is a prominent member. A simple rank ordering of country positions on these aggregate indicators
of power and capabilities tends to disguise the gaps that
separate the industrial countries from the industrializing
countries, and the developed from the advanced developing
countries.

It is important to place Brazil's present position in
perspective on a number of indicators less dramatic than
aggregate size, but more revealing in terms of capability
and performance. This can be demonstrated with a more detailed examination of Brazil's relative position on measures of wealth, trade, and production. For example, although Brazil ranks seventh in the world in population and

tenth in gross national product, it ranks only 75th in the
world in GNP per capita (World Bank, 1982). Moreover,
though Brazil occupies nearly half of the South American
continent, 43 percent of its population (as of 1970) resided in four states of the southeast part of the coun-
try--Rio de Janeiro, Minas Gerais, Espirito Santo, and
São Paulo. Only 9.3 percent resided in the northern and
western regions. Two-thirds of government receipts are
collected in just two states, São Paulo and Rio de Janeiro
(Brazil, IBGE, 1977).

The value of Brazil's world trade is greater than
that of any other non-oil-exporting developing country,
but Brazil's total trade is equal to less than 2 percent
of the industrial countries' trade and less than 10 percent of U.S. trade. While Brazil was the United States'
13th largest market for exports and 18th-ranked supplier
of imports to the United States, those imports represented
only 1.5 percent of all U.S. imports in 1977. The Brazilian market in turn represented only 2 percent of all U.S.
exports in the same year.

Brazil ranks among the top ten world producers of re-
claimed rubber, commercial and passenger vehicles, primary
tin, cotton, phosphate fertilizers, television sets, tires,
and cement. It is the world's second most important producer of iron ore and fourth producer of manganese. It
ranks among the top 20 producers of magnesite, tin ore,
asbestos, chromium, tungsten, bauxite, gold, nickel, and
phosphate rock. In 1976 Brazil was the world's sixteenth-
ranked producer of raw steel but contributed only 1.4 percent of the world total. Its production was comparable to
that of India or Spain, but less than half that of Italy,
and one-tenth that of Japan or the United States (United
Nations, 1977). Brazil has the second largest shipbuilding industry in the developing world, after South Korea.
However, in 1977, it completed construction of only 379,000
gross registered tons (GRT) or 1.1 percent of the total
world GRT produced that year (H. P. Drewry, 1978).

Much of the developed world's fascination with Brazil
has been based on projections of its absolute size without
considering the tremendous gap that continues to separate
Brazil from the older industrial countries. Expectations
about Brazil's role in present world affairs have been
based largely on estimates of Brazil's potential, not cal-
culation of its actual performance and ability. Nevertheless, Brazil occupies a unique position in the present-day
world economy. It has far outdistanced most developing
countries in the rate of its economic growth and degree of
its economic sophistication. It lags far behind most developed countries in terms of the mobilization of its full
resource potential. Until the gap that separates it from

the developed world is narrowed much further, Brazil will
not be able to play its anticipated role of world power.

CONSTRAINTS ON BRAZIL'S FUTURE GROWTH

Although the forecasts of Brazil's future growth
prospects are quite optimistic, a number of factors impede
it from rapidly bridging the gap that separates it from
the developed world. The principal constraints on Brazil's
continued growth include its heavy dependence on imported
petroleum; its large foreign debt that absorbs up to two-
thirds of the country's foreign exchange in debt service
payments; and its capital-intensive development model that
relies on imported technology and financing. Moreover,
Brazil's high population growth rates create pressure for
new jobs at the rate of over 1 million per year and place
tremendous burdens on the public sector for support of
health, education, and welfare services. The unequal distribution of income, reflected in low domestic market demand, creates increasingly strong political pressure on
the government for greater responsiveness to the needs of
the masses. Brazil's debt situation was described above.
The constraints imposed by high population growth rate
and energy dependence are examined below.

Energy Dependence

Energy is Brazil's Achilles heel. In 1976 it was the
world's ninth-largest importer of crude petroleum with 2.6
percent of the world total. At the same time, it ranked
12th in installed electricity capacity, 19th in energy
consumption, 36th in energy production, and 64th in per
capita energy consumption (Selcher, 1979). Energy dependence is one of the principal constraints on Brazil's
rapid recovery from the world economic recession of the
early 1980s and on its early escape from external dependence in general.

Brazil has few options for resolving its energy dependence, and this problem is the root of one of its most
serious disagreements with the developed countries, particularly the United States. No other Latin American
country is as heavily (up to 80 percent) dependent on imported petroleum as is Brazil. In 1977 Brazil imported
62 percent of all the petroleum imported by Latin American
countries; consumed 35 percent of all petroleum and petroleum derivatives in Latin America; and was the ninth largest petroleum importer in the world--first in the developing world.

As noted in an earlier section, approximately 44 percent of Brazil's energy needs are provided by oil and gas
and Brazil currently imports approximately 75 percent of

its petroleum requirements (BOLSA, 1978). In 1975 Brazil broke with 20 years' tradition of exclusive national involvement in petroleum exploration and opened its offshore fields (and later, onshore fields) to exploration by international firms. To date, finds have been relatively small and far from adequate to reduce Brazil's import bill in the near future. The 1973 and subsequent OPEC price increases effectively terminated the Brazilian growth "miracle" as oil imports began to absorb more and more of Brazil's foreign exchange earnings, reducing the country's ability to purchase the goods and machinery needed for further industrial development and prolonging its reliance on foreign investment capital to stimulate growth. Inflation, which had been brought down from nearly 100 percent in 1964 to 15 percent a year in the early 1970s, escalated to over 40 percent by 1978, partly as a result of the first round of oil price increases. In the 1980s, following a second round of price hikes and subsequent global recession, inflation climbed to over 120 percent and persisted at that level in spite of government austerity measures.

Because of its very heavy oil import dependence and its equally heavy reliance on automobiles and trucks for movement of goods and services about the nation, the Brazilian government adopted policies designed to curtail gasoline demand, including Sunday closings, sharp increases in the pump price of gasoline, and development of alcohol substitutes and additives for gasoline. These measures succeeded in reducing the growth in gasoline demand to about 7 percent per year to 1980. However, the government was not able to stem demand for industrial fuels, diesel, and fuel oil, and demand for those products increased by about 50 percent over the same period. Without the economic slowdown that began in 1980, demand would have continued to increase, and the increased cost and volume of petroleum imports would have further fueled Brazil's current inflationary spiral. Brazil was one of the principal beneficiaries of the decline in oil price that began in mid-1982.

Hydroelectric Resources. Brazil does have enormous hydroelectric power potential, estimated conservatively to be approximately 209,000 megawatts (MW), as compared with 158,000 MW for all of Europe. In 1979 its energy development plan called for renewed emphasis on development of hydroelectric potential as one component of the country's effort to reduce its dependency on petroleum imports. The 1979 plan called for increasing installed hydroelectric generating capacity from a national level of 22,000 MW to 69,000 MW by 1990. The Brazil-Paraguay bi-national hydroelectric project at Itaipu, the largest hydroelectric dam in the world with an installed capacity of 12.6 MW, will generate 2.5 megawatts of electricity for the southern

industrial region of the country when it becomes fully operational in 1983. Even this will not satisfy the burgeoning energy demands in the industrial south. Much of
Brazil's hydroelectric potential is located in the north
and northeast, far from areas of high usage. To develop
those resources will require prior installation of access
roads, and long-distance transmission lines. Full utili-
zation of the country's hydroelectric power potential will
not occur for decades.

Nuclear Energy. In addition to trying to exploit its
hydroelectric potential, Brazil has explored several other
alternatives to petroleum, including nuclear energy, biomass, and coal. Brazil's interest in nuclear energy was
evidenced as early as 1951 when Brazil sought secretly to
purchase centrifuges developed in Germany during World War
II. The plan was ultimately quashed by allied occupation
authorities who refused to allow the disassembled machinery to leave Germany. As a result, Brazil did not acquire
even the core of a nuclear research capability until late
in the 1950s.

In the 1960s Brazilian scientists prepared several
position papers urging that Brazil adopt a natural uranium
reactor model, which would not place the country in a dependency position vis-a-vis the nuclear powers. Decisions
on the nuclear program were delayed by the turbulent political events at the beginning of the decade, however.
It was not until after the 1964 revolution that nuclear
energy was placed under authority of the Ministry of Mines
and Energy's state authority, Electrobrás, and more concentrated attention was given to selecting an appropriate
power plant.

Brazil's national pride became involved in the nuclear
decision with the promulgation of the Non-Proliferation
Treaty (NPT) in 1968. Sponsored by the nuclear powers--
the United States, Soviet Union, and Great Britain--the
NPT called on signatory non-nuclear countries to renounce
production of nuclear weapons, a position that, by exten-
sion, meant foregoing active research and development of
nuclear energy. The Third-World reaction to the NPT was
strong and negative, particularly as research at the time
indicated a multitude of possibilities for peaceful uses
of nuclear explosions. Moreover, conventional wisdom promised that nuclear energy could be produced at a fraction
of the cost of either hydroelectricity or even petroleum.
Nuclear energy appeared to be a cheap and easy solution to
many developing country problems. It was, in short, the
key to the dilemma of nonrenewable resources.

In the aftermath of the NPT debate, Brazil began to
focus more attention on its nuclear program and in 1972
the Brazilian press noted that plans for developing

nuclear power generation called for 50 reactors by the end
of the century to attend to the burgeoning industrial and
urban power demands. A number of factors prompted Brazil's greater interest in nuclear energy at this time.
Brazil's principal rival in Latin America, Argentina,
early on had undertaken to develop an independent nuclear
capability. Argentina was widely recognized to be far
ahead of Brazil in research and development of nuclear
technology and Brazil was impelled to catch up as a result. In addition, Brazil's leaders' perception of the
country's potential as a global power required that the
country acquire at least the domestic technological expertise to become a member of the nuclear club.

When the 1973 oil price increase occurred, Brazil had
begun construction on one nuclear reactor, a Westinghouse
facility at Angra dos Reis on the São Paulo coast, and it
was discussing bids with both United States and European
firms for a second and third facility at Angra. The 1973
oil price increase created an immediate heavy demand for
nuclear power plants and enriched nuclear fuel supplies
by suggesting an imminent world energy shortage. The
United States' own reaction to the oil price hike--step-
ping up nuclear plant development at home and withdrawing
guarantees to both Brazil and West Germany for nuclear
fuel--spurred Brazil's and other countries' interests in
developing independent capabilities. Brazil was particularly incensed at the U.S. Atomic Energy Commission's refusal to provide additional fuel guarantees for Angra I,
because its commitment to the Westinghouse facility had
been undertaken with the knowledge that the country would
be dependent on the United States for future fuel supplies.
Scientists and politicians who had argued for an independent capability were vindicated and Brazil broke off
talks with Westinghouse on its second and third facilities
in favor of West Germany's Kraftwerkunion.

On June 27, 1975, Brazil signed an agreement with
West Germany for the purchase of "between two and eight
reactors, together worth from $2 billion to $8 billion,
that would accelerate (Brazil's) nuclear energy program
toward the goals of 10,000 megawatts of electricity generating capacity by 1990 and of producing 41 percent of
her total energy supply by 2010" (Gall, 1976). Because
it was sweetened with a promise of enrichment and reprocessing technology, the nuclear package was hailed as the
largest transfer ever made of nuclear technology to a developing country. Critics envisaged it threatening to
establish:

> a new kind of commercial rivalry for interna-
> tional sales of power reactors that could accel-
> erate nuclear weapons proliferation in the final
> decades of this century. If fully implemented

over the next 15 years, it would give the German
reactor industry desperately needed export sales
and fuel supplies. It also would meet Brazil's
projected demand for atomic energy through 1990
and provide much of the technological base for
Brazil to make nuclear weapons if she wished
(Gall, 1976).

Brazil's mid-decade nuclear policy was thus a complex
result of political and economic motivations. In the long
run the program had to be defended in economic terms. Because of continued problems both with the nuclear program
itself and with the overall balance of payments, Brazil
now seems unlikely to develop the nuclear potential envisioned in the 1975 accord with Germany. The 1979 energy
plan mentioned only Angra I, II, and III Reactors. Nuclear plant construction fell far behind schedule. The
American Westinghouse-built reactor at Angra dos Reis in
Rio de Janeiro state was not completed on time. The site
for the second and third reactors at Angra had to be altered and reinforced because of unstable foundation. Construction was delayed by years, and Brazil will have only
one power plant operational through the first half of the
1980s.

Germany's initial agreement to provide reprocessing
technology was contingent on Brazil's final purchase of
eight power plants. Even under the initial optimistic assumptions, it would have been well into the 1990s before
this construction would have been completed. By 1981 it
was clear that Brazil would not finally purchase all of
the plants. Its domestic scientific community vociferously opposed the program which had been undertaken without consultation with them. Economists complained that
the nuclear program was absorbing too many federal funds
when other programs had been cut back. In 1981 President
Figueiredo visited West Germany to put a quiet end to the
large plan and such other ways of cooperation in the energy field.

Biomass. In October of 1975 the Brazilian president
announced a National Alcohol Program (Pro-Álcool) designed
to use one of Brazil's richest natural resources, its vast
sugarcane growing lands, to reduce need for imported fuels.
The pro-alcohol program was justified both in terms of the
nonrenewability of fossil fuels, Brazil's own deficiencies
in petroleum reserves, and economic incentives that would
create jobs in agriculture and distilling in Brazil's
sluggish rural sectors. The alcohol program has gone
through several cycles of expansion and contraction due,
in large part, to government stimulus and world oil and
sugar prices. Never intended to replace petroleum use
completely, the alcohol program was gauged to cover growth
in demand for gasoline over a prolonged period of time.

Optimistic analysts predicted that Brazil could continue
to grow industrially while holding petroleum imports constant (U.S.-Brazil Commission, 1979). Most of Brazil's
overland transportation was powered by diesel fuels, which
are less readily substitutable by alcohol. In contrast,
the automobile sector, which had been growing at dramatic
rates in the early to mid-1970s, was more easily convertible. Brazilian economists predicted that if gasoline consumption could be held constant or reduced, the petroleum
import problems would be manageable.

Under early government stimulus, Brazil's alcohol
production rose by 50 percent between 1976 and 1977 and
reached 4 billion liters in 1980 with projected production
at 10 billion liters by 1985. The program initially envisaged a 20 percent gasoline-alcohol "gasohol" fuel mix
that was usable in most internal combustion engines with
little or no adjustment. Wholly alcohol-powered vehicles
followed, as the São Paulo automobile industry got on the
alcohol bandwagon. The industry giant, Volkswagen, had
converted 80 percent of its production line to alcohol-
driven cars by 1980, and other manufacturers followed
suit. Although shortages of alcohol and bugs in the first
engines created problems, government encouragement and a
substantial price incentive (fully subsidized, as alcohol
continued to cost more to produce than did gasoline) kept
the program on track. In 1980, one of the last buoyant
years for the Brazilian automobile industry, one-fourth
of automobile sales were alcohol-driven cars, and gasoline
consumption dropped by 10 percent from 1979 to 1980.

By 1980 serious disequilibria emerged in the alcohol
program. Production of fuel lagged far behind demand and
owners with alcohol-fueled cars found they could not drive
them. Distribution of alcohol, controlled by the state
oil company, Petrobras, was irregular. Financing for the
small distilleries that were to create jobs in the interior was hard to come by. The heavy government subsidy to
alcohol became onerous as oil prices hovered about the
$30 per barrel range at which the alcohol program was only
marginally economic. World gasoline prices stabilized
well below comparable alcohol prices, and scientists were
unable, in the short term, to overcome the lesser fuel efficiency of alcohol.

Brazil's deepening recession relieved a good deal of
the pressure on the alcohol program as fewer people bought
cars and demand for gasoline slackened in major urban areas.
The world price of sugar plummeted as well, reducing the
government's costs for alcohol production. The program
seemed to stabilize at a modestly successful plateau by
the end of 1981, when oil prices began to slide, slowly at
first, but then more rapidly throughout 1982. Continued
subsidy of the program became more and more difficult.

The alcohol program provided Brazil with moderate re-
lief from high-priced oil imports but its long-term viability depends on continued world petroleum shortages and
price in the mid-$30 per barrel range. To date, the eco-
nomic prerequisites necessary to signal aggressive implementation of the program have not existed. While Brazil
will likely continue to promote alcohol usage on a low
priority, alcohol has not proved the solution to Brazil's
long-term problem of energy dependence.

Population Growth

During the 1970s Brazilian population grew at an
average annual rate of 2.8 percent (IDB, 1977), slightly
lower than had been projected at the beginning of the decade. In contrast, population growth rates in the developed countries were 0.8 percent (Washington Post, 19 October 1978). Because of the high population growth, the
government has to attempt to maintain a constantly expanding economy with a high rate of job creation. At present,
1 million new jobs per year are required to absorb new en-
trants to the labor pool. This situation has traditionally fueled inflation and is one of the most serious constraints on government economic management.

Past government policy emphasized economic expansion
with forced savings to create investment funds. The policy resulted in an increasing concentration of income and
reduced purchasing power within the population. Beginning
with the late 1970s and paralleling the beginning of debate on the political opening in Brazil, Brazilian economists began to discuss the need for policies to generate
a more equitable distribution of income. The economists
recognized that such policies might result in a slowdown
of economic growth, as less capital becomes available for
investment and incentives to invest are reduced.

A slowdown in the rate of growth could have serious
political repercussions, as unemployment would probably
increase along with domestic political tension. In 1978
Brazil experienced its first manifestations of labor discontent since the 1964 revolution. Most of the strikes
occurred in industrial areas of São Paulo and were intended to extract wage increases higher than the government had been allocating.

POLITICAL STABILITY AND POLITICAL OPENING:
BRAZIL'S TRANSITION FROM AUTHORITARIANISM

Despite the obvious constraints that energy dependence, high population growth, and a large foreign debt
present to Brazil's future growth, the conditions are

present for Brazil to become a power of global proportions.
This will not happen overnight, however. In the short
term, domestic economic and political matters will occupy
the national attention. To date, events of the late 1970s
and early 1980s have served to slow Brazil's emergence on
the world scene. Whereas in the early 1970s in the heady
days of the Brazilian economic miracle, scholars wrote of
Brazil Ascendant (Roett, 1972) or Brazil on the verge of
being a world power (Schneider, 1976), in recent years expectations have become more sober. With the brief exception of Brazil's role during the Falkland Islands war between Argentina and Great Britain, Brazil's foreign policy
role has attracted little attention in recent years. Economic circumstances have not been alone in slowing Brazil's
march toward an activist world role. Domestic political
change--gradual political opening and movement toward a
return to civilian government--have had a profound influence on the level of attention Brazil has given to international issues.

Distenção and Abertura

Brazil is now approaching the end of its second decade of military rule. When the Brazilian revolution of
1964 took place, the revolution's military leaders intended to make an early exit from the political scene just
as the military had done in previous political crises
throughout Brazilian history. For a variety of reasons--
political and economic--this proved difficult. Nevertheless, as each new government came into office, the leadership indicated its "hope" to be able to hand over the government to civilian leaders. President Ernesto Geisel
(1974-1979) made a public commitment to liberalize the political regime in Brazil and begin the process of disten-
ção--or gradual relaxation of authoritarian control of the
system. The government of Joao Baptista de Oliveira Figueiredo, inaugurated in March of 1979, continued the forward momentum under the rubric of political opening or
abertura. Contrary to the expectation of many, the Brazilian political system has made tremendous strides in
accomplishing the gradual political transformation. Since
April 1977, when an initial, and seemingly hard line,
package of political reforms was announced, Brazil has
abolished the extra-constitutional legislation that was
the underpinning of the authoritarian regime; a new political party system has emerged; an amnesty has permitted
political exiles to return and nearly buried the question
of reprisal against those who participated in repression
in the 1960s and 1970s. Direct election for local, state,
and federal officials occurred for the first time in 1982
and the government party lost control over every level of
government except the Federal Senate and the electoral
college which will elect the next president.

The economic slowdown and leveling-off of growth that occurred in Brazil following the 1973 oil price hike was accompanied by a resurgence of national political activity. The opposition party, the Brazilian Democratic Movement (MDB), made impressive electoral gains in direct elections for the Congress in 1974 when the MDB won 16 of the 22 seats contested in the Federal Senate and increased its representation in the Chamber of Deputies from 87 to 165. Moreover, the MDB won a majority in six state assembly elections, whereas it had controlled only one before. In 1976 municipal elections, the government's National Republican Alliance (ARENA) party received 55 percent of the votes cast, but the MDB gained control of the municipal councils in a number of major cities, including several important capitals. Roett (1978) observed that these "election results were widely interpreted as a vote against the government, . . . less in favor of the MDB (than) a statement in favor of political liberalization."

Important interest groups within Brazilian society encouraged the political transition under President Geisel. The church became increasingly outspoken about violations of human rights and was supported by an assertive Brazilian Bar Association that insisted on a return of the right of habeas corpus and other legal principles excepted under the Institutional Acts that gave authority to the military government. The business community protested vigorously against the continued concentration of economic decision-making in the hands of government and the concentration of national investment capital in state-run enterprises. Growing middle-class discontent with falling real wages, a resurgence of inflation, and other economic adjustments caused by changing international economic conditions provided additional impetus for a return to competitive politics. A number of individuals within the armed forces began to express openly their beliefs that a "return to the barracks" was in order. Toward the end of the decade of the 1970s, Brazil's traditionally quiescent labor movement became suddenly activist, protesting government decisions that had resulted in the steady erosion of workers' real income.

Constitutional Reforms

The transition was not uncontested. Hardliners in the military and government protested strongly against outspoken criticism of the regime, and reprisals against opposition elements followed opposition electoral victories. The Congress was closed over a minor disagreement in April 1977, but at the same time, President Geisel responded to the pressure for liberalization by promulgating a series of political reforms that became known as the April Package (pacôte de Abril). The measures announced included cancelling scheduled direct elections for state

governors in favor of indirect elections by electoral colleges composed of state legislators and municipal council
members; nomination of one-third of federal Senators by
the state electoral colleges (these Senators soon came to
be known as "bionic" senators); reapportioning representation in the Chamber of Deputies on the basis of state
population, not voter registration; and limiting the size
of state delegations in the Chamber to no more than 55.
In addition, the law prohibited the use of radio and television for political campaigning, extended the term of
president from five years to six years, and reduced the
required number of votes for constitutional amendments to
a simple majority rather than the previous two-thirds' majority of the legislature.

The April reforms were intended to strengthen the
government party's control and representation at the national and state levels while simultaneously opening the
door to greater political discussion in anticipation of
national elections in 1978. The appointment of "bionic"
senators by state electoral colleges assured the government party a majority in the Federal Senate. The changes
in the electoral law were designed to give greater representation to rural, conservative, northern states where
the government enjoyed greater support than it did in the
more developed, more urbanized, and more activist states
of the center south (Rio de Janeiro, São Paulo, and Minas
Gerais, in particular).

On the first of December 1977, President Geisel took
a major step forward in the political opening and announced
to members of his party that the time had come for ending
the special powers accorded the Executive under Institutional Act No. 5 and that "efficient defence mechanisms
designed to maintain order and peace" would be written
into the Constitution instead (Latin America Political Report, 9 December 1977). The April package of reform measures facilitated government efforts to accomplish this
task, and government support for liberalization was expected to earn the government party additional backing in
1978 elections. While the Institutional Acts were not to
be revoked until January of 1979, the promise of political
liberalization gave rise to vigorous political debate.

In June 1978 when the Geisel government introduced
its promised package of legislative and constitutional reforms, the proposal called for abolishing the Institutional Acts and abolishing the death penalty, life impris-
onment, banishment, and other penalties used against
political detainees; cassados (individuals whose political
rights had been denied) were allowed to return to political life after 10 years. The president's right to close
the Congress and to suspend political rights was also
abolished. Procedures for the forming of new political

parties were specifically included. In a number of cases, the government left itself with ample recourse to maintain control over the political system and to punish or silence political critics if necessary. Nevertheless, the net result of the proposal was to free the political process of the heavy burden of executive tutelage (Latin America Political Report, June 30, 1978).

In spite of heroic efforts to capture the center with its liberalization policies, Brazil's government party lost the popular vote again in November 1978. The opposition MDB won approximately 15 million of votes cast for Senate candidates, while ARENA candidates won only 10 million. In the Chamber of Deputies elections, about 15 percent of the electorate cast blank or spoiled ballots, a share of which, at least, represented a protest against the choices offered. The election did not affect the government's control of the federal legislature, however, because the "bionic" senators continued to constitute one-third of the Senate. At the same time, the Chamber of Deputies majority was reduced to approximately 30 seats. The opposition MDB party saw its outspoken autêntico wing strengthened substantially. The election results promised more heated political debate to come as the two parties sought to reorganize themselves under different labels.

Despite the setback experienced in the November 1978 elections, the gradual opening continued. As Geisel had promised, the Institutional Acts were abolished on 5 January 1979. President-elect Figueiredo announced his own commitment to an expanded political opening (abertura) that would include greater attention to improvement in the wages and quality of life of working-class Brazilians, concentration on stimulating the moribund Brazilian agriculture sector, amnesty for political exiles and cassados, and more freedom for political parties to organize and campaign. The combination of reduced restrictions on political expression and the promise of more liberties to come unleashed the pent-up energies of the Brazilian press, which for the first time in 16 years was able to criticize the government. The opposition party began to test its ability to attract new adherents with the hopes of replacing ARENA as the majority party. The labor movement in São Paulo became suddenly more active and independent, aggressively pressing demands for adequate wage increases and other job-related benefits. An independent labor leadership emerged in the large and well-organized automobile sector and called for change in existing labor laws. Strikes, illegal under existing law, began to take place with regularity as auto workers, white collar workers, and civil servants all sought to test the government's ability to withstand and respond to domestic political pressure.

Amnesty

Brazil's experience with political terrorism and repression had been milder by far than Chile's or Argentina's. Nevertheless, the means used by Brazil to put
that past behind and reintegrate political exiles and cassados into the political life of the nation was exemplary.
Brazil's amnesty bill was presented to the nation in June
of 1979 following detailed behind-the-scenes negotiations
with political leaders and the military. It was a compromise that was acceptable to most, if not as far-reaching
as some would have liked. The principal benefit of the
amnesty went to the political exiles who were allowed to
return home. Amnesty was not granted to individuals engaged in armed resistance, and only a limited olive branch
was extended to individuals imprisoned under the national
security law. Members of the armed forces, approximately
20 percent of those cassados by the revolution, were offered only a token opportunity to return to the military
ranks.

Brazil's amnesty law artfully bridged the gap that
separated liberals, including liberals in the armed forces
who argued with the president that the law "should signal
that the debate was over, leaving nothing for later" and
the hardliners on the left, who wanted to open a painful
inquiry into armed forces responsibility for the repression of the late 1960s and early 1970s, and on the right,
who did not want to yield an inch to demands that the
military relinquish power. It brought back to Brazil many
of the figures who had led the leftist mobilization in the
1960s and proved they had little appeal in the new Brazil.
Others were sobered and looked for ways to participate
within the electoral system.

The law was not accepted in all quarters. In general, the left welcomed the opportunity to engage in politics again. The hard-line right wing reacted negatively,
however, and bombings and threats to politicians increased
as political debate in the country became more public. At
the same time, the divisions within the armed forces over
the abertura issue became more visible. While compromises
with more hard-line elements continued to be necessary as
the Figueriredo government sought to maintain the maximum
consensus behind its policy, the moderate line increasingly prevailed and a new political regime began to emerge.

Political Party Reforms

The government's principal preoccupation in engineering the abertura was to assure minimal loss to the government party itself. Initially, the architects of abertura
had envisioned the emergence of an institutional political
party like the PRI of Mexico. But that had not been the

political tradition in Brazil, and not even a majority of the government party could be persuaded to go along with such a program. Therefore, in October of 1979, and again following in-depth, behind-the-scenes political negotiations, the government introduced a party reform bill establishing the ground rules for the reorganization of the political party system. The legislation abolished existing parties and required that new parties would have to meet stiff electoral requirements such as receiving at least 5 percent of the nationwide vote in a minimum of nine states. Candidates would have to run on a single party slate, and parties themselves had to testify their allegiance to the democratic system and could not represent racial, religious, or class biases. The latter two provisions were intended to discourage the participation of the Communist party (outlawed in Brazil since 1949) and the emergence of working-class parties, although one was forming in São Paulo as the law was being written.

The party reform bill passed the legislature with minimal discussion by a vote of 269-202. Immediately, four groupings emerged, one representing the government party and three representing divisions within the opposition MDB. Political jockeying continued about these poles until elections in November 1982. Over time, the government party saw its own support whittled at by parties claiming to represent a moderate opposition to the military. Their appeal was to change away for the controlled environment of the military regime, and for greater autonomy for business, for the States, and for other individual interest groups. The strongest segment of the opposition and the one that attracted the majority of defectors from the government party was the Party of the Brazilian Democratic Movement (PMDB), formed of the core of moderate opposition that had been participating in the political process ever since the 1964 revolution.

The government responded positively to strong pressure from within its own party for a return to direct elections; and when an ARENA deputy introduced legislation to this effect, the government resisted only briefly before responding with its own proposal. In exchange for cancellation of municipal elections scheduled for 1980, elections for all levels of government except president would be by direct vote in 1982. The system of bionic senators would end, and the laws governing political campaign activity were modified substantially. The Constitutional amendment introduced in March of 1980 would become law only in 1981, but it signalled the end of the political system invoked in 1965 when, in the last direct elections, opposition candidates had resoundingly defeated parties supporting the military revolution. Brazilian political parties read the new law as giving them license to build their constituencies.

Political debate in Brazil from mid-1980 through the end of 1982 was marked by two themes--the political party campaigns and the rapidly deteriorating economic situation. The latter dominated. At the beginning of 1981, the government imposed severe austerity measures designed to bring Brazil's raging inflation under control. The measures hit directly at the constituency of blue- and white-collar workers whose political support the government most hoped to attract to its ranks of followers. The economic crisis provided ample themes for opposition party campaign platforms and seemingly played directly into the hands of the government's most extreme critics. Nevertheless, although a series of efforts was made to form broad-based parties on the left end of the political spectrum, the dominant weight of political opinion remained with the government and more conservative opposition elements, not with the extremists most feared by the military right wing. Several measures were taken to insure the government party's continued electoral success. In November 1981 and in the spring of 1982 new measures governing political party activities were introduced, in each case to make an opposition electoral victory more difficult.

Return to Direct Elections

Brazil's elections were held on November 15, 1982, and on all measures the government lost by a small margin. Of 21.7 million votes cast, the moderate opposition party, PMDB, captured 16 million votes, while the pro-administration party won 15 million votes. 5.7 million votes went to three parties that competed for the working-class vote. Leonel Brizola, one of the principal figures in the unrest leading to the coup of 1964, was elected governor of the State of Rio de Janeiro, and, in spite of last-minute hesitation, his winning vote was announced and he was allowed to take office. The government lost control of 10 of Brazil's 23 governorships, including governorships of the most populous States--the anticipated result of conceding to direct elections at that level. The opposition PMBD won control of 75 of the 100 largest town councils. One Brazilian journalist, still amazed at the tremendous success of the political opening that the elections represented, commented, "It seems that we have stumbled upon democracy!"

The return to democratic government is not complete. The present government must continue to cope with pressing social problems, rising labor unrest, and an intractable financial situation that continues to escape government control. In 1985 Brazil will hold elections for president. For the first time since 1965, civilian candidates are being discussed seriously. Whether political opening will continue to occur in the gradual and evolutionary way that it has been orchestrated to date will

depend largely on the continued commitment of Brazilian
business, labor, and political leaders to a consensus solution to the social and economic problems of the country.
Concerns remain that too bold a move toward populism will
prompt a reaction by conservative military officers still
reluctant to concede authority to civilian leaders. To
date that faction has been a small minority and it has
been controlled by the President. No one knows what support it would have if serious unrest and instability again
infected the country as it did in the 1960s.

Rationale for Political Opening

Brazil's political opening was brought about largely
by the efforts of political advisors within the executive
branch and not, as has occurred elsewhere, as a result of
government giving in to undeniable pressures from its opposition. This explains, in great part, the relative
tranquility with which the transition occurred. Pressures
were present and irresistible, but for the most part the
government was able to co-opt and mute them, maintaining
control over the pace of the liberalization so that a
basic consensus accompanied each major step forward.

The political transition that was first called distenção and then abertura was largely the brain child of
one of Brazil's most distinguished contemporary political
strategists, General Golbery do Couto e Silva, chief ad-
visor to both President Geisel and President Figueiredo
until his surprising departure from office in August 1980.
Golbery was a founder of Brazil's senior military school,
the Superior War College (Escola Superior da Guerra), the
author of several books on Brazil's geopolitical interests, and a principal figure in developing the behind-the-
scenes rationale for the revolution of 1964. It is therefore interesting that as an architect of the authoritarian
regime of post-1964, he should also be the principal architect of its disengagement. In June of 1980 Golbery presented a lecture to the Superior War College in which he
explained the rationale for political opening. While describing Brazilian political history as a process of episodic movements toward more centralized government and
then away from centralization, Golbery maintained that the
principal characteristic of the authoritarian regime installed in 1964 had become one of extreme centralization.
Because of the extreme tendency, the government apparatus
had become ponderous, unresponsive, and defensive of its
prerogatives, rather than an efficient machine serving the
interest of the nation. Such privilege and inefficiency,
coupled with social and economic problems that emerged independently of government policy, resulted in the government becoming the exclusive target of criticism of a great
variety of groups whose grievances were, in fact, quite
different one from another. So long as press censorship

existed and political parties were suppressed, the government would remain the sole target of criticism, for there
was no way of exposing the differences or purposes of the
various oppositions.

The regime installed in 1964 was, in Golbery's mind,
an institutionalized revolution. Criticism of the government should then come from anti-revolutionary forces; but
because of the lack of opportunity for expression, the
government itself was made to appear the anti-revolutionary.
The only choice for the regime to further institutionalize
the processes launched with the 1964 revolution was to
open the political system to free expression in which opposition to government policy would be weakened as its
heterogeneity was exposed. "Less radicalization, more
liberalization on the part of the regime and more tolerance on the part of government will contribute broadly to
the emergence of strong impulses toward atomization of the
oppositionist front," Golbery predicted (Veja, 10 September 1980). To date, this reasoning appears to have been
sound for the Brazilian case.

If Brazil successfully makes the transition to civilian government and greater political participation in decision making, its national confidence will be greatly
bolstered. Brazil will also probably feel much more con-
fident in its international relations and demonstrate increasing independence. The United States will need to exercise greater diplomacy to achieve a common vote with
Brazil on international problems of mutual interest.

218

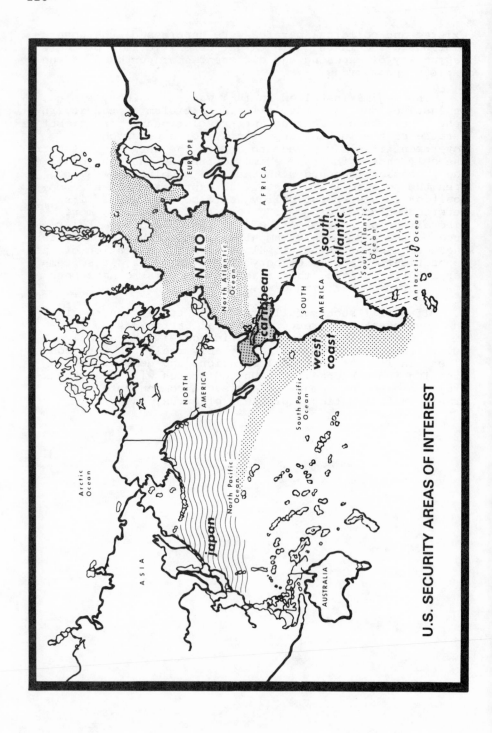

U.S. SECURITY AREAS OF INTEREST

6
Dimensions of U.S. Security Interests in Latin America

U.S. security interests have been dominated by a concern to maintain a strategic balance of power between the United States and the Soviet Union. In this strategic context, Latin America has historically had only a marginal role, in part because the countries in the region had little power and because the region itself has been relatively isolated from the world's political and military conflicts. The Latin American nations, with few exceptions, have been firmly in the U.S. camp in the East-West conflict, but largely on the sidelines of that conflict.

UNITED STATES' SECURITY INTERESTS IN
LATIN AMERICA

Although Latin America has played only a minor role in U.S. strategic planning to date, this country does have clear security interests in the hemisphere--interests that are often overlooked in assessing the region's importance. At least three separate areas of U.S. security interest in Latin America can be identified. The intensity of U.S. interest in each of the regions is determined by proximity to the continental United States and to other areas of security concern, and by the independent political, military, and economic capabilities of the nations in each subregion. On this basis, the three regions of U.S. security interest would be, in order of decreasing importance, the Caribbean basin and Gulf of Mexico, East Coast South America, and finally, West Coast South America. These are depicted in Figure 6.1.

U.S. Security Interests in the Caribbean Basin

The Caribbean basin represents the southern flank of the United States--its strategic rear--and it has traditionally been defined as the region of highest U.S.

security concern in the hemisphere. The United States' principal interest in the area is to maintain its unchallenged and unconstrained freedom of movement through the region. The principal threat to U.S. security lies in the emergence of governments that would provide bases from which the United States' enemies might operate to constrain U.S. freedom of access throughout the region. In addition,

- The Caribbean is an area of important economic interests; it provides a number of critical raw materials for the U.S. economy and transships the bulk of U.S. petroleum imports. It also is the principal route for commercial and naval traffic between the Atlantic and Pacific oceans.

- The region is a critical link in a number of military activities that serve U.S. global defense purposes.

- As an ocean region, the Caribbean is vulnerable to external penetration. Concern about penetration is intensified by the expansion of the Soviet bluewater fleet with basing arrangements in Cuba and by Cuba's own military buildup.

- The region is economically the poorest and politically the most unstable in the hemisphere. Political institutional breakdown offers a base for the expansion of Cuban or Soviet activities encouraging further instability and promoting the emergence of anti-American regimes.

- Because the region is within the United States' historical sphere of influence, the decline of U.S. preeminence in the region or of its ability to deny the region to other powers may be interpreted as a sign of U.S. weakness.

For all these reasons, a key goal of U.S. security policy is to deny access in the region to hostile foreign powers or to hostile political regimes that would challenge interests in the region.

U.S. interest in the Caribbean was initially defined in the 19th century by plans to build a Central American canal to provide U.S. military and commercial ships access to the Pacific. The 1823 Monroe Doctrine as interpreted by the 1904 Roosevelt Corollary was applied almost exclusively in the Caribbean. Between 1904 and 1936 (when Franklin Roosevelt replaced Theodore Roosevelt's interventionist corollary with the noninterventionist Good Neighbor Policy), the United States intervened frequently in the Caribbean principally in defense of economic interests. In the Cold War period after World War II, the United States used military force as an instrument of political policy on at least 217 occasions. More than one-fourth of these events took place in the Western Hemisphere, mostly in the Caribbean basin, largely to impede the coming to power of presumably hostile leftist governments (Blechman, 1978).

Present-day widespread instability in the Caribbean basin poses a serious challenge to U.S. security interest and policy. The instability reflects on the solidarity and viability of the informal hemisphere alliance system, and U.S. inability to assure regional political stability directly challenges presumed U.S. leadership in the region. At the same time, the instability results from deep social and economic problems and political institutional weaknesses that cannot be cured easily or rapidly.

The variety of longstanding social and economic inequities have made leftist revolutionary solutions attractive and recent Marxist successes in Grenada and in Nicaragua have encouraged revolutionary activities and Cuban support for them. Historically weak governments have fallen or look to the United States to solve their problems.

The principal U.S. goal in dealing with regional political instability is to discourage or prevent the emergence of hostile governments in the region. However, the overriding U.S. preoccupation with Communist revolution and with Cuban or Soviet support for revolution in the region has diverted attention from the political weaknesses of existing pro-American governments and parties. Only casual and episodic attention has been given to underlying social, economic, and institutional problems that contribute to regional instability. The United States' strong reaction to revolution has often appeared to signal a lack of concern with the social and economic causes of unrest. Indeed, U.S. intervention in the Dominican Republic in 1965 generally undermined U.S. efforts to develop a credible hemispheric alliance, even though a successful democratic government has emerged out of that episode. The United States' hesitant response to the Nicaraguan crisis in 1978 and 1979 appeared to run counter to Latin American preferences for encouraging progressive governments and ideological pluralism. Policies toward political change in El Salvador and Guatemala have been widely misunderstood.

The United States does have specific national security interests in the Caribbean basin. Caribbean stations provide critical links in the network of U.S. listening posts for monitoring ship and submarine activities in the Atlantic Ocean and approaches to the Caribbean Sea. A variety of military training activities take place at

Panama, Puerto Rico, and Cuba. Communication, tracking,
and navigation facilities are located throughout the region and particularly in the eastern islands. The Navy's
Atlantic Underseas Test and Evaluation Center in the Bahamas has been critical in the development of antisubmarine warfare capabilities.

A continuing high volume of interoceanic and hemispheric trade moves through the Caribbean on North-South
trade routes and to and from the Panama Canal. Lighter-
ing operations in the Antilles are critical to the supply
of petroleum imports to U.S. ports that cannot handle
large tankers.

The Caribbean basin is also the main source of U.S.
raw materials imports from the Western Hemisphere. Mexico
is the United States' second most important supplier of
critical raw materials after Canada, and the principal
supplier of silver, zinc, gypsum, antimony, mercury, bismuth, selenium, barium, rhenium, and lead (see Chapter 2).
With new petroleum capacity, Mexico could supply up to
30 percent of U.S. petroleum import requirements and up to
2 billion cubic feet of natural gas per day. In 1980
Venezuela provided 10 percent of U.S. iron ore imports,
down from 28 percent in the mid-1970s, and 7 percent of
its petroleum products and crude petroleum, down from 23
and 8 percent, respectively, five years earlier. Refineries in the Caribbean, especially the Antilles, supply over
50 percent of U.S. petroleum products from crude imported
from the Middle East and Africa. In better times, nearly
50 percent of U.S. bauxite imports came from Jamaica; today the figure is 25 percent. No other region in the Western Hemisphere except Canada is so important to the U.S.
supply of raw materials, and many of the important suppliers are countries susceptible to political instability.

The presence of a Soviet-backed regime in Cuba is a
profound irritant to the United States both because it
represents an undeniable crack in hemispheric solidarity
and because it provides a base of operations for Soviet
fishing, naval, satellite intelligence, and other activities in the region. Moreover, Cuba is a source of support
for revolutionary and anti-American movements in the Caribbean and elsewhere, as was demonstrated in the early 1960s
and more recently in the support Cuba has given to terrorist groups and guerrilla leaderships in the Caribbean basin.
While Cuba kept a low profile in the region in the 1970s,
confining its efforts to social and economic exhanges, its
activism in other world regions threatened U.S. interests
abroad, increased opportunities for a U.S.-Soviet confrontation, and served as a constant reminder of what could occur
closer to home. Events in Nicaragua following the Sandinista victory in July 1979 have contributed to heightened
concern that "other Cubas" could emerge in the hemisphere.

Despite the close attention the United States seems to have paid to the Caribbean, the U.S. vital interest in the region should not be exaggerated. Many argue that the region's "importance...is psychological--the Caribbean is important because we think it is" (Blechman and Kaplan, 1978). With the exception of the raw materials supplies already mentioned, the region indeed is economically insignificant to the United States (see Chapter 4). The individual countries depend heavily on the U.S. market for their raw materials and agricultural exports. Because of the ready availability of world supplies and comparative transportation costs, they would be hard pressed to find attractive alternative markets should they decide not to trade with the United States. The Panama Canal is becoming less important in world trade, and less important in supply to the United States. Nevertheless, it continues to play an important role in the transport of U.S. commodities, especially grain and coal to Pacific markets. Recently, the Canal was especially active in the transshipment of Alaskan crude petroleum from the Pacific to the Caribbean where it could be carried to U.S. Gulf ports. This activity should decline with the inauguration, in 1982, of Panama's oil pipeline. Militarily, the Canal's uses are limited. Its principal role in conflict since World War II has been in logistics supply to the Pacific. In the event of global conflict with the Soviets, it could not transit U.S. carriers and would pose a risky choke point for other naval ships using it (Hayes, 1977). It nevertheless remains a critical link in the United States' ability to respond rapidly and efficiently in a variety of contingencies.

U.S. concern in the Caribbean basin currently focuses on the possibility that unstable political situations there might provide an entree for further Soviet encroachment in the hemisphere. The Soviets recognize the psychological victory that Cuba represents and have exploited it on every occasion, despite detente (Theberge, 1974). As the missile crisis of 1962 and the Cienfuegos submarine base incident of 1969 suggest, however, the Soviets appear not willing to confront the United States directly in its sphere of influence. In part, the Soviets recognize that a price for additional clients in the Caribbean would be for the Soviet Union to substantially underwrite the Caribbean economies as they have in the case of Cuba. Experience in Chile under Allende and more recently in Nicaragua, where the Soviets have provided arms but little direct economic assistance, demonstrates that this is unlikely. Cuba itself has limited resources, though important psychological ones, to offer Caribbean basin countries. Moreover, major Soviet support would be required for the Cubans to underwrite Caribbean and Central American economic development on their own. This appears unlikely in an area so far from the Soviet sphere of

influence, and, to date, neither Cuba nor the Soviet Union
has indicated a willingness to underwrite new economies.
Indeed both seem to have cautioned revolutionary regimes
in Central America and the Caribbean to not break off
their ties to western economies. Until the recent turmoil
in Jamaica, Nicaragua, and El Salvador, the United States
also gave relatively little economic or diplomatic attention to its interests in the area.

Most Caribbean countries have felt threatened by the
increased leftist agitation in the region. However, their
forces are small and often poorly trained and are ill-
prepared to contribute to their own internal security. As
a result, the United States holds a major responsibility
for providing timely aid and training to regional defense
forces. Moreover, because these countries lie so close to
the United States, there is little need for them to develop
a major defense capability. Of the countries in the region, only Mexico and Venezuela have the population and
the economic wherewithal to support a sizable military
capability. Venezuela also defines its region of security
interest in the Caribbean and is increasing its political
and economic activity in the region (see Chapter 4). Venezuela has embarked on a prolonged modernization program in
which it will increase its air and naval capabilities in
particular. Colombia, too, concentrates its naval capabilities along its Caribbean coastline and has cooperated
closely with the United States in surveillance of drug
traffic. Mexico has concentrated its capabilities in the
areas of coastal patrol (for drug traffic surveillance,
contraband control, and defense of its ocean resources).
Because of its proximity to the United States, Mexico is
not expected to develop a major defense capability in the
foreseeable future. Nevertheless, increasing instability
in Central America has prompted Mexico to modernize and
expand its military forces.

The factors to be considered in weighing U.S. security interests in the Caribbean basin can be summarized
as follows:

1) • U.S. interests in the Caribbean are defined chiefly
by the region's importance in the supply of raw
materials to the United States itself and by the
gateway it presents to the Atlantic Ocean.

2) • The Caribbean must remain secure for the transit
of vessels. Such security is largely dependent on
the quality of political relations that the United
States can establish and maintain with Caribbean
regimes that are in political and economic transition and therefore relatively unpredictable.

- Anti-Americanism in the region poses a major test 3)
of U.S. tolerance for political experimentation
and a challenge to the concept of hemispheric
solidarity. However, anti-Americanism is often
exaggerated.

- In spite of anti-American rhetoric, the Caribbean 4)
region is economically heavily dependent on the
United States and this dependence limits the
countries' ability to move out of the U.S. sphere
of influence.

- Soviet activities in the Caribbean have been lim- 5)
ited and in general have been sensitive to U.S.
reactions. Nevertheless, the Soviets will continue to test U.S. tolerance for Russian military
activities in the Caribbean.

- The Soviet Union will continue to support Cuba and 6)
Cuban military buildup, and will give cautious encouragement to Cuban efforts in support of revolution in the Caribbean basin.

In sum, the Caribbean basin does represent an area
of high security interest. With the exception of U.S.
forces, the region is largely undefended and highly unstable politically. Regional resentments of U.S. political and economic hegemony have led to efforts to reduce
traditional ties and dependence. However, the very strong,
natural economic link to the United States market (see
Chapter 3) places real limits on the extent to which ties
can be diminished. Economic problems provide the greatest
cause for political instability and in the early 1980s
seemed to draw most of the Caribbean basin countries into
closer cooperation with the United States as all parties
sought to find ways to stop the sharp economic decline of
the previous decade.

U.S. Security Interests in the
South Atlantic

The South Atlantic and particularly the Atlantic
narrows has been an area of U.S. concern since World War
II. More recently, the whole area of the South Atlantic
ocean has attracted new U.S. security consideration. The
reasons for this increased attention include the following:

- The importance of the Cape of Good Hope as a supply route for Western European and North American
petroleum supplies because of the increasing employment of supertankers too large to use the
Suez Canal;

- Political instability in southern Africa coupled with Soviet and Cuban participation in that area;

- The persistent aspirations and increasing capability of South Atlantic nations to exercise political-military power in the Southern Hemisphere, paralleled by perceived U.S./NATO disinterest in the region;

- Increasing interest in deep seabed resources and offshore petroleum exploration as well as future development of Antarctican resources;

- Intensified concern with maritime control stemming from claims of sovereignty over 200-mile territorial seas;

- Growing Soviet blue-water naval capability, coupled with the relative stagnation in U.S. fleet size;

- Rapid development of commercial maritime traffic by the countries bordering the region as they extend their economic relations to include Europe, Japan, the Middle East, and Africa;

- Recent substantial upgrading of military capabilities by nations in the region, through purchase of sophisticated weapons and development of indigenous arms industries.

The South Atlantic region is defined geographically as the Atlantic Ocean south of the equator, and strategically as the area south of the line Natal (Brazil) - Dakar (Senegal), or, in a more extended definition, as the area south of the Tropic of Cancer, the southern limit of NATO. The South Atlantic has always been a major maritime trade route, but the 1967 closure of the Suez Canal caused it to become a vital route for supplying petroleum to Europe and the United States as tankers from the Persian Gulf were forced to take the long route around the Cape of Good Hope. Recent figures indicate that approximately 25 percent of U.S. petroleum imports, nearly 60 percent of Western Europe's, and an equal share of Brazil's, move on the South Atlantic Cape of Good Hope sea lanes (OECD, 1979). Approximately 22,000 ships per year, including the oil tankers, move on the trade route (Rondeau, 1976). Although the Suez is again open to traffic, the supertankers developed for the longer route cannot pass through the canal and will continue to go around the cape. In 1978 more than 70 percent of world tanker fleet deadweight tonnage (dwt) was held in ships of over 100,000 dwt (OECD, 1979).

In addition to the petroleum trade, the nations bordering the South Atlantic, particularly African nations,

are rich in raw materials crucial to the industrial economies of northern Europe, the United States, and Japan.
Six of the critical raw materials required by industrial
societies--chromium, cobalt, industrial diamonds, manganese, platinum group metals, and vanadium--are produced
in southern Africa, particularly Rhodesia and South Africa
(International Economic Studies Institute, 1976). The nations bordering the South Atlantic are, moreover, among
the most rapidly expanding of the developing countries,
and their economic growth is increasingly dependent on
international oceanborne trade. Not only has their commerce with the industrial countries expanded in geometric
proportions in recent years, but also trade between Africa
and South America has expanded. Brazil, in particular,
has targeted the West Coast African market as a priority
development area. Since 1976, trade with the African
economies has become an increasingly important element of
Brazil's total foreign trade. By far the largest component of that trade has been petroleum.

For the North Atlantic states, the major concern in
the South Atlantic is the security of petroleum shipping
and raw materials supplies. South Atlantic countries,
particularly Brazil, which imports 90 percent of its
petroleum requirements from the Eastern Hemisphere (see
Table 5.6), share this concern, but are also interested
in a variety of other commercial shipping routes and
trade relations linking South America with Japan, West
Africa, and Europe. The major powers have a minimal
presence in the region. The United States has no air or
naval bases in either Africa or South America. The Soviet
Union has access to the port and air fields at Conakry,
Guinea, but to date has maintained a relatively low profile in the area (Ginsburg, 1977). Nevertheless, this
presence is regarded as a major Soviet foreign policy offensive in Africa. The prime factors focusing U.S. attention on the South Atlantic have been Soviet support of
political unrest in southern Africa, either independently
or via logistic supply to Cuban forces, and Soviet naval
activity off Guinea and Angola.

A cursory reading of recent literature on naval policy considerations underscores the concern with which
U.S. policymakers view the rapid expansion of Soviet blue-
water naval capabilities. In 1976, the Secretary of the
Navy noted that

during the past decade the Soviet Union has established itself as a formidable maritime power.
Today its navy is the world's largest (and is
deployed) on a worldwide basis. Soviet ships
and submarines in the Mediterranean Sea and the
Indian Ocean usually outnumber our own forward
deployed units. In recent months we have seen

increased employment of Soviet surface combat-
ants, and emphibious ships with embarked naval
infantry, used to support Soviet policies in
world trouble spots, most recently off West
Africa. For example, since late November 1975,
Soviets have maintained an Alligator class LST
with Naval infantry aboard in the Gulf of Guinea
generally operating to the north of Angola.
These factors in conjunction with the emergence
of the Soviet Union as a leader in the other
aspects of maritime power, such as merchant
marine shipping, fishing, and oceanographic
research, indicate that they not only recognize,
but are using sea power as an essential element
of national strategy (Middendorf, 1976).

A Navy Admiral has noted that

Soviet aircraft frequently operate from Conakry,
Guinea, and can cover the South Atlantic Ocean
as far as the Central Coasts of South America,
threaten sea interdiction along the West African littoral as far as Capetown, or reach north
to Gibraltar. A base at Angola would extend
aircraft radii to the sea approaches of Buenos
Aires and, around the Cape, north into the Indian Ocean over the sea lanes as far as Kenya...
Bases in Cuba, close to the Panama Canal, give
air coverage south to Natal and eastward into
the Atlantic, overlapping with air coverage
from Conakry (Bagley, 1977).

The Soviet naval buildup reflects a shift in Soviet
thinking about the missions of its navy and the uses of
sea power (see McGwire, 1974, 1975, 1977). Traditionally,
the Soviet Navy has been concerned with defense of the
homeland. During the 1960s, along with building up its
fleet, the Soviet Union adopted a forward-deployed strategic defense posture to counter U.S. and NATO capabilities
in the North Atlantic and Mediterranean. Since the late
1960s, however, the Soviet fleet has been engaged as an
"active instrument of Soviet foreign policy, protecting
and promoting Soviet interests...in the third world"
(Weinland, 1975).

Analyses of Soviet political uses of seapower have
focused on global activity, much of which has taken place
in areas much closer to home than the South Atlantic, for
example, the Mediterranean, Red Sea, and Indian Ocean
areas (McGwire, 1977). Soviet navy port visits around
the world have increased substantially in the past 15 to
20 years (McGwire, 1975; Blechman and Levinson, 1977).
The majority of port calls by combatant vessels in the
South Atlantic were in western Africa (Morocco, Senegal,

Guinea, and Sierra Leone). While some were associated
with political events ashore, most were related to ship
transfers between the Soviet North Atlantic and Pacific
fleets. Relatively little Soviet naval activity involved
South America directly. Port calls by Soviet vessels almost ceased during the mid- and late 1970s, and merchant
and fishing fleet activities off Latin America are, according to many analysts, almost nonexistent (Kravanja,
1976). Port calls resumed in the 1980s as tensions resulting from an aggressive human rights policy, events in
Central America and then from the Falkland Islands war
appeared to invite further cracks in hemisphere security
relations. This situation probably will continue since
the South American states have adopted a 200-mile territorial water limit and increasingly insist that fixed
percentages of their foreign trade be carried in domestic
bottoms (Drewry, 1974). Only a small portion of South
American trade (mostly grain exports) occurs with the Soviet Union (see Chapter 2).

In the late 1970s the United States began to focus
more attention on the South Atlantic region. At issue
are the continuing political instability in Africa, coupled with the Soviet and Cuban participation in the area,
the security of vital raw materials supplies, the capabilities for rapid deployment of forces in crises, the
defense of vital shipping lanes, the surveillance of Soviet activities in the South Atlantic and on the NATO
flank, and the bolstering of support capabilities for
some wartime contingencies. Similar considerations, particularly Soviet and Cuban activities in Angola, combined
to raise the issue of a potential South Atlantic Treaty
Organization (SATO) among regional powers in 1976.

Soviet-assisted Cuban activities in Angola, in particular, provided conservative anti-Communist regimes in
South America with their first "credible" external threat
since World War II. This, coupled with a downgrading of
U.S. military sales and assistance programs in the region,
and perception of greater U.S. concern with U.S.-Soviet
detente than with Communist advances in the Third World
(Grondona, 1976) provided the background to the discussion of the regional defense organization. The logical
parties to a South Atlantic defense organization would be
Argentina, Brazil, and South Africa. Because of an earlier agreement (1956) between Argentina, Brazil, Uruguay,
and Paraguay, the latter two countries are also potential
signatories to a SATO agreement. Chile might be also,
because of its sympathy to anti-Communist causes and its
strategic position at the Strait of Magellan/Cape Horn.
Nigeria, on the African side, would also be a candidate.
The United States, a European power, or both would be
necessary partners because of the limited military capabilities of the South Atlantic countries.

230

The diverse, and frequently divergent, interests of
these prospective partners make agreement on and definition of South Atlantic security interests extremely difficult, if not impossible. These conflicting interests
on Brazil's part led Foreign Minister Antonio F.
Azeredo da Silveira to dismiss the South Atlantic defense alliance notion in September 1976, arguing, "There is not
the slightest possibility of establishing a collective
defense system in the South Atlantic, especially with the
awkward and undesirable presence of South Africa" (Foreign Broadcast Information Service, September 23, 1976).
Shortly thereafter, Navy Minister Azevedo Henning stated
publicly that "the Soviet presence in Africa is a problem
which exclusively concerns the African countries...."
(Jornal do Brasil, October 14, 1976). Admiral Henning
also noted that Brazil had no intention of creating new
alliances to defend the South American continent (Jornal
do Brasil, October 14, 1976), thus scotching rumors that
Argentina and Brazil were about to upgrade the South Atlantic Pact from a joint training and exercise agreement
to an offensive and defensive agreement.*

Whether or not a South Atlantic defense organization
is a viable option for the future, the South Atlantic
countries of Latin America potentially are able to make
an important contribution in U.S. contingency planning for
regional defense. Brazil and Argentina share U.S. vital
concerns in the region. Both have important commercial
interests in the security of maritime trade. Nearly
40 percent of their exports and one-third of their imports
cross the South Atlantic Ocean to Western European markets. Both countries have growing commercial relations
with Africa. Both have already embarked on a major merchant marine and naval buildup. By 1985, one observer
noted, Argentina could have the core of a carrier strike
force, and Brazil's Niteroi-class destroyer fleet will
represent a major antisubmarine warfare force, "even by
superpower standards" (Scheina, 1978; 1983).

Both Brazil and Argentina define the South Atlantic
region as their sphere of influence and of defense

*Apart from the 1947 Inter-American Treaty of Reciprocal
Assistance (Rio Treaty), defense agreements between Latin
American countries are primarily agreements to conduct
joint training exercises and do not entail offensive or
defense commitments for continental defense. This arrangement has permitted the South Americans to rely upon
the U.S. "umbrella" for defense of the region in case of
external threat. However, both major South Atlantic powers have sought to develop independent capabilities over
the past decade. Commitments under the Rio Treaty received their greatest test in the 1982 Falklands war, in
which the Rio Treaty did not apply.

responsibility. Argentina's interests are more closely
linked to those of South Africa, the Antarctic region,
and the southernmost reaches of the South Atlantic, which
is the area of greatest shipping activity. Both countries have claimed sovereignty over a 200-mile territorial sea which implies a quantum increase in responsibil-
ities for ocean defense and surveillance.

Brazil's military interest in the South Atlantic
stems in part from its vantage point at the Natal-Dakar
"channel," the narrowest (1,400 nm) point between the
South American and African continents. Northeast Brazilian naval and air bases were used extensively in convoy
escort, coastal patrol, ocean surveillance, and logistic
staging in World Wars I and II. The Brazilian Navy participated actively in both of these conflicts, and Brazil
foresees a similar role for itself in future global conflicts, as well as a greater need to defend its own highly
developed coastal industrial complexes against hostile
attack.

Neither Brazil nor Argentina now has the capability
to exercise a much-expanded security role in the South
Atlantic. Their forces are both configured primarily for
coastal defense of major population centers from Rio to
Buenos Aires and for defense against attack by each other
rather than a broader ocean role. They probably could
not engage in coastal patrol and escort or other activities simultaneously. Both currently have limited anti-
submarine capabilities but are actively seeking to upgrade
them. This upgrading will require substantial increase in
electronic detection capability, but neither European nor
American suppliers have been willing to cooperate in this
area.

Neither Brazil nor Argentina yet has the logistic
capability to support prolonged action. Both also suffer
extreme resupply vulnerability as a result of their reliance on U.S. and European suppliers for their more sophisticated weapons. In this respect, weapons standardization
issues more often addressed in the context of NATO also
are important in the Latin American context and become
more difficult because of long distances involved. More
reliable access to spare parts and maintenance assistance
would be critical in any more active employment of current forces. Over the long run, Brazil's and Argentina's
own defense industries will bridge some of these gaps in
less technical areas, but gaps are likely to remain in the
areas of sophisticated weapons and electronics (recently
determined as a priority development area for the Brazilian Navy).

In short, for either Brazil or Argentina to engage
in regional defense roles that are complementary to those

of the United States or its allies, a major defense acquisition program that looked toward building such complementarity would be needed. Purchases to date have not been so coordinated. Brazil's acquisitions have tapered off as a result of the country's economic difficulties. Argentina's purchases responded to the political and military ambitions of a narrowly based regime and may not be sustainable.

Within the South Atlantic region, South Africa, the pariah, continues to possess the best facilities for monitoring and servicing commercial and military traffic. Its Simonstown naval base provides extensive repair and dry-dock facilities. South African airfields can accept the most modern strategic and tactical aircraft. The country possesses a modern meteorological system and sophisticated navigational facilities. The Silvermine Command and Control Center can track and provide continuous information on ships from South America to Bangladesh and from North Africa to Antarctica (Rondeau, 1976). Again, a major effort would be required to develop similar capabilities in Brazil or Argentina.

Also of growing importance in the South Atlantic equation is Nigeria, clearly the regional power on the West African coast. Like the South American powers, Nigeria has engaged in a major upgrading of its military capabilities. Brazilian relations with Nigeria, especially economic relations, are increasingly close and cooperation between the two countries is more probable in the short term than is cooperation between Brazil and South Africa.

In summary, the United States has clear interests in keeping the South Atlantic open to uninterrupted commerce that provides critical resources to its own and its allies' industrial economies. Moreover, the United States seeks to minimize the impact of expanded Soviet presence in the area, particularly as it influences global perceptions of the East-West political balance. The South Atlantic regional powers share both these concerns, though to different degrees and for different reasons. The United States has clear interests in maintaining close working relations with the South Atlantic regional powers themselves, as they represent several of the most important developing powers. Brazil and Nigeria are regarded as emerging Third World powers with ability to exercise leadership in their respective regions and each has increasing awareness of the importance of the region itself to world economic well-being and security. Argentina, despite prolonged political and economic difficulties, remains a political force in South America. Each of these regional powers is developing military capabilities that complement those of the United States and could

reinforce U.S. forces, thus freeing the United States for
action elsewhere in a variety of contingencies.

Several constraints work against early close cooperation between the South Atlantic countries and the United
States:

- The Latin Americans' unwillingness to undertake
  additional defense burden and responsibility because of domestic political and economic
  considerations;

- Their unwillingness to commit themselves to a
  role of ideological and military opposition to the
  Soviet Union or to Third World liberation movements backed by the Soviets, in a period when the
  Third World disposition is toward nonalignment
  with the superpowers. In this regard Brazil has
  stated its own policy as one of "not-automatic
  alignment";

- U.S. and European unwillingness to provide developing countries with high-technology equipment
  necessary to upgrade their capabilities so that
  they represent a credible force.

U.S. Security Interests in West Coast South America

The United States has less important security interests in west coast South America than in the Caribbean
basin or the South Atlantic. The west coast countries do
not guard major ocean trade routes as the east coast
countries do; nor do the west coast countries provide the
launching platform to the Pacific Ocean that the east
coast countries provide to the Atlantic. Their economic
and political ties to Europe and the United States are
stronger than their ties to the Pacific region, though
the latter are growing rapidly. The west coast countries'
principal role in U.S. contingency planning is in providing access to ship repair and refueling facilities in the
event of contingencies that require the movement of ships
between the Atlantic and Pacific oceans. In this regard,
west coast forces are relatively well prepared to provide
for the defense of these facilities.

The west coast countries supply the United States
with a number of important raw materials, including tin,
tellurium, antimony, barite, and copper. While they are
not the chief supplier of any of these materials, their
ability to substitute for more distant suppliers in the
event of conflict or cutoff is important in overall U.S.
economic security considerations.

The west coast countries represent an important political bloc within the hemisphere and, with Venezuela,
have been the leaders of the movement for greater Latin
American independence from the United States within the
framework of the inter-American system. Frictions in U.S.
relations with the west coast countries have resulted in
an intensification of their military disengagement from
the United States, which has been accompanied by a rapid
increase in arms acquisitions and intensification of sa-
bre rattling in traditional rivalries and border disputes.

A series of border disputes between west coast countries makes the prospect of conflict more likely in this
area than in other regions of Latin America. In 1982 Argentina went to war over its claim to the Malvinas (Falkland) Islands. In 1978 the Argentine-Chilean disagreement
over the arbitration of the Beagle Channel led to the
largest troop mobilization in South America since the
Chaco War in the 1930s. Peru and Ecuador, Peru and Colombia, Colombia and Venezuela, Venezuela and Brazil,
Peru, Bolivia and Chile all have serious border-related
disputes that occupy military force and attention. Peru
has armed itself well beyond the requirements of domestic
defense. With acquisitions from the Soviet Union, Peru
now has an air strike capability against its neighbors, a
formidable Soviet SA-3 SAM air defense network, the most
modern and powerful tank force in South America (arrayed
against Chile), and the strongest fleet in the subregion,
second in size and power only to Brazil's (Nolde, 1979).
In response to this buildup, Ecuador and Chile have both
upgraded their air defense capabilities. Chile would currently be hard pressed to defend both its northern and
southern (Beagle Channel) border regions simultaneously.

Until the outbreak of hostilities between Peru and
Ecuador over a disputed border region in the remote jungle,
and more recently the war between Argentina and Great Britain over the Falkland Islands, most authorities regarded
the possibility of wars in the subregion as a low probability. Political and economic uncertainties and ideological differences between governments nevertheless increase
concern over regional tensions. Should conflict break
out again, it will also likely be short-lived, as none of
the Latin American countries has staying power to conduct
a prolonged war effort. Generally inadequate road and
airfield infrastructure, maintenance difficulties, and
problems of resupply by foreign manufacturers all serve
to constrain adventurism. Moreover, external engagements
would undoubtedly give rise to domestic instabilities
which the military establishments would have difficulty
coping with simultaneously. All of these constraints
were made profoundly evident in the Argentine war with
Great Britain in 1982 and will likely receive much closer
attention in the future.

Like the east coast countries and Mexico, the west
coast South American countries are forging increasingly
strong ties to other world regions. Peru and Ecuador have
made successful overtures to Japanese investors, while
Chile has been able to replace trade lost to the United
States during the Allende government with European markets. The Andean countries have been particularly strong
supporters of the concept of ideological pluralism as
demonstrated by their support in 1979 in the Organization
of American States (OAS) for political change in Nicaragua,
and their continued promotion of economic "Latin Americanism" as represented by the Latin American Economic
System (SELA). As is described in a subsequent section,
the west coast countries have been at the forefront of
efforts to turn the forces of the inter-American system
itself away from military and ideological issues and toward economic development goals. In recent years military
governments in the region are increasingly demoralized
and enjoy less legitimacy as a result of their inability
to deal with domestic problems. The trend begun in Peru
and Ecuador to transfer government to civilian authorities
may be repeated elsewhere, but is likely to be accompanied
by less predictable political and economic decision making
as political leaders seek to be responsive to divergent
interests. Both domestic and intraregional tensions may
be compounded.

Because of political differences over the past decade
and political and economic change within the region itself,
the United States has diminished leverage with the west
coast countries. Its influence is now exercised principally through international lending agencies, the Export-
Import Bank, and other agencies providing long-term aid to
underwrite economic development in the region. At the
same time, other Latin American powers, Venezuela and Brazil particularly, have extended their own contacts with,
and sought to establish leadership of, the west coast
countries.

The factors influencing U.S. security interests in
west coast South America can be summarized as follows:

● The United States has less vital interests in west
  coast South America than in other regions of Latin
  America because the region is more isolated from
  external events, has less economic importance in
  the world, and has less (though still significant)
  economic importance to this country.

● The United States' main security interest in the
  subregion is in the availability of port facilities for global war contingencies, particularly
  in the event the Panama Canal could not be used.

- There is real potential for conflict among west coast countries or between Argentina and Chile. The consequences of such conflict would be of serious concern to the United States.

- West coast countries represent an important political bloc within Latin America and have been leaders in efforts to disengage Latin America politically, militarily, and economically from the United States. The possibilities for such disengagement are limited, however.

- Despite the relatively slight security importance of the west coast countries to the United States, continued efforts to improve the quality of U.S. relations with them are important for future hemispheric cooperation.

LATIN AMERICAN SECURITY INTERESTS

In contrast with the United States' global security perspective, until very recently the Latin American perspectives have been narrowly focused at the domestic or subregional levels. Latin American definitions of security concerns and of military mission have tended to emphasize nationalism, political-ideological conformity, and economic growth and development. The traditional military mission of defense of territory has been less important, but has been used to justify acquisition of increasingly sophisticated arms and development of indigenous arms production capabilities that lessen dependence on foreign suppliers. Nuclear energy programs undertaken for economic reasons have acquired political justification as well.

The United States' ability to pursue its interests successfully in Latin America depends on the degree to which those interests coincide with the interests of the Latin American countries. As Latin American nations develop politically and economically, the coincidence of security interests appears increasingly narrow. Nevertheless, the United States has a profound interest in maintaining the close working relationship it has developed in the past with Latin American leaders even though the bases of relations may be different. This section examines the different emphases and changing focus of Latin American security concerns and relates them to future U.S. policy concerns.

Economic and Political Dimensions of
Latin American Security Interests

In the 1960s and 1970s, development and counterinsurgency received the Latin American political and military leaders' greatest attention. In the 1960s guerrilla and terrorist forces with both domestic bases and support from abroad, posed real threats to established Latin American political systems, particularly those in South America. Beginning in 1964, a generation of modernizing, authoritarian military governments came to power to deal with the problems of political instability and of political and economic development. By 1968, in South America only Venezuela and Colombia still had civilian governments. The counterinsurgency efforts undertaken by these military governments were successful for the most part. The Latin American political scene of the 1970s was considerably more stable than it had been in the 1960s. Governments began to focus on development and modernization.

The pattern in the 1980s appears to be for a return to elected civilian governments. While some degree of political instability can be predicted with confidence in the current process of political liberalization, many Latin American military governments appear to have diminishing confidence in their ability to solve national political and economic problems. Slowly, but steadily, nearly every country in the region but Chile has begun the process of political opening.

The authoritarian regimes were considerably less successful in mobilizing economic development than they had been in controlling insurgency. Brazil experienced remarkable growth, but the pattern was not repeated either in Peru (Stepan, 1978) or in Argentina. Chile experienced a dramatic recovery from its near collapse during the Allende period but by 1980 was beginning to show signs of serious dislocations once again. Development progress was erratic in both Ecuador and Bolivia, and the economic results and political and social costs of military rule in those countries are yet to be assessed. In Uruguay the quality of life deteriorated under military governments. In Central America, emphasis traditionally was placed on authority rather than development, and the resistance to military dictatorships that began to emerge in the late 1970s recalled the pattern of conflict in South America in the 1950s and 1960s.

Military Dimensions of Latin American
Security Interests

In spite of the attention that Latin American military leaders have focused on development and internal security, it would be an error not to recognize their

continuing concern with political-military image abroad
and with the political-military balance in the hemisphere.

National prestige is an important determinant of arms
acquisitions. Beginning in the 1960s, Latin American
countries have sought to acquire military capabilities
that are commensurate with their perceptions of their political and economic development achievements. They have
increasingly had the industrial and financial wherewithal
to acquire modern hardware and technology on the world
market. In seeking to bolster their national images,
Latin American military regimes increasingly lobby for
state-of-the-art equipment that previously had been denied
to them. Competition between the world arms suppliers
means that countries willing to agree to suppliers' terms
or to pay cash for weapons are often able to get the
equipment they want, even when its appropriateness is
questionable in the regional military context. Indeed,
Pierre (1982) notes that "Latin America is the most competitive market, in commercial rather than political
terms, in the world."

While the prestige factor is important in determining
arms purchases, Latin American countries also pay close
attention to the military balance with their bordering
neighbors, which they have traditionally perceived as
their major external "enemies." Unresolved disputes over
border demarcations and regional rivalries for preeminence
are longstanding issues in the region (see Dominguez,
1979). An examination of Latin American strategic writing, expressed in the language of geopolitics, reflects
this narrow regional security focus (see Child, 1979, for
a thorough review of Latin American geopolitical bibliography).

Within the region, Brazil and Argentina have especially well-developed bodies of literature reflecting
military strategic thought. This literature is dominated
by the writing of one or two authors--Gugliamelli (Estra-
tegia, various issues) in the case of Argentina, and Golbery (1957, 1967) and Meira Mattos (1975, 1977) in the
case of Brazil. Brazilian geopolitical writing has traditionally emphasized the continental base of Brazil's projection as a regional power. Only recently has attention
been given to Brazil's maritime projection in the South
Atlantic. In contrast, Argentine writing has been more
externally oriented, focusing on Argentina's maritime position in the South Atlantic and Antarctica and on the
perceived threat from Brazil. Similarly, Chilean geopolitical writing, although substantially less developed
than that of Brazil or Argentina, focuses on Chile's maritime projection and on Chile's role in the South Pacific
and in the control of the Straits of Magellan. Chile's
principal rival for preeminence in the southern cone is

perceived to be Argentina, although in fact Chile's armed
forces are situated to fend off land attack from Peru to
the north. Peru, which has a strong military academic
tradition, has concentrated primarily on social and economic development issues, while nevertheless preparing for
conflict with either Chile or Ecuador. By comparison with
its neighbors, Peru is the most heavily armed force in the
region. Other military establishments in Latin America
have written less about their perceived aspirations on the
continent but nevertheless have concentrated on building
up their defense capabilities against their neighbors (see
Nolde, 1980).

Latin American Arms Acquisitions and Arms Production

Latin American countries made major arms purchases in
the late 1960s and early 1970s, when strong overall economic growth facilitated cash purchases of sophisticated
weapons in the European marketplace. While their initial
preferences had been for U.S. weapons, congressional and
executive restrictions on the sale of sophisticated materiel caused the Latin Americans to turn to more willing
suppliers. Along with making overseas purchases, several
countries began to develop their own arms production capabilities. Brazil and Argentina have developed domestically designed weapons. Brazil now ranks among the top
five Third World suppliers of weapons to the world market.
Chile, Venezuela, Peru, and Colombia also have begun to
develop production capabilities through both research and
licensing agreements with other suppliers.

Arms purchases and indigenous arms production in
Latin America since the late 1960s, when first orders were
placed by newly installed military-authoritarian governments, reflected efforts (1) to replace outmoded and
costly-to-maintain weapons of 1960s and earlier vintage,
(2) to acquire military capabilities commensurate with
each country's growing economic and political capabilities, and (3) to minimize and eventually eliminate dependence on external suppliers that are increasingly regarded as unreliable and likely to use weapons dependence
as instruments of political leverage. Indigenous production capabilities also have been viewed as a logical spin-
off of industrial development in other areas such as
steel, automobiles, and electronics. They are justified
on grounds of potential foreign exchange savings, as well
as for the prestige that accrues to independent producers.
In addition, Latin Americans view arms production agreements, particularly joint production and licensing agreements, as avenues to acquisition of the advanced technology necessary for further industrial development in other
areas. In spite of the emphasis on security, in most

cases Latin American production lines serve both civilian
and military needs, with the former predominating.

Arms Acquisitions. The Appendix to this book con-
tains tables describing the kinds, origin, and year of
acquisition of the major weapons systems held by the major
South American militaries. A comparison of the data permits an overview of the comparative military strengths,
as well as their acquisition patterns over the past two
decades.

The core of each Latin American country's military
arsenal has been, and for some continues to be, U.S.
equipment of World War II and Korean vintage acquired
under the military assistance programs (MAP) in the 1950s.
The MAP program equiped armies with essential items to ensure their mobility and developed small navies and air
forces. The military roles for which the equipment was
intended were (1) support to U.S. efforts, (2) self-
defense efforts, and (3) internal security. Beginning in
the 1960s this equipment became increasingly difficult to
acquire and to maintain, and countries began to "trade up"
(Einaudi, 1970). Emphasis initially was given to replacing equipment with comparable materiel of a later generation. Later, Latin Americans began to engage in a quali-
tative upgrading of both air and naval arms. Beginning in
the late 1960s and continuing through the first half of
the 1970s, orders were placed for state-of-the-art aircraft and modern ships and submarines as well as more sophisticated land vehicles and air and ground defense
systems.

In the mid-1960s several countries, including Brazil
and Peru, approached the United States to indicate interest in the supersonic F5 airplane. The United States,
under heavy pressure from the Congress, refused the sales
on the grounds that Latin American countries did not need
such an advanced aircraft. The Latin Americans persisted,
however, and made their purchases in Europe. The French
sold their Mirage to Brazil and subsequently to nearly
every other Latin American country. After long negotiations, Peru purchased 36 Soviet SU22s, the first Soviet
sale in the region outside of Cuba (see Pierre, 1982, for
a discussion of the impact of U.S. arms sales restraint in
the Latin American and the global context). In 1981 Latin
American countries again challenged U.S. assumptions of
the need for advanced weaponry in the region. Venezuela,
a close regional friend and oil supplier, sought and was
granted authority to purchase 24 state-of-the-art F16
fighters. Peru approached the U.S. government somewhat
later with a similar request, but was denied. The Peru-
vians decided to purchase the French Mirage 2000 instead.

During the period of U.S. arms sales restraint, the United States' share of the Latin American arms declined from 35 percent in 1963 to only 13 percent in the 1975-1979 period (Arms Control and Disarmament Agency (ACDA), 1973, 1982). By the end of the 1970s, both the Soviet Union, with 20 percent of the market, and France, with 14 percent, topped the United States in sales to Latin America. During their decade-long arms buildup, the Latin Americans acquired 23 surface combatant ships, 25 submarines, 165 supersonic aircraft, and 895 surface-to-air missiles (ACDA, 1982). The purchases served both to deter neighbors' possible hostility and, more importantly, as symbols of national sovereignty and independence.

Two serious problems resulted from the Latin American pattern of purchases. First, as noted in the earlier discussion of Brazilian and Argentine readiness, the broad range of suppliers created a series of maintenance and logistics problems for the Latin Americans because of the large and costly inventory of spare parts that must be stocked, and different mechanical operation procedures with which maintenance personnel must be familiar. Second, the still-vintage character of much of the Latin American military force created maintenance and logistics problems of a different nature. Spare parts continued to be difficult to find, especially for the vintage aircraft, and maintenance became increasingly time-consuming and costly. Parts were frequently pirated from one craft to another so that what looked like a powerful and flexible force on paper was far from that when tested in actual performance. Long after the Latin Americans began to upgrade their inventories, Argentina discovered that both of these problems seriously hampered its air and naval capabilities during the Falkland Islands conflict (Scheina, 1982, and English, 1983).

The lessons of the Falklands war were not lost on the Latin American countries. They had been content with slow transition from vintage 1950s equipment to 1970s equipment just short of state-of-the-art. Moreover, in the latter half of the 1970s the military establishments accepted the economic constraints imposed by inflation and deteriorating markets and postponed purchases. Argentina's loss of its 1950s vintage Canberra and Skyhawk aircraft and the success it experienced with the French Super Etendard airplane and Exocet missiles clearly will motivate further purchases of those items. Argentina's experience with its two modern submarines was also instructive. Without the sophisticated anti-submarine warfare (ASW) electronics that suppliers have refused them, the submarines were not able to play an effective role in the war. The Argentine experience may prompt Brazil, Chile, and other countries to examine their own inventories and develop new shopping lists of weapons.

Argentina is reported to have invested several billion
dollars in replacing lost equipment with more modern items
items. Finances permitting, there is likely to be a new
round of Latin American orders for sophisticated equipment and electronics in the mid-1980s. One analyst suggests that the Latin American navies must conclude that
fleets of two or three submarines are inadequate and will
opt for larger submarine components for their navies.
They may begin to plan for a nuclear submarine complement
for the future (Scheina, 1983). They will likely seek a
greater anti-submarine capability. Civilian governments
that have recently replaced authoritarian military regimes
will have to be sensitive to military demands for more
adequate equipment.

Indigenous Arms Production. In addition to upgrading
their forces through purchase of sophisticated materiel
from developed countries, a number of countries, notably
Brazil, Argentina, and to a lesser extent Chile and Venezuela, have developed indigenous production capabilities
to supply their lower level technology needs. Latin
America's indigenous arms industries started in the World
War II period when Brazil and other countries all sought
to assure themselves of an independent supply of ammunition and arms as a hedge against involvement in the mounting war threat. Brazil established its war materials department in 1937 to manufacture ammunition, and this
industrial base expanded over the years to include small
arms production and, later, military vehicles. The Brazilian automotive industry was initially conceived during
the 1930s effort to ensure independence of supply of military vehicles in the event of emergency.

Thus, concern for the security of supplies from distant sources and, beginning in the 1960s, growing nationalism combined with industrial world restrictions on sales
of modern equipment prompted Brazil, Argentina, and other
states to develop indigenous production capabilities for
aircraft, missiles, and armored vehicles and ships. In
1979, the Stockholm International Peace Research Institution (SIPRI) reported that Brazil was the fifth largest
Third World arms supplier after Israel, Iran, Jordan, and
Libya. Brazil also produced more different types of major weapons than any other Third World country. Brazil
and Argentina together held licenses to produce more than
17 different European weapons systems in their domestic
factories and shipyards and held several indigenous designs (SIPRI, 1978). Brazil has found its aircraft and
armored cars to be particularly attractive to other Third
World countries because of their easy maintenance and low
price tags. Major sales have been made to Libya, Algeria,
Nigeria, Iraq, and several South American countries.
Total Brazilian arms exports amounted to $24 million in
1975 and increased to $100 million by 1978. By 1982

Brazil's arms export industry was able to generate about $500 million in foreign exchange for the country (Latin America Regional Report). In contrast, Argentina, which also has strong indigenous production capabilities, does not export its production.

The prospects for continued development of the indigenous arms industries in Brazil and other Latin American countries are excellent. The domestic industries receive considerable government financial support, enjoy an active government-supported marketing apparatus, and have developed systems with applications tailored to the needs of smaller, less sophisticated forces in Third World countries. In addition, the indigenous weapons industry satisfies the desire for greater supply independence from the major powers. Licensed production agreements with European suppliers are expected to provide Argentina, Brazil, Chile, Venezuela, and other countries with the necessary technology to support increasingly sophisticated weapons development programs in the future.

The same economic necessities that have led European manufacturers to sell to Third World countries stimulate Latin Americans to sell abroad. Brazil has set the example. None of the Latin American countries has a domestic military establishment large enough to support an indigenous arms industry alone. Additional markets are needed to realize economies of scale and reduce the costs of expanding procurements. The logical targets of opportunity for Latin American arms sales will continue to be the other developing countries which do not need the ultra-sophisticated mechanical and electronics packages that increasingly characterize the weapons systems of the major powers. Brazil and Argentina have both exploited the surrounding Latin American market for armored vehicles, and small aircraft and trainers. Brazil has recently been criticized for its heavy dependence on politically undependable Middle Eastern markets such as Libya and Iraq. Both countries regard their transactions as purely commercial and resent efforts to impose restrictions.

Arms acquisitions in Latin America will respond to domestic political and economic realities rather than to external pressures in the future. It is unlikely that any of the countries presently having indigenous arms industries will relax their emphasis in this area. However, it will be important to make sober assessments of the contributions these industries make to military power projection capability or to real arms independence. Competition among developed world arms industries will provide Latin American militaries with a wide choice of more sophisticated weaponry in the future. Restrictive arms policies such as the United States followed in the 1960s and 1970s will not succeed in limiting arms flows, and rather will

limit U.S. access to and influence with Latin American
military leaders. Future U.S. arms policies will have to
deal realistically with the competition from the international arms market and with indigenous production ambitions. More accessible financing of U.S. arms purchases,
co-production arrangements with selected Latin American
industries, and joint long-range planning of military
needs would all contribute to strengthening U.S.-Latin
American security relations.

Trends in Nuclear Development

Argentina, Brazil, Mexico, and Chile all have installed nuclear power reactors and have major plans for
developing indigenous nuclear power programs in the coming
years. Nearly every other Latin American country has an
active nuclear research program and pilot reactors operating or under construction. As in armaments policy, the
major Latin American countries have resented efforts on
the part of developed, nuclear powers to control and
supervise their acquisition of nuclear technology. Of the
four countries with near-nuclear status in the region,
only Mexico is a signatory to the 1968 Non-Proliferation
Treaty (NPT). Chile is not a party to the Tlatelolco
Treaty that creates a nuclear weapons free zone in Latin
America.

The United States was the principal collaborator in
the development of Latin American nuclear research programs beginning in the 1950s with the Atoms for Peace program. Initially, Argentina was the only Latin American
country to decide to develop a fully independent nuclear
capability without developed-country collaboration. The
Argentine nuclear program is presently the most sophisticated in the region. It is thought that Argentina is near
to having the ability to explode a nuclear device should
it choose to do so. Until 1982, when Brazil's first reactor at Angra dos Reis came into operation, Argentina was
the only country in the region with an operating power reactor. Its program remains far more developed than that
of any other country, including Brazil.

In spite of early close U.S. association with Latin
American nuclear programs, the trend, since the late
1960s, has been in the direction of (1) movement away from
cooperation with the United States; (2) more bilateral
nuclear cooperation among Latin American countries; and
(3) growing instances of cooperation between Latin American and non-Latin American countries (Reddick, 1982). The
major countries in Latin America have demonstrated a clear
preference for working with European suppliers rather than
American suppliers in the nuclear area. They blame U.S.
policies, beginning with promotion of the NPT in the late
1960s and subsequently in passage of the Nuclear

Non-Proliferation Act (NNPA) in 1978, for discouraging U.S.-Latin American cooperation in nuclear energy research and development. Both of these instruments are regarded as promoting policies of technological denial and supply dependence and have generated resentment in the region. European countries have been willing to accept Latin American de facto agreements to full scope safeguards under the International Atomic Energy Agency (IAEA) rather than demand de-jure acceptance prior to selling equipment or fuel. West Germany has been the principal benefactor at the United States' expense, for Germany's nuclear industry won contracts for both Argentina's and Brazil's second- and third-generation reactors. British, French, Swiss, Dutch, and Spanish suppliers are also active in various phases of Latin America's nuclear program. In 1981 Argentina turned to the Soviet Union for heavy water supplies when it could not reach accord with U.S. negotiators on this issue.

The West Germans have also supported establishing nuclear power support industries in both Argentina and Brazil that will ultimately permit both countries to provide the equipment to other Latin American countries. Both Argentina and Brazil have established agreements for cooperation in the nuclear energy field with Peru, Bolivia, Chile, Ecuador, Venezuela, Colombia, Uruguay, and Paraguay. Brazil, along with Argentina, was involved with Iran's nuclear program prior to the fall of the Shah. In 1980 Brazil signed a broad nuclear agreement with Iraq that called for collaboration in the development of the Iraqi nuclear energy program. The agreement raised concerns that Brazil might be led to transfer some of the sensitive technology it hoped to gain from its purchases from West Germany. Argentina also has cooperative agreements outside the hemisphere with Libya, India, and South Korea. In 1980 Argentina and Brazil signed a joint agreement for nuclear cooperation on the historic occasion of exchanges of visits between presidents Videla and Figueiredo. The agreement envisages extensive cooperation and exchange of know-how between the two countries, and, if fully implemented, could have an important effect on their historic nuclear rivalry. At the same time, it lays the groundwork for the emergence of a nuclear industry complex that will be fully independent of U.S. control and, as a result, fairly insensitive to U.S. pressures.

Latin American countries defend their rapid acquisition of nuclear energy know-how as an integral part of their efforts to solve their energy supply problems for the future, as well as an undeniable sovereign right and responsibility. Latin America will continue to face dramatically rising demands for energy over the next several decades. Most Latin American countries can provide a substantial portion of their energy requirements through domestic oil and gas production (Brazil and the Caribbean

basin countries are the exceptions). Hydroelectric and
coal power will be major energy sources for other countries. In the mid-1970s nuclear energy was regarded as a
necessary component of Latin American countries' planned
energy mix. In 1978 it was predicted that by 1985 more
than 5 percent of Latin America's energy would be derived
from nuclear power plants (Reddick, 1981).

With the substantial delays in construction, cost
overruns, and growing recognition that nuclear energy is
not the cheap source of abundant power it was once thought
to be, many Latin American countries will follow Brazil's
lead and likely delay heavy investment in their nuclear
industries. Nevertheless, in spite of a growing recognition that nuclear energy will not be a major source of
power in the near future, nearly all Latin American countries are proceeding with reactor development programs.
Their reasons are similar to those offered for pursuing
development of steel industries and acquisition of sophisticated weapons--nationalism and national prestige.

Because the Latin American countries have resisted
nuclear supplier countries' efforts to impose restrictions
on the technology available to them, and their refusal to
sign the NPT, which most believed denied them access to a
technology necessary for their full and rapid development,
it is feared that each program ultimately will result in
development of nuclear weapons capabilities and the subsequent acquisition of nuclear weapons arsenals within the
region. Until recently, the undisguised competition between Argentina and Brazil contributed to such concern.

Since 1969, the Treaty for the Prohibition of Nuclear
Weapons in Latin America (Tlatelolco Treaty) has been the
most important instrument for assuring non-proliferation
of nuclear weapons in Latin America. The treaty requires
that Latin American countries pledge to keep their territories completely free of nuclear weapons and that they
neither develop, test, nor import such weapons. No foreign bases are permitted in the region, and the nuclear
weapon states and states with territorial interest in the
Americas have been solicited to sign protocols binding
them to the same terms subscribed by the Latin American
countries. Twenty-two Latin American countries are full
parties to the treaty, while Argentina, Brazil, Chile, and
Cuba are not. Brazil and Chile have signed and ratified
the treaty, but do not regard it to be in effect until all
parties have signed and ratified. Argentina announced its
intention to ratify in 1977, but has delayed that action.
Some have suspected that Argentina hopes to have a full-
scale nuclear program in place before it joins the treaty.
Full implementation of the treaty will occur when Argentina ratifies the treaty, when Cuba signs and ratifies it,
and when France ratifies Protocol I. The United States

ratified Protocol I in 1982 after protracted debate in which the regional non-proliferation treaty became enmeshed in discussion of the strategic arms limitation (SALT) treaties.

Most Latin American countries deny that they have any intention to develop nuclear weapons and most agree with the interpretation that the spirit if not the letter of the Tlatelolco Treaty even precludes explosion of a peaceful nuclear device. However, both Brazil and Argentina have stated publicly that their interpretations of the treaty view peaceful uses of nuclear energy, including explosions, to fall within the range of activities permitted under the treaty.

Until recently, supplier countries, particularly the United States, have concentrated their efforts on controlling access to nuclear technology, particularly state-of-the-art technology. In the 1970s, however, the economics of the nuclear industry became such that supplier countries were forced to make sales abroad in order to support their own indigenous nuclear industries. The Latin American countries, notably Argentina and Brazil, were among the principal beneficiaries of the competition.

Because national pride is so deeply involved in Latin America's development of its independent nuclear capabilities, there is little to be gained by seeking to limit or control access to nuclear technology. The Latins resented such efforts and became more determined to develop their own capabilities in an unsafeguarded environment. Many argue that the best opportunities to engage the Latin American countries in nonproliferation activities is to cooperate with their programs and enlist their support in regulating the international nuclear regime. Reddick (1981) suggests an agenda for discussion that could respond to both U.S. concerns about proliferation and Latin American desires for access to technology. The agenda would include (1) full implementation of the Tlatelolco Treaty; (2) development of a consensus among supplier nations on the transfer of technology, protection of materials and defenses against terrorism; (3) cooperation with Latin American countries in fuel cycle development in a regional context (like Euratom) if possible; and (4) support for the development of regional institutions to regulate and coordinate development and implementation of safeguards and technical assistance.

Such a proposal concedes the inevitability of transfer of nuclear technology and the development of nuclear weapons production capabilities among a number of Third World countries in the future. It presumes that nationalism will prompt many countries to acquire weapons technology. However, it also recognizes that few, if any,

Latin American countries are anxious to engage in a regional nuclear weapons arms race, or are anxious to expose their nuclear sectors to accident or terrorist actions. Under such circumstances, the prospects for cooperation among nuclear and near-nuclear countries should be excellent and offer the base for the development of international nuclear regulatory regimes with which developed and near-nuclear countries will feel comfortable. With the Tlatelolco Treaty in place and given the relative absence of conflict potential in Latin America as compared with the Middle East, or the Indian Subcontinent, Latin America continues to be the world region in which constructive efforts to establish a nonproliferation regime hold greatest promise.

Any expansion of the group of nuclear-capable countries threatens the stability and viability of the existing regime of international nuclear controls and safeguards. Nevertheless, exploration of nuclear technology and development of nuclear expertise is very likely inevitable among advanced developing countries, including the major powers in Latin America. The United States no longer can control the transfer of fuels or technology to these countries. Policies of denial tend to reduce the United States' voice in the internal decision making of countries acquiring nuclear expertise. Yet it is in the United States' clear interest to maximize its influence over nuclear policy choices of its neighbors and to seek to persuade them against proliferation and promote their maximum responsibility and restraint in the nuclear area.

LATIN AMERICAN INTERESTS IN THE INTER-
AMERICAN COLLECTIVE SECURITY SYSTEM

Because of their increasing political independence, growing economic capabilities, and diverging security interests, Latin American countries are no longer comfortable with the traditional framework within which inter-American security relations have been considered. Latin Americans want a larger share in regional decision making; less U.S. interference in purely Latin American political, economic, and security affairs; and greater U.S. commitment to regional economic development as a quid pro quo for continued close security relations. At the same time, the Latin Americans do not want to sever relations with either the United States or with the inter-American system. They recognize the benefits of the U.S. strategic umbrella and continue to seek U.S. training and assistance. They recognize that relationships within the framework of the inter-American system have costs but also allow them maximum opportunity to exact concessions from the United States.

Atkins (1977) describes the inter-American system as
developing in four phases during which political, economic,
and military priorities have shifted several times. A review of that evolution provides a better understanding of
current dissatisfactions with U.S. leadership of the system.

The first phase of the regional system spanned the
years from 1889, the First International Conference of the
American States, to 1928, the sixth conference. The
United States was primarily interested in expanding commercial relations with Latin America and secondarily in
establishing procedures for the pacific settlement of regional disputes. The Latin American states shared these
interests, but viewed Pan Americanism foremost as a way
to achieve security against outside intervention, first
from Europe and then from the United States itself.

The second phase was characterized by general harmony
of interests and spanned the period from the late 1920s to
World War II. The principal developments involved the
progressive acceptance of nonintervention by the United
States between 1930 and 1936, and the building of regional
security arrangements between 1938 and 1945.

The third phase, from 1945 to the mid-1960s, was
characterized by a return to divergent goals. The United
States and Latin America reversed their views as to the
purpose of the inter-American system. The United States
pursued primarily mutual security goals in the context of
a global cold war, while the Latin Americans viewed regional organization essentially as a means to promote economic goals.

The fourth phase of the inter-American system's evolution began in the mid-1960s and has been characterized
by a growing Latin American assertiveness within the system for a redefinition of hemispheric concerns. The Latin
Americans increasingly have challenged the U.S. concept of
a hemispheric "anti-Communist alliance." Through the
1970s security issues became less important to members who
preferred to focus on economic development and openly expressed dissatisfaction with U.S. regional dominance and
impatience over the issue of Cuba.

Latin American complaints about the inter-American
system tend to reflect differences in emphasis, not a
preference for abandoning the system itself. Since the
mid-1960s, Latin Americans have been seeking to revise the
juridical structure of the system to strengthen its economic and social functions and deemphasize political and
security issues. Atkins notes that the Latin Americans
have long felt that their economic and social welfare was
being neglected by an overemphasis on hemispheric peace
and security. Amendments to the Organization of American

States (OAS) charter submitted in 1967 specifically down-
graded security considerations by downgrading the security-
related agencies and upgrading the economic and social
agencies. A 1973 OAS General Assembly resolution referred
to the inter-American system as "outmoded" and "unreal-
istic," and sought proposals for its restructuring. In
1975 the Protocol of San Jose reiterated the concept of
ideological pluralism within the hemisphere stating as one
of the purposes "to reaffirm and strengthen the principle
of non-intervention as well as the right of all states to
choose freely their political, economic, and social organization" (Atkins, 1977b). At the same time, the Latin
Americans succeeded, over U.S. opposition, in including
amendments to the charter and to the Rio Treaty establishing the concept of collective economic security for development, with Peru noting that "security is founded in development and without development there is no security"
(Atkins, 1977b).

More recently the Latin American countries resisted
U.S. leadership when they rejected the U.S. call for collective action by the OAS membership to intervene in the
Nicaraguan revolution. The Organization membership gave
public support to democratic principles and elections in
El Salvador, but declined to play an official role in
bringing that conflict to an end. During the Falkland
Islands crisis of 1982, the OAS convened an emergency
meeting of its council of ministers but did not play a
decisive role in the conflict. U.S. support for Great
Britain in the conflict presented the most serious challenge of all to hemispheric relations as the Latins chose
to interpret the U.S. action as abandoning its commitment
to the region and to the Rio Treaty.

In sum, in the recent ranking of Latin American security concerns, economics have taken precedence. In
part, this ordering results from Latin America's long isolation from the crossroads of external conflict, many
countries' recent successes in dealing with domestic political instability, and their increasing awareness of the
importance of economic development as the basis for political and economic growth and stability. In part, too,
the Latin American position reflects disagreement with the
U.S.-dominated security policy that has resulted in only
sporadic U.S. attention to Latin American problems that is
perceived to place U.S. interests in Latin America subor-
dinate to U.S. global interests and that restricts Latin
American options for independent action.

While the Latin American countries have indicated
their disagreements with the structuring of priorities in
the inter-American system, they have not rescinded their
fundamental commitment to collective security if and when
a real threat to their interests is perceived. They

recognize the benefits of the U.S. security umbrella and find continued dialogue in the context of the inter-American system useful for pursuing their development goals. Atkins notes that the system's framework of consultation allows them to "constrain the United States while extracting rewards from it" (Atkins, 1977b). At the same time, the Latin Americans resent the need to bargain for concessions they regard as critical to their own national interests.

A major challenge to the United States in reconstructing its relations within the hemisphere is to be more responsive to Latin American demands from the relationship while at the same time eliciting more responsible participation by the Latin Americans in dealing with regional security, economic, and political problems. In spite of their formal participation in regional institutions, the Latin American nations often have not used those institutions constructively. The United States has at times abused its leadership role in the region. Conflicting interests may make the regional forum less attractive to Latin American leaders in the future. Yet it is increasingly important to the United States as a framework within which to assess and hopefully influence Latin American support for U.S. positions in the region and on global issues. Whereas in the past the United States could often assume general Latin American support for U.S. positions, such support will more likely be determined an issue at a time in the future. A rigorous inter-American system can facilitate consensus-building.

The Falkland Islands Crisis: Challenge to Inter-American Security Relations

On April 2, 1982, Argentina invaded the Falkland Islands--or Islas Malvinas--, achieved the surrender of the 18-man British marine garrison there, and announced its intention to annex the Malvinas as the twenty-third political department of the Republic of Argentina. Great Britain, which had ruled the Falklands as a colony for nearly 150 years, immediately mobilized the largest naval task force to be organized in 25 years to retake the Falklands. Britain successfully called upon the United Nations Security Council to adopt a resolution condemning Argentina's use of force to resolve the long-standing dispute over the sovereignty of the Falklands. It also imposed an economic embargo on Argentina that affected Argentina's exports to the European Common Market, and large financial holdings in British and European banks. Following Britain's lead, the members of the European Common Market took the unprecedented step of imposing a total ban on Argentine imports, thus depriving Argentina of about $10 million in Western European trade each week (New York Times, April 11, 1982).

Argentina did not enjoy similar support. Latin American countries in general supported Argentina's claim to sovereignty over the islands, although many were uncomfortable with Argentina's use of force to assert that sovereignty. Peru and Venezuela were the only countries to give strong support, both moral and logistic, to Argentina in the conflict. The United States initially sought to play the intermediary role, recognizing that it had friends on both sides of the dispute.

By the time hostilities ended, Argentina had lost over 1,000 men, a cruiser, a submarine, from 3 to 9 lesser ships, between 19 jets, 1 helicopter, and 74 planes and 7 helicopters. In contrast, the British suffered 243 dead or missing and lost 2 destroyers, 2 frigates, a civilian supply ship and 2 landing ships, 10 other ships, and 28 aircraft (the Washington Post, June 16, 1982).

The Argentine Air Force performed well during the conflict. In contrast, the Navy, which, having gotten the original force onto the Malvinas, withdrew to the sidelines following the sinking of the cruiser General Belgrano. The Argentine Army proved unable to handle even the rudimentary problems of occupation. Overall, the Argentine military was disgraced both by its undertaking the adventure and by its performance throughout. Ultimately the Falklands adventure brought about the collapse of the Argentine military government as an exasperated and embarrassed population gradually took stock of the military high command's poor handling of the crisis.

Sovereignty over the Falkland Islands has been disputed by several countries. The islands were first "discovered" by the British in 1592, but no one landed there until 1690, and no British settlement was established until 1765. A French settlement was established in the islands in 1764, but when Spain protested the settlements, the French obligingly ceded their colony to the Spanish. First Spain and then, after its independence from Spain, Argentina made efforts to oust the British and assert claims over the territory, but did not actually establish a settlement in the Falklands until 1830. In January 1833, the Argentine garrison left the islands, which from that day were administered as a colony by Great Britain.

Argentina again began to protest British control over the islands immediately after World War II, partly in conjunction with increasing United Nations activity and support in behalf of decolonization. Argentina rejected a proposal to refer the dispute to the International Court of Justice in 1954. In 1965 United Nations Resolution 2065 passed, inviting Argentina and the United Kingdom to proceed without delay with the negotiations to find a peaceful solution to the problem of the Falklands.

Preliminary talks at that time established the clear lines
of enduring differences between the two countries.

After years of unproductive discussion, in February
1981 Argentina and United Kingdom representatives met at
the United Nations and Argentina formally rejected the
British proposal (based on decisions by the Falkland Islands residents) that the status quo be frozen for 25
years. Another meeting followed in February 1982 with no
progress in resolving the dispute. This prompted the Argentine foreign minister to issue a statement saying that
"unless the Falkland Islands issue was resolved quickly,
the Argentine government would 'put an end' to the negotiations and consider itself free to choose a procedure
which better suited its interest." Argentina chose to
take the islands by force.

The United States was torn in a number of different
directions in reacting to the Falklands invasion. On the
one hand, through the many rounds of negotiation on the
sovereignty issue, the United States had assumed the position that it "had no position" and encouraged the parties
to work out their differences. On the other hand, the
United States, as well as Britain and Argentina, were all
signatories to the United Nations charter and therefore
subscribe to its cardinal principle of non-use-of-force
to resolve disputes. Moreover, Britain was the United
States' closest ally in a region far more important strategically and geopolitically than the South Atlantic.
However, Argentina recently had been the target of special
attention from a U.S. government seeking to rebuild a
strong hemispheric security alliance. Responding to these
different pressures, the United States Secretary of State
engaged in a 20-day round of shuttle diplomacy. The ulti-
mate failure of that diplomacy and subsequent U.S. material, as well as moral, support for the British raised
serious questions about U.S. commitment to the inter-
American "alliance" and forecasts of the imminent collapse
of the hemispheric system.

Argentina sought to invoke the Rio Treaty to mobilize
regional support behind its military effort and to neu-
tralize the United States. However, the Treaty had dealt
with the Falklands sovereignty dispute only in that during the drafting Argentina had expressed its challenge to
British sovereignty and asserted its own claim (some say
for the first time) to the South Georgia and South Sand-
wich Islands. The United States took the position at the
Rio Conference that the Treaty had no effect on the sovereignty or status of any territories in the region.

The Organization of American States also skirted the
question of Rio Treaty involvement. On April 29, 1982,
the OAS passed a resolution supporting Argentina's claim

to sovereignty over the Falkland Islands, but at the same
time calling upon Argentina and Britain to comply with
U.N. Resolution 302, which called on Argentina to withdraw
from the islands; on both sides to exercise restraint and
to engage in negotiations to find a peaceful resolution
of the dispute. The OAS resolution underscored the dilemma felt by many Latin Americans who held little love
or respect for Argentina and its repressive military government but who were loathe to engage in public display
of non-solidarity within the region.

Many thought that United States support for the British in the disputes would result in the collapse of the
inter-American system and signal an end to the myth of
U.S.-Latin American commonality of interests. However,
behind the rhetoric of Latin American solidarity on the
legitimacy of Argentina's claim to the islands there was
very little agreement. While the Latins were forced to
confront the bald demonstration of U.S. foreign policy
priorities, few were genuinely surprised at the U.S.
choice. Most Latin Americans adhered to the strict construction of the U.N. Charter's prohibition against use of
force and recognized the dangerous precedent that Argentina's use of force in the dispute could set for the region. Moreover, the Argentine military regime enjoyed
relatively little support elsewhere in Latin America, especially among those countries embarked on a return to
democracy. Chile feared that Argentine success in the
Falklands crisis would translate sooner or later to further difficulties in the Beagle Channel. Brazil was
anxious lest Argentine adventurism be turned into greater
competition for leadership in Latin America itself and
played a major role in drafting the ambiguous OAS resolution. Although Peru provided Argentina with replace-
ment military equipment, including the highly successful
Exocet missiles, it also worked actively to find a resolution after the United States desisted. Mexico maintained a low public profile but privately indicated its
disapproval of the Argentine move. Only Venezuela, which
had its own similar border dispute with neighboring Guyana, and Panama defended Argentina vociferously in public.
The Central American countries had other problems to worry
them, and the new members of the Organization of American
States--the English-speaking Caribbean countries--backed
Britain and expressed amazement at their Latin neighbors'
reaction to the invasion of the Falklands and subsequent
British mobilization to regain them. In short, sentiment
in the region was considerably more divided than appeared
at first glance.

In retrospect, the Falkland Islands crisis is not
likely to have a serious lasting effect on inter-American
relations, and particularly on U.S.-Latin American relations. Other issues, such as economic recovery and the

regional debt crisis, to which the United States responded
generously, quickly replaced the Falklands issue on the
regional agenda. The thoroughness with which Argentina
failed in its effort to deal with both military and diplomatic dimensions of the crisis cost it the remaining sympathy it may have had in the region.

The Falklands crisis did cause Latin American militaries to examine more seriously the value of the inter-
American system and their commitment to it. As a consequence of this more detailed examination, Latin Americans
will not take for granted a U.S. role in the hemisphere
politics in the future. The Falklands crisis was the
first time Americans and Latin Americans found themselves
so divided on a regional question. The range of issues
on the agenda of hemispheric security issues will be nar-
rower in the future than in the past, and will likely focus in greater detail on security commitments. Nevertheless, Latin American countries will remain committed to
the alliance in the future, as they have in the past.
The Argentine territorial dispute with Great Britain has
little transcendental meaning for other Latin American
countries.

More importantly, the Falklands war has forced Latin
American militaries to examine their own stock of equipment and their own potential performance in combat roles.
Clearly, in spite of nationalistic posturing and U.S. ambitions that the South Atlantic militaries play a complementary role to NATO, Argentina was not prepared to fight
a major power. It did perform well with some of the high
technology equipment it had purchased recently, however,
and it is likely that Latin American militaries will focus
their future attention on purchasing the kind of equipment
that bridged the gap between the major power and the regional power. Such equipment will include Exocet missiles,
Super Etendard aircraft, more and more sophisticated submarines, radar, and electronics tracking systems. Future
regional wars will have much more destructive potential as
a result. The Latin Americans will not likely be re-
strained by admonitions against arms races in the hemisphere. Rather, they will perceive their current arsenals
as clearly inadequate to challenges in the future. A regional arms buildup is almost a certainty over the next
several years.

Latin America's military leaders are also likely to
begin to examine their own combat readiness more critically. The Falklands engagement pointed clearly to a number of flaws in organization and command that may well
characterize other regional military powers. Argentina's
reliance on a conscript army was one of the principal
flaws in its organizational structure, for it was impossible to field large numbers of experienced and seasoned

troops. Officers had little experience at command in the field. Logistical support was flawed and inadequate for the numbers of troops left on the islands, and there was little effective coordination between services. Since the Argentine Air Force and Navy performed credibly well and the Army, the dominant service, performed very badly, Army leaders in the region are likely to take note. Training units for their military function may become a more important element in overall regional military planning, and the tendency for soldiers to retreat from politics to return to the barracks may be reinforced.

APPENDIX
Armaments of Latin American Military Forces

The following tables of armaments of Latin American military forces are intended to provide a basis for comparison of the relative level of armament and degree of sophistication of individual Latin American countries and their principal rivals in the hemisphere. The data underscore the conclusion that Latin American militaries are increasingly diversified in terms of source of arms supplies, and have focused recently on acquisition of high technology and state-of-the-art equipment.

Data in the tables have been taken from the latest available volumes of The Military Balance 1982/1983 (London: International Institute of Strategic Studies (IISS), 1983), Jane's Fighting Ships, 1982 (London: Jane's Publishing, 1982), and Jane's All the World's Aircraft, 1982-1983 (London: Jane's Publishing, 1983). These different sources do not always agree one with another, and there are variations in estimates of numbers of items held by different countries. For these reasons, the data should be considered illustrative, and not confirmed, final figures.

Designation of ships and aircraft follow those used by IISS in The Military Balance. Information as to origin, year of origin, and acquisition date (provided in parentheses) is generally taken from Jane's various volumes. Where two countries of origin are provided, it is usually the case that the weapon was designed by the first country for the second country. In some cases the weapon was also assembled in the second country.

	ARGENTINA		
Category	#	Special Equipment	Origin, Year of Origin, and (Acquisition Date)

NAVAL FORCES

Category	#	Special Equipment	Origin, Year of Origin, and (Acquisition Date)
Submarines	2 209 (Salta	--	Germany/Argentina, 1974 (1974)
	1 Guppy	--	U.S., 1945 (1971)
Carriers	1 Colossus	--	Britain, 1945 (1968)
			U.S., 1939 (1951)
Destroyers	2 Type 42	Exocet Sea Dart Lynx Helo	Britain/Argentina, 1970 (1976, 1982)
	3 Sumner	Exocet	U.S., 1944 (1972, 1974)
	1 Gearing	Exocet	U.S., 1945 (1973)
	2 Fletcher	--	U.S., 1943 (1971)
Frigates	3 A-69	Exocet	France, 1976 (1978)
Fast Attack	2 TNC-45 (G)		Germany, 1946 (1974)
Craft	4 Dabur (P)		Israel, 1946 (1978)
	2 Higgins (T)		U.S., 1946

NAVAL AIR

Category	#	Special Equipment	Origin, Year of Origin, and (Acquisition Date)
	28*Combat aircraft		
	1 Attack sq.	11 A-4Q (Skyhawk)	U.S., 1954
		4*Super Etendard	France, 1977 (1981)
	1 Marine recon.	5 S-2E (ASW)	U.S., 1961
		5 S-P2H	
		3 P95 (EMB-111)	Brazil, 1978 (1982)
		7 S-61D/NR (Sea King)	
		9 Alouette A-103	France, 1953
		4 WG13 (Sea Lynx)	Anglo/French, 1977
	Anti-submarine missile	AM-39 (Exocet)	France, 1976

AIR FORCE

Category	#	Special Equipment	Origin, Year of Origin, and (Acquisition Date)
	97*Combat aircraft		
	1 Bomber sq.	7 Canberra B-62	Britain, 1949
		2 T-64	Britain, 1949
	5 Fighter ground attack sq.	3/40 A-4P Skyhawk	U.S., 1954
		2/15 MS-760 A Paris-II	France/Argentina, 1954
	3 Fighter/interceptor sq.	14 Mirage-III	France, 1969
		6 Dagger	Israel
	2 Counterinsurgency sq.	31 Pucará	Argentina, 1974
	1 Counterinsurgency helo sq.	14 Hughes 500M	U.S., 1968
		6 UH-1H	U.S., 1967
	1 SAR helo sq.	6 Lama	Italy, 1971
		2 S-58T (Seabat)	U.S., 1954

ARGENTINA (cont'd)

Category	#	Special Equipment	Origin, Year of Origin, and (Acquisition Date)
AIR FORCE (cont'd)			
		Air-to-air missile	R-530 Matra	France, 1965
		Air-to-surface missile	AS-11/-12	France, 1957/1962
LAND FORCES			
	285	Medium tanks	
	110	Light tanks	

ON ORDER: (Naval Air) 8 Super Etendard, 6 WC13 (Sea Lynx); (Air Force) 10 Mirage V, 24 Skyhawk, 11 1A-5A Pucará.

*Numbers uncertain due to combat casualties in the Falkland Islands conflict.

BRAZIL

Category	# Class	Special Equipment	Origin, Year of Origin, and (Acquisition Date)
NAVAL FORCES			
Submarines	3 Oberon	--	Britain, 1961 (1973-1977)
	5 Guppy	--	U.S., 1945/1946 (1972-1973)
Carriers	1 Colossus	--	Britain, 1945 (1961)
Destroyers	5 Sumner	1 Seacat SAM	U.S., 1944 (1972, 1973)
	2 Gearing	ASROC; WASP helo	U.S., 1945 (1973)
	5 Fletcher	--	U.S., 1943 (1961-1968)
Frigates	6 Niteroi	2w3 Seacat SAM	Britain/Brazil, 1976 (1976-1978)
		2w Exocet	
		4w Ikara/ASW	
NAVAL AIR			
	13 Combat helo	4 SH-3D Sea King	U.S., 1961
	2 ASW sq.	9 Lynx MK-89	Anglo/French, 1977
	Anti-submarine missile	ASROC	
AIR FORCE			
	227 Combat air		
	1 Interceptor sq.	13 Mirage III BR	France
		2 DBR	France
	2 Fighter ground attack sq.	32 F5-E	U.S., 1972
		4 F5-B	U.S., 1964
	8 Counterinsurgency recon.	139 AT-26 Xavante	Italy/Brazil
		8 RC-95	Brazil, 1977/1978
	1 ASW sq.	8 S-2E	U.S., 1961
		9 S-2A	U.S., 1961
	1 Marine recon. sq.	12 P95 (EMB 11)	Brazil, 1978
	4 Search and recovery sq.	3 RC-130E	U.S., 1962
		8 SC-95	Brazil, 1972
		2 Bell 47G	U.S., 1947
		6 SA330 Puma	France, 1968
	Anti-air missile	R530-Matra	France
		Piranha	Brazil
LAND FORCES			
	161 Medium tanks		
	107 Light tanks		

ON ORDER: (Navy) 1 submarine, 4 corvettes; (Air Force) 88 AM-X (Italy, 1982), 12 EMB 120 Brasilia, 100 YT 17 Tangara (Brazil, 1981), 8 UH-1H Iroquois (U.S., 1961); (Army) 50 X-1A2 light tanks, 55-60 rocket launchers.

VENEZUELA

Category	# Class	Special Equipment	Origin, Year of Origin, and (Acquisition Date)
NAVAL FORCES			
Submarines	2 209	--	(1976, 1977)
	1 Guppy	--	U.S., 1945 (1972, 1973)
Frigates	4 Sucre (Lupo)	Otomat SSM	Italy/Venezuela, 1979 (1979+)
		Aspide SAM	
	2 Almirante Clemente	--	Italy/Venezuela, 1956 (1956, 1957)
Fast Attack Craft	3 Vosper/Thorny-croft/M	Otomat SSM	Britain (1974, 1975)
	3 Vosper/Thorny-croft/G	--	Britain
NAVAL AIR			
	6 Combat air		
	1 ASW sq.	6 S2E	U.S., 1961
	1 ASW helo sq.	6 AB-212	U.S.(Italy), 1971
	1 SAR sq.	2 C212	Spain, 1971
AIR FORCE			
	87 Combat air		
	2 Light bomber/ recon.	20 Canberra	Britain, 1949
	1 Fighter/ground attack sq.	16 Mirage III/5	France
	2 Interceptor/ fighter sq.	14 CF5A	U.S./Canada, 1963
		4 CF5B	U.S./Canada, 1963
		18 F86K	U.S., 1949
	1 Counterinsur-gency sq.	15 OV-10E	U.S., 1966
	2 Helo sq.	13 Alouette III	France, 1959
		20 UH-1D/H	U.S., 1961
		9 UA-19	U.S.
		2 Bell 212	U.S./Canada, 1970
		2 Bell 214ST	U.S., 1977
		2 Bell 412	U.S., 1981
	Anti-air missile	R-530	France
LAND FORCES			
	75 Medium tanks		
	40 Light tanks		

ON ORDER: (Naval Forces) 2 209 submarines, 2 Sucre frigates; (Naval Air) 4 AB-212; (Air Force) 18 F16A, 6 F16/B/D (U.S., 1978).

		CHILE	
Category	# Class	Special Equipment	Origin, Year of Origin, and (Acquisition Date)

NAVAL FORCES

Category	# Class	Special Equipment	Origin, Year of Origin, and (Acquisition Date)
Submarines	2 Oberon	--	Britain, 1961 (1976)
	1 Balao	--	U.S., 1944 (1961)
Cruisers	2 Brooklyn	1 Helo	U.S., 1938 (1951)
	1 Gota Lejon	--	Sweden, 1947 (1971)
Destroyers	2 Almirante	Exocet SSM Seacat SAM	Britain, 1960 (1960)
	2 Sumner	1 Helo	U.S., 1944 (1974)
	2 Fletcher		U.S., 1943 (1963)
Frigates	2 Leander	Exocet SSM Seacat SAM 1 Helo	Britain, 1974/1974 (1973, 1974)
	3 Lawrence	--	U.S., 1943 (1966)
Fast Attack Craft	4 Lürssen-type (T)	--	Chile, 1965 (1965, 1966)
	2 Reshef (M)	6 Gabriel SSM	Israel, 1973 (1981)

NAVAL AIR

	6 Combat air		
	1 ASW sq.	6 EMB-111	Brazil, 1978 (1980, 1981)
	1 SAR/liaison sq.	3 EMB-110C(N)	Brazil, 1968
		4 CASA-C212	Spain, 1971
		1 Navajo	U.S., 1964
	1 SAR-liaison helo sq.	10 Alouette-III	France, 1959
		2 S-58	U.S., 1954
		4 Bell 206	U.S., 1966
		12 Bell 47-G	U.S., 1947

AIR FORCE

	84 Combat aircraft		
	3 Fighter ground attack sq.	16 Hunter F-71	U.S., 1953
		4 Hunter T-77	U.S., 1953
		15 F-5E	U.S., 1972
		3 F-5F	U.S., 1972
	3 Counterinsurgency sq.	34 A-37B	U.S., 1967
		6 AT-26 Xavante	Italy (Brazil), 1970
	1 Fighter sq.	8 Mirage 50C	France, 1969
	1 SAR helo sq.	6 S-55	U.S., 1950
	1 Helo sq.	1 Puma	France, 1968
		10 UH-1H	U.S., 1967

LAND FORCES

	120 Medium tanks		
	107 Light tanks		

ON ORDER: (Navy) 2 209 submarines, 1 County destroyer; (Air Force) 12 Mirage 50, 20 T-25, 7 C-101; (Army) Piranha.

		Special	Origin, Year of Origin,
Category	# Class	Equipment	and (Acquisition Date)

COLOMBIA

NAVAL FORCES

Submarines	2 209	--	Germany, 1975 (1975)
Destroyers	2 Holland	--	Dutch/Colombia, 1958
	(1 in reserve)		(1958)
	1 Sumner	--	U.S., 1944 (1973)
Frigates	1 Crosley	--	U.S., 1945 (1969)
	1 Courtney	--	U.S., 1957 (1972)

NAVAL AIR   No naval air

AIR FORCE

	26 Combat air		
	1 Fighter recon.	12 Mirage 5 COA	France, 1969
	sq.	4 Mirage 5(COR/D)	France
	1 Counterinsurgency sq.	10 AT-33A	Brazil
	1 Recon. helo sq.	10 Hughes OH-6A	U.S., 1966
	1 Search and recovery sq.	27 Lama	Italy, 1971
		6 HH-43B	
	Miscellaneous helo	--	
	Anti-air missile	R-530 Matra	France, 1963

LAND FORCES

12 Light tanks

ON ORDER: (Navy) 4 FV-1500 Corvettes; (Air Force) 12 Kfir C-2, air-to-air missiles, air-to-surface missiles; (Army) medium tanks.

		ECUADOR	
Category	# Class	Special Equipment	Origin, Year of Origin, and (Acquisition Date)

NAVAL FORCES

Submarines	2 209	--	Germany, 1974 (1978)
Destroyers	2 Gearing	--	U.S., 1946 (1978)
Frigates	2 Lawrence	--	U.S., 1943 (1967)
Fast Attack Craft	3 Lürssen-type	Exocet SSM	Germany/Ecuador, 1976 (1976, 1977)
	3 Manta-type	Gabriel SSM	Germany/Ecuador, 1971 (1971)

NAVAL AIR

	2 Alouette III	--	France, 1959
	11 Miscellaneous fixed wing		

AIR FORCE

	40 Combat aircraft		
	1 Light bomber sq.	3 Canberra B-6	Britain, 1949
	1 Fighter ground attack sq.	10 Jaguar S	Britain, 1978
		2 Jaguar B	Britain
		10 Kfir	Israel, 1975
	1 Interceptor sq.	15 Mirage E-1JE	France, 1974
		2 Mirage F-1JB	
	1 Counterinsurgency sq.	5 A-37B	U.S., 1967
	Anti-air missile	R-550 Magic	France, 1975

LAND FORCES

	120 Light tanks		

ON ORDER: (Navy) 1 destroyer, 6 Corvettes, Exocet SSM; (Air Force) 10 F-5E, 2 F-5F.

PERU

Category	# Class	Special Equipment	Origin, Year of Origin, and (Acquisition Date)
NAVAL FORCES			
Submarines	4 209	--	Germany, 1974 (1974)
	2 Guppy	--	U.S., 1944 (1974)
	4 Abtao	--	U.S., 1954 (1965, 1968)
Cruisers	2 De Ruyter	1w Exocet, 3 Helo	Dutch, 1953 (1973, 1976)
	1 Ceylon	--	British, 1943 (1960)
Destroyers	2 Daring	8 Exocet SSM, 1 Helo	British, 1953 (1969)
	2 Fletcher	--	U.S., 1943 (1960, 1961)
	1 Holland	--	Dutch, 1954 (1978)
	5 Friesland	--	Dutch, 1956
Frigates	2 Lupo (Carvajal)	Otomat SSM, Aspide SAM, 1 Helo	Italy, 1978 (1981)
Fast Attack Craft	2 PR-72	Exocet SSM	France, 1976 (1981)
NAVAL AIR			
	12 Combat air		
	1 ASW sq.	9 S-2E Tracker	U.S., 1954
	1 ASW helo sq.	4 SH-3D Sea King	U.S., 1959
		6 AB-212	U.S. (Italy), 1971
	1 Marine recon. sq.	2 F-27 MPA	Germany, 1976
		1 Casa C-212	Spain, 1971
	1 Helo util.	10 Bell 206B	U.S., 1966
		6 UH-1D/H	U.S., 1961
		2 Alouette III	France, 1959
AIR FORCE			
	114 Combat aircraft		
	2 Light bomber sq.	20 Canberra	Britain, 1949
	4 Fighter ground attack sq.	2/24 Mirage 5P	France, 1969
		2/36 Su-22 Fitter-C	USSR, 1971 (1977)
	2 Counterinsurgency sq.	25 A-37B	U.S., 1967
	4 Helo sq.	6 Alouette III	France, 1959
		15 Bell 47G	U.S., 1947
		17 Bell 212	U.S. (Canada), 1970
		8 Mi-6	USSR, 1967
		6 Mi-5	USSR, 1967
LAND FORCES			
	510 Medium tanks		
	110 Light tanks		

ON ORDER: (Navy) 2 209, 2 Lupo frigates, C-212 marine recon. air; (Air Force) 20 Mirage 2000, 14 MB-339 (Italy, 1977), 1 DC8; (Army) 50 M-48A2 medium tanks.

Bibliography

ACDA. See U.S. Arms Control and Disarmament Agency.

Aspen Institute for Humanistic Studies (1982). <u>Governance in the Western Hemisphere</u>. New York: Aspen Institute for Humanistic Studies.

Atkins, G. P. (1977a). <u>Latin America in the International System</u>. New York: The Free Press.

_____ (1977b). "Mutual Security in the Changing Inter-American System: An Appraisal of the OAS Charter and Rio Treaty Revisions." Carlisle Barracks, Pa.: Strategic Studies Institute, U.S. Army War College.

Baer, W. (1979). <u>The Brazilian Economy: Its Growth and Development</u>. Columbus, Ohio: Grid Publishing, Inc.

Bagley, W. H. (1977). <u>Sea Power and Western Security: The Next Decade</u>. Adelphi Papers No. 139. London: International Institute of Strategic Studies (IISS).

Bank of London and South America (1978). <u>BOLSA Review</u>. London: Bank of London and South America, Ltd.

Blechman, B. M., and Kaplan, S. S. (1978). <u>Force Without War: U.S. Armed Forces as a Political Instrument</u>. Washington, D.C.: The Brookings Institution.

Blechman, B. M., and Levinson, J. (1976). "Toward a New Consensus in Defense Policy," in H. Owen and C. L. Schultz (eds), <u>Setting National Priorities: The Next 10 Years</u>. Washington, D.C.: The Brookings Institution.

BOLSA. See Bank of London and South America.

Brasil, Banco Central do Brasil (1978, 1981). <u>Central Bank Bulletin</u>. Brasilia, D.F.: Banco Central do Brasil.

Brasil, Instituto Brasileiro de Geografia e Estatistica
(IBGE) (1977). Anuario Estatistico do Brasil. Rio
de Janeiro: Instituto Brasileiro de Geografia e
Estatistica.

Brasil, Ministerio da Fazenda (1976). Comercio Exterior.
Brasilia: Ministerio da Fazenda.

The Brookings Institution (1976). Setting National Priorities: The Next 10 Years. Washington, D.C.: The
Brookings Institution.

Bustamante, J. A. (1979). "Emigración Indocumentada a los
Estados Unidos," in El Colégio de México (ed), Indocu-
mentados: Mitos y Realidades. Mexico: El Colégio de
México.

CACI (1977). Planning for Problems in Crisis Management.
Washington, D.C.: CACI, Inc.

_____ (1978). Market Assessment for Transportation
of Trade with Developing Countries. Washington, D.C.:
CACI, Inc., for Office of Maritime Technology, Maritime Administration.

Calvert, P. (1982). "The Causes of the Falklands Conflict," Contemporary Review 24(July): 6-11.

Chernick, S. E. (1978). The Commonwealth Caribbean, the
Integration Experience. Baltimore, Md.: The Johns
Hopkins University Press for the World Bank.

Child, J. (1979a). "From 'Color' to 'Rainbow': U.S. Strategic Planning for Latin America. 1919-1945," Journal of Inter-American Studies and World Affairs 21
(May).

_____ (1979b). "Geopolitical Thinking in Latin America," Latin American Research Review 14, 2: 89-112.

_____ (1980). Unequal Alliance: The Inter-American
Military System, 1938-1978. Boulder, Colo.: Westview
Press.

Clement, N., and Green, L. (1978). "The Political Economy
of Devaluation in Mexico," Inter-American Economic
Affairs 32, 3(Winter): 47-75.

Cline, W. R. (1976). "Brazil's Emerging International
Economic Role," in R. Roett (ed), Brazil in the Sev-
enties. Washington, D.C.: American Enterprise Institute for Public Policy Research.

Commission on United States-Brazilian Relations (1980).
"The Brazilian Fuel-Alcohol Program." Report of the
Rapporteur. Mimeograph.

Commission on United States-Latin American Relations
(1975). The Americas in a Changing World. New York:
Quadrangle Books for the Center for Inter-American
Relations.

The Committee of Santa Fe, Council for Inter-American Security (1980). "A New Inter-American Policy for the
Eighties." Manuscript.

Cornelius, W. (1977). "Illegal Mexican Migration to the
United States: A Summary of Recent Research Findings
and Policy Implications." Background Paper No. 3,
Council on Foreign Relations. May 9.

_____ (1978). Mexican Migration to the United
States: Causes, Consequences, and U.S. Responses.
Cambridge, Mass.: MIT Center for International Stud-
ies. July.

_____ (1979a). "La Migración Illegal Mexicana a los
Estados Unidos: Conclusiones de Investigaciones Re-
cientes, Implicaciones Políticas y Prioridades de
Investigación," in El Colégio de México (ed), Indocu-
mentados: Mitos y Realidades. Mexico: El Colégio de
México.

_____ (1979b). "La Nueva Mitologia de la Emigración
Indocumentada Mexicana a Los Estados Unidas," in Cen-
tro de Estudios Nacionales (ed), Indocumentados.
México: El Colégio de México.

de Vries, R. (1983). "Global Debt." Statement prepared
for hearings before the subcommittee on International
Economic Policy, Senate Foreign Relations Committee,
The World Economic Situation. Washington, D.C.: U.S.
Government Printing Office.

do Couto e Silva, G. (1967). Geopolítica do Brasil. Rio
de Janeiro: Editôra José Olympio.

Dominguez, J. I. (1978). "Cuban Foreign Policy," Foreign
Affairs 57(Fall): 83-108.

_____ (1982). "Cuba's Relations with Caribbean and
Central American Countries," in A. Adelman and R.
Reading, Stability and Instability in the Caribbean
Basin. Boston, Mass.: Lexington Books, forthcoming.

Drewry, H. P. (1974). The Rise of National Fleets. London: H. P. Drewry (shipping consultants).

_____ (1978). The Emergence of Third World Ship-building. London: H. P. Drewry (shipping consultants).

Einaudi, L. R. (1973). "Arms Transfer to Latin America: Toward a Policy of Mutual Respect." Santa Monica, Calif.: The Rand Corporation (June, R-1173-D05).

Embassy of Brazil (1979). Boletim. March 8.

English, A. (1983). "The Argentine Navy: Post Falklands," Navy International 88, 3(March): 148-152.

Euromoney (1978). April: 1-37.

Fagen, R. R. (1978). "Mexican Petroleum and U.S. National Security." Unpublished manuscript. Dept. of Political Science, Stanford University, Palo Alto, Calif. June.

_____ (1979). "An Inescapable Relationship," The Wilson Quarterly III, 3(Summer): 142-150.

Fagen, R. R., and Nau, H. (1978). "Mexican Gas." Paper prepared for Conference on the United States Foreign Policy, and Latin American and Caribbean Regions, Washington, D.C., March 27-31. Mimeograph.

Ffrench-Davis, R. (1982). "External Debt and Balance of Payments in Latin America: Recent Trends and Outlook," in Inter-American Development Bank, 1982.

Fishlow, A. (1978). "The Latin American Economy in the 1980's: Implications for the United States Policies." Statement before the subcommittee on Western Hemisphere Affairs, Senate Foreign Relations Committee. October. Washington, D.C.: U.S. Government Printing Office.

_____ (1979). "Flying Down to Rio: Perspectives on U.S.-Brazil Relations," Foreign Affairs 57, 2(Winter): 387-405.

_____ (1982). "The United States and Brazil: The Case of the Missing Relationship," Foreign Affairs 60, 4(Spring): 904-923.

Gall, N. (1976). "Atoms for Brazil, Dangers for All," Foreign Policy 23(Summer): 155-201.

_____ (1979). "The Twilight of Nuclear Exports: Brazil and Iran," American Universities Field Staff Reports: 1979/No. 12 South America. Hanover, N.H.: American Universities Field Staff.

Ginsbergs, G. (1977). "The Soviet Quest for Influence and Military Facilities in the Third World," in M. McGwire and J. McDonnell, Soviet Naval Influence: Domestic and Foreign Dimensions. New York: Praeger.

Gonzalez, E. (1974). Cuba under Castro: The Limits of Charisma. Boston: Houghton Mifflin Co.

Grabendorff, W. (1979). "West Germany and Brazil: A Showcase for the First World-Third World Relationship?" Washington, D.C.: Occasional Paper No. 4, Center of Brazilian Studies, The Johns Hopkins University School of Advanced International Studies.

Grayson, G. W. (1977). "Mexican Foreign Policy," Current History 72, 425(March): 97-101, 134-135.

Grondona, M. (1976). "South America Looks at Detente . . . Skeptically," Foreign Policy 26(Spring): 184-203.

Gurr, T. R. (1970). Why Men Rebel. Princeton, N.J.: Princeton University Press.

Halperin, M. (1981). The Taming of Fidel Castro. Berkeley and London: University of California Press.

Hayes, M. D. (1977). U.S. National Security Interests in the Panama Canal: Projections Over Time. Washington, D.C.: CACI, Inc.

_____ (1978). "The South Atlantic: Changing Perspectives on an Emerging Issue." Washington, D.C.: Occasional Paper No. 7, Center of Brazilian Studies, The Johns Hopkins University School of Advanced International Studies.

Hayes, R. E. (1972). "The Effect of Changes in Level of Civil Violence on Political Regulation Policy." Unpublished Doctoral Dissertation, Department of Political Science, Indiana University.

Hilton, S. E. (1975). Brazil and the Great Power, 1930-1939. Austin: University of Texas Press.

Holt, D. D. (1979). "Why the Bankers Suddenly Love Mexico," Fortune 100, 2(July 16): 138-139.

Huntington, S. P. (1968). Political Order in Changing Societies. New Haven, Conn.: Yale University Press.

IDB. See Inter-American Development Bank.

272

Inter-American Development Bank (IDB) (1978). "OECD and Latin America: Trade Trends and Prospects." Mimeograph.

_____ (various years). Economic and Social Progress in Latin America. Washington, D.C.: Inter-American Development Bank.

International Economic Studies Institute (IESI) (1976). Raw Materials and Foreign Policy. Washington, D.C.: International Economic Studies Institute.

International Institute for Strategic Studies (IISS) (various years). The Military Balance. London: International Institute for Strategic Studies.

International Monetary Fund (IMF) (various years). Direction of Trade Statistics. Washington, D.C.: International Monetary Fund.

Jane's All the World's Aircraft (various years). London: Jane's Publishing Company.

Jane's Fighting Ships (various years). London: Jane's Publishing Company.

Jornal do Brasil (1976). October 14.

Kissinger, H. A. (1974). American Foreign Policy (exp. ed.). New York: W. W. Norton & Company, Inc.

Krasner, S. D. (1978). Defending the National Interest: Raw Materials Investments and U.S. Foreign Policy. Princeton, N.J.: Princeton University Press.

Kravanja, M. (1976). "The Soviet Fishing Industry," in Soviet Ocean Developments. Washington, D.C.: U.S. Government Printing Office.

Kuczynski, P. P. (1977). "The Economic Development of Venezuela: A Summary View as of 1975-1976," in R. D. Bond, Contemporary Venezuela and Its Role in International Affairs. New York: New York University Press.

Latin America Commodities Report (1980). "Sugar: Fear of Lost Market if Prices Rise Sharply." May 9, p. 7. London: Latin American Newsletters, Ltd.

Latin America Economic Report (LAER) (various issues). London: Latin American Newsletters, Ltd.

Latin America Informe Semanal (LAIS) (various issues).

273

Latin America Political Report (LAPR) (various issues).
London: Latin American Newsletters, Ltd.

Latin America Regional Reports: Brazil (1982). "Carajas:
Myth and Reality." September 17, pp. 4-5.

Latin America Weekly Report (LAWR) (various issues).
London: Latin American Newsletters, Ltd.

Leogrande, W. M. (1982a). "Cuba Policy Recycled," Foreign Policy 46(Spring): 105-119.

_____ (1982b). "Letters: Cuba," Foreign Policy 48
(Fall): 175-184.

Lowenthal, A. F. (1976). "The United States and Latin
America: Ending the Hegemonic Presumption," Foreign
Affairs 55, 1(October): 199-213.

Marcella, G. (1977). "Cuba and the Regional Balance of
Power." Carlisle Barracks, Pa.: Strategic Studies
Institute, U.S. Army War College.

Martin, J. B. (1978). U.S. Policy in the Caribbean (A
Twentieth Century Fund Essay). Boulder, Colo.:
Westview Press.

McGwire, M., Booth, K., and McDonnell, J. (1975). Soviet
Naval Policy: Objectives and Constraints. New York:
Praeger.

McGwire, M., and McDonnell, J. (1977). Soviet Naval Influence: Domestic and Foreign Dimensions. New York:
Praeger.

Meira Mattos, D. de (1975). Brasil: Geopolítica e Destino.
Rio de Janeiro: Livraria José Olympio.

_____ (1977). A Geopolítica e as Projeções do Poder.
Rio de Janeiro: Livraria José Olympio.

Meissner, D. (1979). Mexico-United States Relations.
Racine, Wis.: The Johnson Foundation.

Meyer, L. (1977). "La Resistencia al Capital Privado Ex-
tranjero: El Caso del Petroleo, 1938-1950," in Ber-
nardo Sepulveda Amor et al. (eds), Las Empresas In-
ternacionales en México. Mexico: El Colégio de México.

Middendorf, J. W. (1976). "The Posture of the Navy."
Statement before the U.S. Senate Armed Services Committee, Hearings on Fiscal 1977 Authorization for
Military Procurement. Washington, D.C.: U.S. Government Printing Office.

274

Moore, B., Jr. (1966). Social Origins of Dictatorship and Democracy: Lord and Peasant in the Making of the Moddern World. Boston: Beacon Press.

Murphy, P. J. (ed) (1978). Naval Power in Soviet Policy: Studies in Communist Affairs, Vol. 2. Washington, D.C.: U.S. Government Printing Office.

The New York Times (various issues).

Nogee, J. L., and Sloan, J. W. (1979). "Allende's Chile and the Soviet Union: A Policy Lesson for Latin American Nations Seeking Autonomy," Journal of Inter-American Studies and World Affairs 21, 3(August): 339-368.

Nolde, K. (1979). "Arms in South America." April. Manuscript mimeograph.

O'Flaherty, J. D. (1978). "Finding Jamaica's Way," Foreign Policy 31(Summer): 137-158.

Oil and Gas Journal (various issues).

Organization for Economic Cooperation and Development (OECD) (1978a). Development Cooperation: 1978 Review. Paris: Organization for Economic Cooperation and Development.

_____ (1978b). Economic Outlook, No. 24. December. Paris: Organization for Economic Cooperation and Development.

_____ (1979). Maritime Transport: 1978. Paris: Organization for Economic Cooperation and Development.

_____ (various years). Trade by Commodities: Series C. Paris: Organization for Economic Cooperation and Development.

Pagliano, G. J. (1979). "Mexico's Oil and Gas Resources: Implications for the U.S." Washington, D.C.: Library of Congress, Issue Brief No. IB 79015. June.

Pan American Union (1952). The Foreign Trade of Latin America Since 1913. Washington, D.C.: Pan American Union, Division of Economic Research.

Pellicer de Brody, O. (1976). "El Acercamiento de México a América Latina: Una Interpretación Política," in J. Wilkie et al., Contemporary Mexico. Los Angeles: University of California Press and El Colégio de México.

_____ (1979). "Relaciones Exteriores: Interdependencia con Estados Unidos o Proyecto Nacional," in P. G. Casanova and E. Florescano (eds), Mexico Hoy. Mexico: Siglo XXI.

Pierre, A. (1982). The Global Politics of Arms Sales. Princeton, N.J.: Princeton University Press.

Poitras, G. E. (1974). "Mexico's 'New' Foreign Policy," Inter-American Economic Affairs 28(Winter): 59-77.

Purcell, J. F. H., and Purcell, S. K. (1976). "The State and Economic Enterprise in Mexico: The Limits of Reform," Nueva Política. May-July.

Reddick, J. R. (1981). "Nuclear Trends in Latin America," in Aspen Institute for Humanistic Studies, Governance in the Western Hemisphere. Background papers. June 1982.

Rico, C. F. (1978). "Las Relaciones México-Norteamericanas y la Retórica de la Interdependencia," Proceso 112. December 25.

_____ (1979). "Algo de lo que Está en Juego," Proceso 113. January 1.

Rodriguez, C. F. (1981). "Fundamentos estratégicos de la política exterior de Cuba," Cuba Socialista (second period) 1, 1(December), cited in Dominguez, 1982.

Roett, R. (1975). "Brazil Ascendant--International Relations and Geopolitics in the Late 20th Century," Journal of International Affairs (Fall).

_____ (1978). Brazil: Politics in a Patrimonial Society (rev. ed.). New York: Praeger.

Rondeau, J. A. (1976). "Apartheid: Shadow Over South Africa," U.S. Naval Institute Proceedings. September.

Ronfeldt, D. F. (1976). "The Mexican Army and Political Order Since 1940," in A. F. Lowenthal (ed), Armies and Politics in Latin America. New York: Holmes & Meier.

Ronfeldt, D. F., and Einaudi, L. R. (1971). Internal Security and Military Assistance to Latin America in the 1970's. Santa Monica, Calif.: The Rand Corporation (R-924-ISA).

Ronfeldt, D. F., and Sereseres, C. (1978). The Management of U.S.-Mexico Interdependence: Drift Toward Failure? Santa Monica, Calif.: The Rand Corporation.

276

Rooney, J. H. (1978). "The United States-Mexico Trade
Agreement of 1977," Texas International Law Journal
13(Summer): 435-59.

Scheina, R. L. (1978). "South American Navies: Who Needs
Them?" U.S. Naval Institute Proceedings. February.

_____ (1983). "Regional Reviews: Latin American
Navies," U.S. Naval Institute Proceedings. March
1983, pp. 30-34.

Schneider, R. M. (1978). Brazil: The Foreign Policy of a
Future World Power. Boulder, Colo.: Westview Press.

Selcher, W. (1979). "Brazil in the Global Power Systems."
Washington, D.C.: Occasional Paper No. 11, Center of
Brazilian Studies, The Johns Hopkins University
School of Advanced International Studies.

Shapira, Y. (1978). Mexican Foreign Policy Under Echeverria. Beverly Hills, Calif.: Sage.

SIPRI. See Stockholm International Peace Research
Institute.

Smith, A. K. (1970). "Mexico and the Cuban Revolution:
Foreign Policymaking in Mexico Under President Adolfo
Lopez Mateos (1958-1964)." Unpublished dissertation,
Cornell University.

Smith, W. S. (1982). "Dateline Havana: Myopic Diplomacy,"
Foreign Policy 48(Fall): 157-174.

Stepan, A. (1971). The Military in Politics: Changing Patterns in Brazil. Princeton, N.J.: Princeton University Press.

_____ (1978). The State and Society: Peru in Comparative Perspective. Princeton, N.J.: Princeton
University Press.

Stevenson, W. (1976). A Man Called Intrepid: The Secret
War. New York: Harcourt Brace Jovanovich.

Stockholm International Peace Institute (SIPRI) (1978).
World Armaments and Disarmament: Yearbook 1978-1979.
Stockholm: Stockholm International Peace Institute.

Syvrud, D. E. (1974). Foundations of Brazilian Economic
Growth. Washington, D.C.: American Enterprise Institute, AEI-Hoover Research Publications.

Theberge, J. D. (1974). The Soviet Presence in Latin America. New York: Crane Russak and Co., Inc., for the National Strategy Information Center, Inc.

Theriot, L. H. (1978). Cuban Foreign Trade: A Current Assessment. Washington, D.C.: U.S. Department of Commerce, Office of East-West Policy and Planning.

Time (1983). "The Debt Bomb Threat," January 10, pp. 42-51.

Treverton, G. F. (1977). Latin America in World Politics. Adelphi Papers No. 137. London: International Institute for Strategic Studies.

Tugwell, F. G. (1977). "Venezuela's Oil Nationalization: The Politics of Aftermath," in R. D. Bond (ed), Contemporary Venezuela and Its Role in International Affairs. New York: New York University Press.

United Nations (1977). Yearbook of International Trade Statistics. New York: United Nations.

U.S. Arms Control and Disarmament Agency (ACDA) (1974, 1976, 1982). World Military Expenditures and Arms Transfers. Washington, D.C.: U.S. Government Printing Office.

U.S. Bureau of the Census (various years). U.S. Exports/ World Area by Schedule E, Commodity Groupings (FT 455). Washington, D.C.: U.S. Government Printing Office.

_____ (various years). U.S. General Imports/World Area by Commodity Groupings (FT 155). Washington, D.C.: U.S. Government Printing Office.

U.S. Congress, Joint Economic Committee (1978). The Chinese Economy Post-Mao. Washington, D.C.: U.S. Government Printing Office.

_____ (1982). Cuba Faces the Economic Realities of the 1980s. Washington, D.C.: U.S. Government Printing Office.

U.S. Congress, Library of Congress, Congressional Research Service (1978). Mexico's Oil and Gas Policy: An Analysis. Prepared for the Committee on Foreign Relations, United States Senate, and the Joint Economic Committee, Congress of the United States. December.

278

U.S. Department of Commerce (1977, 1978, 1981). "U.S. Direct Investment Abroad," Survey of Current Business. August. Washington, D.C.: U.S. Government Printing Office.

U.S. Department of the Interior, Bureau of Mines (1976a). Mineral and Materials Monthly. July. Washington, D.C.: Bureau of Mines.

_____ (1976b). Mineral Facts and Problems. Washington, D.C.: Bureau of Mines.

_____ (1976, 1978). Commodity Data Summaries: 1977, 1979. Washington, D.C.: Bureau of Mines.

U.S. Department of State (1981). "Communist Interference in El Salvador," Special Report No. 80. February 23.

U.S. Office of the President (1977). International Economic Report of the President. Washington, D.C.: The White House.

U.S. Senate, Committee on Energy and Natural Resources (1979). Mexico: The Promise and Problems of Petroleum. Washington, D.C.: U.S. Government Printing Office.

U.S. Senate (1981). Nomination of Vernon A. Walters, Gen., USA (Ret.) to be Ambassador at Large. Hearings Before the Senate Foreign Relations Committee. Washington, D.C.: U.S. Government Printing Office.

Valenta, J. (1982). "Soviet Strategy in the Caribbean Basin," U.S. Naval Institute Proceedings, The Naval Review (May).

Veja (1980). "A Abertura, por Golbery." September 10.

The Wall Street Journal (various issues).

The Washington Post (various issues).

Watson, B. W. (1982). Red Navy at Sea: Soviet Naval Operations on the High Seas, 1956-1980. Boulder, Colo.: Westview Press.

Weinert, R. S. (1977). "The State and Foreign Capital," in J. C. Reyna, and R. S. Weinert (eds), Authoritarianism in Mexico. Philadelphia, Pa.: ISHI.

Weinland, R. G. (1975). "Soviet Naval Operations: 10 Years of Change," in M. McGwire et al. (eds), Soviet Naval Policy: Objectives and Constraints. New York: Praeger.

World Bank (1979). <u>Mexico: Manufacturing Sector: Situa-</u><u>tion, Prospects & Policies</u>. Washington, D.C.: The World Bank.

_____ (1977, 1980, 1982). <u>World Atlas</u>. Washington, D.C.: The World Bank.

_____ (1978, 1979, 1982). <u>World Development Report</u>. Washington, D.C.: The World Bank.

Index

285